"I had a few minutes yesterday and picked up *Captain of My Ship, Master of My Soul* . . . started reading . . . and now I've finished it! A deep spiritual quest—one we can all go on—in the midst of creating a secret psychic spy program for the government? That's what you'll learn about, and be inspired by, in this fascinating autobiography. This is a must-read for anyone interested in ESP, remote viewing, or the way spirit can be found in modern life."

Charles T. Tart, Ph.D.
Institute of Transpersonal Psychology

Captain of My Ship, Master of My Soul

Living with Guidance

F. Holmes Atwater

Copyright © 2001
by F. Holmes Atwater

All rights reserved, including the right to reproduce this
work in any form whatsoever, without permission
in writing from the publisher, except for brief passages
in connection with a review.

Cover design by Kelly O'Neil, KSO Design
Digital imagery © copyright 2001 PhotoDisc, Inc.

For information write:
Hampton Roads Publishing Company, Inc.
1125 Stoney Ridge Road
Charlottesville, VA 22902

434-296-2772
fax: 434-296-5096
e-mail: hrpc@hrpub.com
www.hrpub.com

If you are unable to order this book from your local
bookseller, you may order directly from the publisher.
Call 1-800-766-8009, toll-free.

Library of Congress Catalog Card Number: 2001091192

ISBN 1-57174-247-6

10 9 8 7 6 5 4 3 2 1

Printed on acid-free paper in the United States

This book is dedicated
to the ONE I love.

"Life is not something physical
and death something spiritual.
Substantive reality is inclusive.
God is really big!
The secret to remembering
your true identity is
simply realizing
All That Is."

Contents

Part Two:

SCIENTIST, EXPLORER, SPIRITUAL "I"

Acknowledgments

I have not written or published this book without the help of others. Two of the most important are my wife, Fay Atwater, and friend (mentor, editor, and publisher) Frank DeMarco of the Hampton Roads Publishing Company.

Joe McMoneagle, Paul H. Smith, and my sister, Sunny Gates, with whom I collaborated, helped me accurately recall portions of my spirit journey that are quickly receding into the distant past. My dear friend Miriandra Rota kindly reviewed previous iterations of this manuscript, supported my determination, and provided a great deal of spiritual insight.

Bob Monroe and the staff of The Monroe Institute exemplify the evolving human spirit expressed throughout this manuscript. Thank you all for your help and service to humanity.

And I would acknowledge gratitude to my parents from beyond the grave and all other nonphysical assistance provided in the writing and publishing of this book. I would, except that being one with God, the I Am of it all, the concept of being separate from such "spiritual" realms is, by definition, not possible. There are not "physical" and "spiritual" realities, worlds, or realms but Oneness. So thank you, God—which would include me and by extension "others" mentioned above, which there can't be because there is nothing outside of or other than God I Am.

Okay, I acknowledge it. I wrote this book.

Preface

Over twenty years ago, I met Dr. Charles T. Tart, professor emeritus, at a conference in California and then later at SRI International in conjunction with the U.S. government remote-viewing program. Through the years I have enjoyed reading his books on consciousness and parapsychology. You can check out his website at http://www.paradigm-sys.com/cttart/.

One day during lunch, on a visit to Menlo Park, California, I asked Dr. Tart how he found the time to write books, given his fascinating and very busy life. He said that there always seemed to be time when it was necessary. "Life," he said, "just seemed to arrange itself—making time available for writing." When I pressed him for a more personal answer, he said, "There comes a moment, or perhaps someplace outside of normal waking consciousness, when a voice inside me says stop, write this down." We both sat in silence for a few minutes, he wondering why he had shared such a personal side of himself and I wondering if I would ever hear such a voice. I did and this book is what I wrote down.

The story tells a spirit journey, a particular life span. Some would say that we pass from spirit into the physical at birth and conversely pass from the physical world into spirit at death. I say that we never pass *from* the spirit, that our reverie of the world around us is just that. The physical world is only a silhouette, a shadow without substance. Everyday life is a mere reflection of spirit experienced as an intention to become aware of *All That Is*. Spirit does not journey through (nonexistent) space/time but across the vastness of knowledge itself, a dimensionless realm of *All That Is*. We are always spiritual beings, even when having a physical experience. Our spiritual selves, enlightened souls, share concurrently what we experience in the physical world with *All That Is* (also known as God).

Well, perhaps I should just get on with the story.

During a time not so long ago, our culture teetered on the brink of an apocalypse with that of the former Soviet Union. I grew up and lived through these troubled times, this era of looming self-annihilation called the Cold War. In elementary school, we hid under our classroom desks during duck-and-cover exercises so that we might survive the coming nuclear holocaust. History bears witness to the fact that we did not destroy ourselves and that *after the war* we have experienced an evolutionary psychic shift in Western culture.

In the midst of a world in conflict over material gain during the height of the Cold War, a military remote-viewing surveillance program emerged—as if to balance the insanity of it all. Because of this program, now known to the world by the code name Star Gate, numerous military and civilian government personnel, highly placed members of Congress, and, without naming names, a few in the executive branch discovered that we are not bound by the confines of our physical perceptions—we are, in fact, more than our physical bodies. The cultural impact of this realization continues to grow as more and more people uncover the details of the government-sponsored work in remote viewing.

For me, all this began with a childhood filled with extraordinary spiritual experiences that led me to a military career as a clairvoyant counterspy. Guided by spirit from within to initiate a unique military remote-viewing surveillance program originally called Grill Flame, I recruited and trained an elite cadre of professional remote viewers for the U.S. government.

Guided again by spirit, I entered a new life in Virginia after retiring from the military. I joined The Monroe Institute, a well-known research and education organization. Using the Institute's facilities, I followed my spiritual yearnings and was able to explore a realm of knowledge seemingly beyond the confines of my physical body. Since then, working in the Bob Monroe Research Lab, I have published technical research on methods for expanding consciousness and, working with the staff at the Institute, assisted thousands of others to realize their own true spiritual identity.

As a middle-aged adult, I now live in a culture busily reconnecting with its spiritual roots as envisioned by our founding fathers. Through this book, I know that you too will realize your own guided spirit journey through life and your true nature as you always have and always will.

Introduction

BY JOSEPH W. MCMONEAGLE

Skip Atwater came into my life back in August of 1978. I was a chief warrant officer assigned to the Emitter Location and Identification (ELI) Office, at the Headquarters for Intelligence and Security, U.S. Army, Arlington, Virginia. At the time it was impossible to tell his rank, since he was serving in a part of army intelligence where they don't usually wear uniforms.

Our initial introduction to one another consisted of meeting in an empty office on the third floor, where he showed me a folder containing numerous newspaper clippings about psychics. The newspaper clippings ranged in believability from the skeptical to the incredulous. In retrospect, I have to admit, that because of the subject matter, I was very concerned about the stability of the man sitting across from me and was uncomfortable with the questions he was asking. This initial assessment proved to be entirely wrong. Subsequently, it was through his efforts that I would be recruited into the army's secret, psychic-spy unit, Star Gate, as Remote Viewer #001.

I was very honored when Skip came to me and asked if I would introduce his book *Captain of My Ship, Master of My Soul.* Since we have been friends for 23 years you would think this an easy task, but it isn't. This is primarily because his book isn't an easy book to describe in its entirety. First, it's a complex history of a human being who is probably one of the most metaphysically attuned individuals I know. It is a story about his life's journey, a journey in which he has operated on a day-to-day basis, almost entirely on faith.

How many times have you heard someone say: "You have to have faith that it will work out," or, "Have faith, trust in God," or, "Faith moves mountains"? Well, how many of us truly operate that way? My guess is not many. Or, at least that is not our primary focus. I can tell you that Skip Atwater is one of the few human beings I've ever met who operates only that way. He not only believes that faith can move mountains, but lives his life with an expectation that it will. And, around Skip, you will see mountains move.

What makes *Captain of My Ship, Master of My Soul* unique is that it chronicles his life from childhood to present, with a focus on how and why he has learned to live his life with such expectation, such a tremendous faith in its ultimate outcome. This isn't a cool story you'll find yourself half-believing. It is a heroic story, filled with incredible demonstrations of faith embedded within the everyday problems of life and living.

In childhood, Skip was taught that we ". . . never pass from the spirit" into the physical, such as at birth. He goes on to say: "We are always spiritual beings, even when having a physical experience." He clearly came to understand this even as a child. He shares with us how he managed to integrate these kinds of understandings into his daily actions, and how they affected his life.

Skip enlisted in the army in 1968, with an expectation that he would never be confronted with the moral issue of taking a life, a laughable expectation for anyone aware of the ongoing situation in Southeast Asia at the time, but for Skip, a simple act of faith. Skip's simple acts of faith constitute a teaching and learning experience, which we can all benefit from.

A significant portion of the book is dedicated to the reasons behind the establishment of the army's secret, psychic-spy program, and how it was done. These are highly original and unique insights, since they come directly from one of the individuals most involved in the initiation of the Star Gate project. As far as army involvement, Skip could be considered one of the originating fathers in its deployment. While Skip would be one of the first to say that it was a team effort and took the involvement of dozens of people to make it work, one can readily see his "acts of faith" deeply interwoven within the pattern or framework of its being. Skip speaks with authority here, since he was not only the project's first, but its only operations and training officer (O&TO) from 1977 to 1987.

As the O&TO, Skip's acceptance and integration of a metaphysical structure to physical reality were key elements that enabled the remote-viewing project to succeed as well as it did. He may not have known at the time, but he certainly intuited, that the role of expectation in the success of remote viewing was also a key element. Since expectation was so well integrated within his consciousness and physical experience, it automatically became a part of the remote viewers' reality, at least for those under his control—mine included. A great deal of his effort as O&TO of the unit infused within me the kind of remote-viewing expertise that I display today.

Using remote viewing to target UFOs is seen by many as having negative connotations and best avoided. Skip has an interesting perspective on this, which is probably one of the best in the field. He is open to certain uses of remote viewing, but cautions about the care that should be exercised in the selection of which protocols should be used. Since he is probably one of the most effective users of remote viewing in its history, one would do well to pay attention to his concerns and follow the kinds of guidance he provides freely within his book. His experience with the application of remote viewing to real-world problems is exceptionally deep.

At the end of his army career, Skip moved to rural Virginia and became a researcher at The Monroe Institute (TMI). This is the world-renowned institute founded by Robert Monroe, author of *Journeys Out of the Body*, the first and now classic introduction to out of the body experiences (OBEs). This was a natural move given Skip's metaphysical focus. Early in the book he explains how he was first introduced to Bob Monroe, and Hemi-Sync, a method that aids in the exploration of altered states of consciousness. This is the juicy part of the read for me. He goes into some detail regarding how he thinks Hemi-Sync actually works within the brain and what its effects might be—more so than I have read in many other articles on this subject. He describes some of his experiences while attending a Gateway Voyage seminar at the Institute, and surprises us with his humble acceptance of things he "never really seriously considered" before. But, this should surprise no one who knows Skip. That is simply the way he is. He accepts things as they appear in his life, he has an expectation that whatever he experiences will be of value and bring him something necessary to his existence. And he does this effortlessly, which of course is probably the most profound aspect about this book.

We've all met someone who claims to have had a particular kind of experience, and in nearly every case they've treated that experience as something exceptional or special. We've also met people who, as we say in the army, can't walk their talk. Skip walks his talk and always has. He's created a life filled with metaphysical experience and has successfully integrated these experiences. In his life there is always something expected, there is always something special, and he always lives what he believes.

I've been connected with the paranormal for almost half of my lifetime, and I have read an enormous amount of applicable literature, but this is one of the best examples of how to integrate one's personal experience. A reader could look at this as a practical guide on how to lead a metaphysical life. Skip Atwater definitely lives his talk. If you are looking for ground-floor examples of how inner guidance can improve your life or bring focus to your existence, then I strongly recommend you take the phone off the hook and settle in for awhile, because it will be hard to put down. But don't just read it, go out and experience it for yourself. This is a beautiful book that comes straight from Skip Atwater's heart. For everyone who might read this book and benefit from it, thank you, Skip.

Joseph W. McMoneagle, CW2, USA Ret.
Author, *Remote Viewing Secrets*

Foreword

BY DEAN RADIN, PH.D.

Some ideas are so paradigm shattering, so unsettling, and so inconceivable, that they remain hidden in plain sight for many years. One such idea is that we can sometimes perceive objects and events beyond the reach of the ordinary senses, unbound by the usual constraints of space and time. This idea, called clairvoyance or, in modern guise, "remote viewing," has persisted throughout history and is known in all cultures.

Until recently, whenever the topic of remote viewing was raised it was typically cast into one of three forms: The religiously inclined saw it as either divine or blasphemous, the entertainment industry used it as an attention-getting plot element, and many scientists considered belief in it as an indicator of mass delusion, or worse. Indeed, many scientists considered remote viewing nonsensical because such phenomena could not exist in the common sense world of local, isolated objects, forces, and fields. Few scientists imagined that remote viewing (or psychic phenomena in general) was actually a reflection, in human experiential terms, of a new, more comprehensive view of reality. Today, physics has revealed a deeply interconnected, nonlocal universe where at some level everything really is connected to everything else. In such a reality, remote viewing not only can, but must exist.

Books on nonlocality and interconnectedness are now proliferating, there is a restlessness in fundamental physics, and previously unthinkable visions of reality are becoming thinkable. Skip Atwater's book plays an important role in the jigsaw puzzle struggling to take shape, and it serves as a powerful indicator of how close we are to a radical shift in our understanding of who and what we are. The fact is that not long ago, while the scientific mainstream was busy ridiculing the mere possibility of remote viewing, Captain Atwater and others were actively using it in highly classified intelligence gathering programs.

I was one of a few scientists who were quietly working on the research side of those secret programs, trying to understand the basic phenomena and to find ways of improving them. It was an enormously stimulating job. We regularly observed so-called "impossible" psychic phenomena under rigorously controlled laboratory conditions, but unfortunately, because the program was classified, we could not discuss our results openly. As a result, I was sometimes amused but more often frustrated when dealing with skeptics who vigorously argued that the phenomena we were studying on a daily basis didn't exist. For many years, my colleagues and I had to wait quietly on the sidelines, knowing that some day the world, or at least a subset of confirmed skeptics, was in for a big shock. They would learn that human beings were capable of far, far more than science textbooks admitted.

I looked forward to the day when the existence of the classified remote-viewing programs would be formally acknowledged, because I knew that this revelation would slowly stimulate a serious reconsideration of our assumptions about what human beings are, and what we are capable of. As it turned out, I only had to wait about ten years.

Now we are beginning to read the personal accounts of individuals involved in the U.S. government's remote-viewing efforts. We'll eventually see similar books published by individuals who were our research and operations counterparts from other countries. The existence of these books is one reason that we're beginning to see significant changes in mainstream scientific opinion about psychic phenomena. Today, only uninformed, hardcore skeptics still argue that these effects are impossible. In contrast, informed skeptics are reluctantly admitting that scientific studies have confirmed the existence of "anomalous" effects that no one can explain. In another decade or two, as more of the stories are told, and especially as more of the scientific research is published, the reality of these phenomena will begin to sink in. And then our ideas about reality itself will begin to change.

Skip Atwater's book is a key chapter in this very important, still-unfolding story. It illuminates a piece of history that until very recently has been shrouded in mystery and intrigue. I trust you'll be as thrilled to read it as I was.

Dean Radin, Ph.D.
Boundary Institute

Part One:

Child, Soldier, Counterspy

Chapter One

The Awakening

In the spring of 1977, I was just getting started in the U.S. Army's secret counterintelligence remote-viewing operations at Fort Meade, Maryland. Seeking information on organizations and techniques that could benefit our military goals, I got in touch with The Monroe Institute of Applied Sciences. Because of the secrecy surrounding my military mission, I could not reveal the true nature of my inquiry at the Institute. I didn't conceal the fact that I was a military intelligence officer but stated simply that I had read Bob Monroe's book, *Journeys Out of the Body*, and was curious about his research and facilities and whether others could be taught his techniques. I was asked to leave a phone number. I asked to meet and talk with Bob Monroe. And in a day or two, much to my surprise, Mr. Monroe himself called back and provided me with directions from my base of operations in the Washington, D.C., area to Whistlefield Farm, a 432-acre estate—his Virginia home.

As I drove around the Washington, D.C., Capital Beltway, west on Interstate 66, and south on U.S. 29, I somehow knew I was headed for another of life's grand adventures. As I drove deeper into the rural Virginia countryside, my thoughts drifted between expectations and daydreams. I wondered about this man. Others had written of their so-called out-of-body experiences, but Monroe's work was somehow different. Monroe went beyond reporting the trivialities of extra-corporeal visits to friends, neighbors, and distant places in the world. He wrote of visiting other dimensions or, as he put it, other locales—realms beyond the physical world reminiscent of my childhood understanding of a "spiritual" domain representative of our true nature. Of course, such thoughts extended beyond my *official* interest in Monroe and the possible application of his techniques for military remote viewing.

The farther south I traveled on U.S. 29, the more I noticed the oncoming spring. Trees seemed fuller, greener, and some filled with blossoms. I stopped at a roadside fast-food restaurant for a cup of coffee. The waitress spoke with a placid southern accent that somehow graced the experience of springtime itself. As I drove south and west of Charlottesville, the homes changed from apartments, townhouses, and real-estate efficient tract houses to rural single-family dwellings surrounded by proportional parcels of open land.

Beyond these modest homes there were working farms, hayfields, and grazing livestock until I approached the Blue Ridge Mountains. Here, the homes reflected an entirely different culture—or at least economic class. These Virginia estates, with their manicured lawns and carefully landscaped properties, had their own names. Apparently this longstanding tradition still persisted here in rural Virginia, something I hadn't noticed along the greater Baltimore-Washington corridor. As I whizzed by these elegant homes at fifty-five miles an hour, I kept reviewing the driving instructions Bob Monroe had given me and wondering what I would find when I finally reached my destination.

The Whistlefield Farm homestead stretched across a broad, open meadow in a receding valley hidden in the foothills of Virginia's Blue Ridge Mountains. It was quite elegant, containing a main house and several outbuildings, including barns for hay, horses, and tractors, a huge, glass greenhouse, and guest quarters, which the family referred to as the Owl House. Near the property entrance was a building with the office and lab facilities for The Monroe Institute of Applied Sciences.

When I approached the house, Nancy Monroe, Bob's wife, met me at the door. Clearly, Nancy was a southern belle. Wearing a beautiful print dress, tasteful jewelry, and fresh nail polish, she exuded a gracious, ladylike manner. She spoke with a gentle, southern accent, a leisurely segue from word to word that mysteriously focused one's attention and stirred the fires of the soul. Her eyes sparkled from within, as though an inner bright light, a knowingness, was somehow leaking out. With a broad smile, Nancy welcomed me into the house and guided me through various rooms and out to a small patio where Mr. Monroe was waiting. This screened-in patio area was part of the house and perhaps a step or two below the main floor level.

Mr. Monroe, sitting on a divan in the patio, wore sweatpants, suspenders, slippers, and a partially unbuttoned, coffee-stained shirt. His appearance presented an interesting departure from Nancy's. As he brushed cigarette ashes off his shirt, he looked up and calmly said, "Well, hello." No southern accent here. No pretentious social niceties either. I thought—as a first impression—that perhaps he was more interested in who he was "out-of-body" rather than what I might think of him or how I might perceive him in the physical.

I introduced myself, telling him that I had read his book and was fascinated with his work. Nancy graciously offered me some iced tea, then withdrew quietly into the main house and left us alone to talk. Thinking back, this was very typical and quite appropriate—for a proper, southern lady raised in the mid-twentieth century.

Bob spoke freely and openly about his book and his personal experiences. At times, an occasional glance from his penetrating blue eyes seemed as though he was seeing beyond my overt military persona and speaking directly to my soul. I felt uneasy about this, somewhat vulnerable, as the official purpose of my visit was considered classified.

Bob asked me to walk around outside with him in the sun-warmed spring air so that we might enjoy the picturesque and fragrant spring blossoms. He showed me the greenhouse and the gardens, and we eventually settled down to continue our talk on a grassy slope near his laboratory and offices. Sitting there at the base of a flowering fruit tree, I found myself thinking about my own out-of-body experiences that I remembered from childhood. Bob encouraged me to share my thoughts with him.

I started by telling Bob about my earliest remembered out-of-body event, which had to do with the fact that I was a bed-wetter until I was about ten years old. I don't remember my parents or my sisters ever ridiculing me or teasing me about bed-wetting. They would casually remind me to go to the bathroom before going to bed. If I had an accident at night, I just told my mom, who would tell me to take a shower or bath and she would change my bed or ask me to put my bedding in the laundry so it could be washed. Even though I was not criticized at home, there was talk at school about bed-wetting and I knew enough to keep this bed-wetting thing a secret.

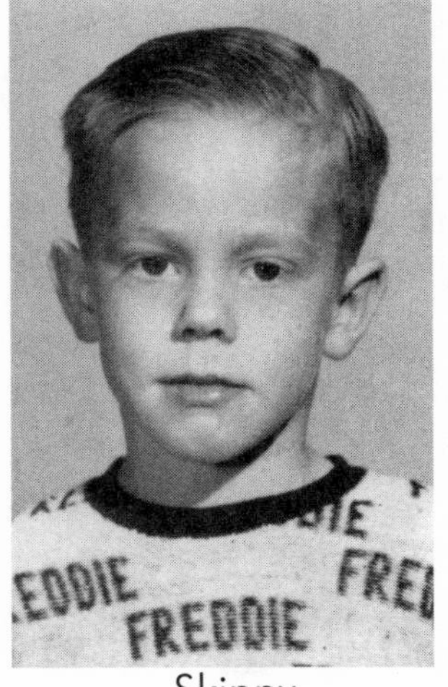

Skippy

As I grew up, I began to have fewer and fewer bed-wetting incidents, but each time it happened it made me angrier. I became more and more frustrated. I didn't like wetting my bed and I didn't like that funny, brown, rubber mat Mom always put under my sheets to protect the mattress. One final time, I woke up wet, yelled out in frustration, and began to cry.

Mom came running into my room and asked what was the matter. I showed her my wet pajamas, sheets, and blankets and began to scream at her, "I went to the bathroom. I went to the bathroom. I went to the bathroom." She told me to calm down and tell her exactly what had happened. I told her that I knew I needed to go to the bathroom and I went in there and sat on the toilet. But when I started to pee, I woke up in my bed and I was all wet. Standing there in my wet pajamas, my crying subsided, only to be replaced with fitful anger.

Mom reached out to me and gently put her hand on my shoulder, smiled, and said simply, "Oh!" I wiped away my tears and asked her what had happened to me. She said that when I went into the bathroom I must have forgotten to take my body with me. I asked her what she meant, and she explained that I only spend part of the time in my body and that when I had gone into the bathroom I probably just went without it. Somehow, this made sense to me and I never did wet the bed again.

Bob smiled and asked if this was the only time that I remembered being out of my body. "No," I said, and went on to tell him that after my mom had told me about being apart from my physical body when I wet my bed, I began to pay attention to what happened when I went to sleep at night. I noticed that I attended some kind of "night school" with others whom I recognized. If I didn't focus too much on this "night school," I could travel out-of-body and go play with neighborhood friends.

When I got a little older, these nightly sojourns changed. I visited school friends and approached people, girls especially, outside the confines of an adolescent social structure that severely limited my interactions with the opposite sex.

I became particularly interested in a blue-eyed girl with curly, auburn hair named Kathy. I found out where Kathy lived by following the school bus to her stop and then casually riding by on my bike while she walked to her house. She lived farther from school than I did but in a familiar area. At the time, I had a paper route and delivered the town paper throughout her neighborhood.

From then on, I could always find her house when I traveled out-of-body. Late at night, I would float in the air outside her house and hope that she would come out. A couple of times, I drifted through the house trying to find her. I never did.

I went on to tell Bob that as I moved deeper into my teenage years and fantasized about living apart from parental oversight, I began to have nocturnal out-of-body sojourns to a particular house in a forested area. I explained to Bob that I would always approach the house from an altitude and was able to see it surrounded by trees on a forest-covered mountainside. As I swooped down to ground level and moved closer to the front of the house, I noticed that it had board-patterned siding (i.e., not stucco or cement blocks) and was nestled into the woods.

Through the years, I visited this location over and over again. On several occasions, I drifted into the house and discovered that it had an antique-looking desk downstairs at the foot of the staircase. There was also a greenhouse attached to the side of the house. I thought I saw two small sets of stairs leading to the greenhouse from the main structure. At the time I was telling Bob of this out-of-body experience, I didn't realize that the structure I was describing was to become my future home, a house I would build myself.

Having taken considerable time telling Bob about these and some other childhood out-of-body experiences, I felt I had said enough and wanted to get on to the purpose for my visit, which, because of military secrecy, I could not fully disclose. I started thinking about how I could turn the conversation.

We sat in silence, which felt awkward to me, for a minute or two. Then Bob began to explain that he had developed a sound technology, a stimulus that allowed people to have experiences under laboratory conditions—experiences that were similar to what he had written about in his book and to those I had been talking about myself. He said that many of these people could talk about or report their experiences while they were happening.

I couldn't imagine how this could be done, given the memory of my own childhood out-of-body experiences. I asked how it was possible, and Bob replied, "Well, kid, I guess we'll just have to show you." And with that, Bob invited me into his laboratory and offices.

We had not yet visited this building, and I had been wondering why he had not taken me there during our walk around the property. As we worked our way up the slope toward the building, I thought, "Maybe he's going to show me an out-of-body experiment in progress. There must be an ongoing experiment in the lab and he's going to let me observe."

As we entered the building, I said a polite hello to the receptionist and followed Bob down a hall, passing a room with a lot of recording equipment, switching panels, and audio-mixing boards.

We turned into a small room with a bed. Bob told me to lie down in the bed and he would play some sounds for me. I was startled by his suggestion and looked quickly around the room.

It was a plain, very plain, room without windows or any regular furniture. The bed did not stick out into the room but was seemingly built into the wall. It was recessed back into the wall surface so that it did not take up any floor space in the rather small room. I moved toward the bed and asked hesitantly, "Do you want me to lie here?" He told me to lie down and put on the stereo headphones that were on the pillow.

As I complied, I asked what kinds of sounds I would be hearing. He said that he would first play some music for me so that I would be comfortable. As I reclined with the headphones on, I noticed something hanging down in front of my face. I asked what this was. He told me not to worry about it, that it was a microphone so that he would be able to hear me in the other room—meaning, I guessed, the room with all the equipment we had passed going down the hallway. He asked me if I was comfortable, then turned out the lights in the room and closed the door.

Within a minute or so, I heard music through the headphones. This wasn't music that I had heard before and I thought it rather strange. (I learned later that the music was from a composer named Tomida, who became well known for his baroque, new-age music.) I relaxed a bit, and after a while the music faded into the sound of waves crashing on the beach.

Bob, speaking through my headphones, said, "This is the sound of surf. It represents the natural power of sound and is a symbol here at the Institute." I liked the surf sound. It reminded me of the beach and of happy times in California, where I grew up. I imagined the waves crashing up on the sand and receding back into the sea, and I thought I could even hear the popping hiss of bubbles in the beach sand when the water receded.

The sound of the crashing waves faded, leaving a warm hiss reminiscent of the gentle whoosh of bubbly foam as it soaks into the beach sand. I waited, thinking there might be another wave, and I began to experience an unusual auditory sensation, a slow, rhythmic pulse. I couldn't tell where it was coming from. It seemed to be in the background, behind or underneath the warm, hissing noise. At one point, I was sure that the pulsing was actually coming from inside my own head.

But I quickly forgot about the sound and my thoughts began to drift—until I noticed that the bed seemed to be moving up toward the ceiling. The sensation of movement was unmistakable, but I couldn't hear the mechanism working to raise the bed. This was really interesting.

I assumed that Mr. Monroe had control of the bed from the room with all the equipment. I thought the mechanism must be like the hydraulic lift that mechanics use on cars when they do an oil change. But I still couldn't hear an air compressor or any other mechanical noise. I wondered how such a device could have been installed at a private residence and thought maybe someday I could have such a device in my garage. As these random thoughts dissipated, I discovered that I was traveling.

My kinesthetic sense of motion (like the feeling you get when flying in an airplane) was accompanied by a strange visual perception. I seemed to be moving through a white tube or tunnel, its walls lined with crystalline forms. My impression was that I must have been flying down the middle of a Flavor Straw.[1] I was going quite fast. In *Star Trek* terms, I would estimate my speed at about warp seven.

Bob's voice came to me over the earphones. "What's happening?"

"I seem to be going somewhere."

"Where are you going?"

"I don't know."

By this time, I had forgotten all about the room and the strange bed. My journey through this passageway continued for what seemed to be a long while. Eventually, I sensed that I was coming to the end of the Flavor Straw and I arched my back, following the upswing curve of the tube. Above me, I could see a vast, open, white area.

---

1 I remembered Flavor Straws from when I was a kid. They were straws with flavored sugar crystals inside, which flavored the milk, water, or whatever I had.

Just as I began to exit the tube, my perspective switched, and suddenly I was standing in the boundless white space watching myself emerge from the end of the Flavor Straw. At almost the same moment, knowingness, a revelation, filled my mind. I had come all this way, only to discover that I was already there.

Realizing this, I must have exclaimed, "Oh!" or something similar, because Bob immediately spoke to me through my headphones, asking, "What happened?" His voice startled me. I had forgotten all about him. For a moment, I thought he must be in this white space with me somewhere. I regained my composure and answered by saying, "I'll have to tell you later."

I explored this white space for some time, but today I do not consciously remember much of what I found there. I am sure it was meaningful in some way, but I cannot recall the particulars.

Bob startled me again. He said that it was time to get some lunch and that we should finish up. The very concept of lunch seemed strange to me in the vast white space. But then he changed the sound patterns, and I became aware of being back in the room in the building in the Virginia countryside. I felt myself, or perhaps the bed, being lowered back down. Again, the sense of motion was obvious, but it was very gentle, and I couldn't perceive any mechanical noise or vibration. I wondered how a hydraulic lift could be so smooth.

The lights came on in the room and I felt disoriented. For a moment, I couldn't quite figure out where I was. Then Bob came into the room and started urging me to get up and move out into the sunshine. I sat up, turned, swung my legs over the edge of the bed, and rested my feet on the floor. I bent over and raised the blanket that was draped over the edge of the bed and looked under the bed. There was no lift mechanism, just a floor. The bed frame was actually rather crudely built out of two-by-four framing lumber and a sheet of plywood.

Seeing me bent over, Bob asked if I had dropped my wallet or watch on the floor. I looked up at him and told him that I hadn't. Again, he urged me to stand and walk outside. As we went down the hall toward the exit, he kept asking me what I wanted to eat for lunch. At the time, his voice seemed loud and somewhat annoying. I told him that it didn't matter to me. Secretly, in my mind I was thinking that if I could get a six-pack of whatever had just happened to me, I would take that for lunch.

We ate at a restaurant a few miles from Whistlefield on top of the Blue Ridge Mountains. Bob explained that I had experienced a sound technology he had developed and patented. He called this technology Hemi-Sync[2] because the two halves of the brain worked together, or in synchrony, to enable the auditory beating or pulsing I had experienced. He said that many people had been able to experience a wide range of expanded states of consciousness with this technology. When I told him about the sensation of rising up to the ceiling, he smiled and assured me that the bed did not move. Recognizing only then what had really happened to me, I asked if everybody had out-of-body experiences with this Hemi-Sync sound. He said that not everybody remembers or reports such experiences and that the Hemi-Sync sounds only encourage a "mind awake—body asleep" state, not necessarily an out-of-body experience. He said that the experiences people have in this state depended on their intent and motivation and can be limited by their fears and belief systems.

At the time, I didn't understand all he was saying and I wondered why I had floated out-of-body so easily. I asked Bob if the Hemi-Sync sounds he had used with me in the laboratory were special in any way. He said that the sounds weren't special and that he suspected that I would be able to get out-of-body rather easily based on what I had told him about my childhood experiences. He went on, "From what you told me, you must have been in contact with or guided by something greater than your physical body for some time now. Surely, you have a sense of self that is greater than your physical body? Children intuitively know this until such awareness is subdued by social conditioning. Apparently this knowing, this awareness, of a greater self was not discouraged during your upbringing."

---

[2] Hemi-Sync is a registered trademark of Interstate Industries, Inc.

I understood what Bob was talking about. We all grow up thinking, believing, and knowing that in whatever the circumstance we find ourselves, it's normal. Poor folks don't think of themselves as poor. They see themselves as normal. Children in horribly dysfunctional families establish a comfort zone of normality in such relationships and strive to recreate similar family units for themselves in adulthood. Heterosexuals think of themselves as normal and measure others' lifestyles by their own reference frame. Until some authority from outside tells us there is something wrong, or different, or strange about our family or us, we grow up under the illusion that we are normal.

I knew my family and myself as normal, regular just like everybody else. I still know that to be true today as a middle-aged adult. But, in the intervening years between then and now, there were mindful reflections, some re-membering (as in realizing wholeness again), and this awakening out-of-body experience at thirty years old with Bob Monroe was helpful, too.

As Bob said at lunch that day, I had a sense of self greater than my physical body, some form of Guidance, greater than my physical, ego-centered self. But just what is this thing called Guidance anyway?

It seems to me that we use the word Guidance as a convenient way to express a notion that is perhaps somewhat beyond a comprehensive, verbal explanation. The term Guidance seems to convey the notion that something outside of ourselves is providing sage advice. But let's not get bogged down in this quagmire, as I suspect that Guidance is metaphoric for something else altogether.

The word trip, as in "LSD trip," says to us that one doesn't really go anywhere yet experiences the world—*All That Is*—differently. This voyage, this journey through earthly life, is a real *trip*. So if what we are experiencing—electromagnetic physical reality, earthly life—is actually a trip of sorts, then who, what, where, and when are we?

This question, of course, has been posed before in other words and in other ways. But the answer is always the same. We are, have always been, and always will be one with God. The illusion of time and space simply provides for a sea of experience. Realizing this, it is easy to see that Guidance does not come from outside us, for there is nothing "outside" of *All That Is*—God. This whole notion of my true spiritual identity has its earthly root in my "normal" childhood, in both my family life and religious education.

For several years, the family was very active in the Unity church. Dad helped build a new chapel, and when the construction was finished the family attended church regularly (should I say religiously?). I went to Sunday school and learned Bible stories. My sisters were involved with the church too. I learned later that my parents, who were very spiritual but not particularly religious, got the family involved with the Unity church expressly to provide us a religious education and some exposure to organized religions. As it turned out, the religious teachings provided a supportive environment, a language framework in which to express and learn things beyond the accepted boundaries of everyday life.

Throughout childhood, we had a wide range of family pets. Dad built a barn and for a time my sister Sandy had a burro named Eleanor for a pet. Over the years, I remember having various dogs, cats, fish, desert turtles, and ducks.

Inevitably, animals died. When this would happen, Mom would usually comment within a day or two that she had seen or communicated with the pet that had died. Mom would casually say something like, "I saw [name of dead pet] in the hall. He told me that he was fine and we shouldn't worry about him anymore." These sorts of comments fit well with the concepts being taught every Sunday in church.

My religious education focused on the importance of a spiritual existence beyond our perception of the physical. The church taught that this spiritual existence was the "real" everlasting reality. What we see around us, as our physical world, constitutes the ephemeral and limited. The act of birth itself positions most of us to view the apparent world through a monocle, a lens through which only the physical world can be perceived. Death frees us from this finite perspective.

Physical existence should not be taken lightly or thought of as unimportant, however. Some would say that we pass from spirit or the spiritual realm into the physical at birth and conversely pass from the physical world into spirit at death. However, I was taught, and it is my own experience, that we never pass *from* the spirit. We are always spiritual beings, even when having a physical experience. Our spiritual selves experience what we experience in the physical world. The Sunday school teachings sought to encourage orienting one's perspective from the spiritual and, therefore, seeing the physical world through spiritual eyes, so to speak.

The family listened to Mom report meetings with dead pets and, later, dead grandparents. This all seemed very reasonable to me, given my formal religious education. But at home this other nonphysical world was not referred to as holy. There was no mention of heaven or God or Christ or some other religious icon. It was just accepted as a matter of fact that the "real" world included more than what we could discern with our five physical senses.

As I got older, the family left the Unity church, and as I approached my teens I was dragged along to the Science of Mind church every Sunday. There was no more Sunday school, Bible classes, or socializing with other kids. I usually sat through the service politely. I wasn't particularly interested in what the minister had to say, but I did enjoy looking at all the people who showed up. As far as I was concerned, the biggest attraction of the Science of Mind church was that the actor Lloyd Bridges, the star of the *Sea Hunt* television series, went there. Every Sunday, I would look for him standing around outside the church just before or after the service. Another attraction was that we always went out to lunch after church.

After my sisters had grown up and left home, I was an only child and Dad's successful dental practice meant that the family was financially secure. There was more discretionary money for going out to eat. This was the late fifties; going out to eat was a meaningful family experience.

One particular Sunday, during the service at the Science of Mind church, the minister caught my ear with something he was saying about taking personal responsibility. As I looked up at him, I noticed what appeared to be a blue light-bubble surrounding his head and shoulders. This was not a spotlight; as he leaned or moved slightly to the right or left the bubble seemed to follow him.

I watched this "*light*" for several minutes until I turned to my mom and asked, "What is that blue light around the minister?" Mom whispered to me, "That's called his aura. I'll tell you about it at lunch. You can pick the restaurant today." She raised her index finger to her lips and whispered, "Be quiet for now so that everybody can hear what he is saying." I looked back at the minister and watched the blue bubble for the rest of the service.

And lunch? I don't remember where we went or if Mom told me anything about the minister's aura. What I do remember, looking back fifty years, is that such subjects were addressed casually, as if to communicate, "Everybody knows that." Such an attitude left no reason to question or to doubt the veracity of such parental guidance.

There was something else, too. The church-oriented religious education of my youth seemed to focus on a spiritual aspect of us, usually talked about relative to a life-after-death existence, and a physical aspect involved with life, as we know it here on Earth. The doctrine of the church did not emphasize a distinction between these two expressions, but, as a practical matter, the church teachings did. At home, there was less separation between these two perspectives. Expectation and realization of a whole being came from a family life, a behavior, treatment of one another, conversations, and an identification with a spiritual self who was, as the expression goes, in this world but not of it.

The teachings of the church would lead one to believe that we are physical creatures that have a soul or a spirit and that these aspects of self are somehow separate. At home, we were taught to realize (to make real) that we are always and always will be spirit and sometimes have physical experiences. These physical experiences never disconnect us from who we really are. Of course, when I was ten or twelve years old, I didn't understand all this. I thought my parents were really dumb and old-fashioned.

Relatives and close friends of my parents spoke of spiritual things as well. My father was raised as a Christian Scientist, and so the concept that healing was connected to the greater spiritual reality beyond the physical filtered into family thinking. Oddly, my father, his father, and his grandfather were all dentists. And I remember going to doctors and getting medical treatment. I don't remember any talk about spiritual healing. I think behavior spoke of healing (and perhaps getting injured or getting sick in the first place) as being a personal responsibility.

Recently, a friend of the family for more than fifty years said that the one thing she remembered was my mother healing the burned hands of our housekeeper. As the story goes, our housekeeper burned her hands in a stove accident and yelled to my mother, "Mrs. Atwater, Mrs. Atwater, come help me! Please come help me!" Mom came immediately and calmly held the housekeeper's hands in her own until the pain disappeared. From that day forward, the housekeeper told everybody how Mrs. Atwater had healed her hands. I was just a toddler at the time.

Until recently, neither my sister nor I recalled this story that was so clear in the memory of our family friend. But such things were just normal around our house. I grew up seeing miracles as normal, regular, and happening to us just like everybody else. I tell people I grew up in a metaphysical or metaphysically oriented family. Some people say, "Oh," or, "Isn't that wonderful." Others ask, "What do you mean?" And to them, I reply with memories and little stories, like the following, of my "normal" childhood.

One of my childhood chores was trimming the ivy that cascaded over a rock wall bordering the driveway. I remember clearly one particular Saturday when I wanted to play with my neighborhood friend, Mike. Before I could go play, I had to finish cutting back the ivy.

On this particular Saturday, my forearms broke out in a rash as I worked on the ivy. I showed my dad and told him that I couldn't cut the ivy. He told me straight out that I had done this to myself because I wanted so much to go play with Mike. "Who, me, Dad? No, really, I want to finish my chores, but I can't," was my retort.

Calmly, without a change in facial expression, he told me to go in the house and tell Mom what had happened. I found Mom and showed her my arms. She asked what had happened and I told her, "My arms broke out in a rash while I was cutting the ivy because I want to go down to Mike's house." Oops! I waited to see if she had heard what I said.

She asked if my arms had ever done this before when I cut the ivy. I answered, "No, never." She told me to wash up with soap and water and go back outside. When I got back outside, Dad was trimming back the ivy.

I said, "I'll do that; it's my chore."

He said, "Not today. Today you had better go see Mike. The ivy will grow back and you can trim it when it does. Today with Mike will never come again." And with that bit of wisdom, he sent me off to play. Dad was right. The ivy did grow back, and I trimmed it many times after that one Saturday. I don't remember what happened to the rash on my arms, but I'll bet it didn't bother me at all while I was playing with Mike.

As a child, what I took away from such family experiences was that you might go to a doctor to set a broken leg or repair an internal organ but *healing*—whatever that was—became the responsibility of one's true spiritual identity.

Another example of the "normalcy" of my upbringing took place on the first days of kindergarten. Mom made a point of showing me that parents brought kids to school and picked them up in cars that were different than ours. We had an Oldsmobile station wagon, circa mid-1950s. The Oldsmobile had a distinctive, exterior visor over the windshield. This was in the days before tinted glass. My mother's point was to ensure that I didn't get into the wrong car and get kidnapped or something.

I recall this car so distinctively because one day when Mom picked me up from kindergarten, she made a U-turn from the curb in front of the school. I went flying out of the door, propelled by the centrifugal force of the turning car. Cars didn't have seat belts back then and the passenger side door had not closed properly. I remember looking desperately into Mom's eyes as I flew out of the car. I somehow never hit the ground, though. I remained suspended in midair until Mom stopped the car, and I then gently floated back into my seat. She asked if I was okay and remarked that we should be more careful. At the time, it didn't occur to me to question why I had not been hurt. And neither Mom nor I thought anything strange of my momentary suspended state.

Throughout her life, Mom would occasionally say, "You will always be taken care of." She never mentioned *who* would be doing this, although today I think she must have been referring to my true spiritual identity. I suppose the kindergarten suspended-in-midair incident must be the earliest memory I have of the validity of her prophetic reminder.

When I was older, my sister told me that Mom always talked about herself and her high school girlfriends practicing levitation in the school gym. Mom said that she and her friends would stand around in a circle, and the person in the center of the circle would lie on the floor. The rest of them would "imagine her being lifted into the air," and she would be.

As a teenager, I became more than just interested in cars. My first car, a 1940 Chevy coupe, was given to me on my sixteenth birthday. I eventually sold the Chevy coupe for seventy-five dollars and bought my Uncle Willie's 1954 Ford sedan for one hundred dollars. Uncle Gene gave me an old 292-Thunderbird engine, and I went to work building a muscle car. I had the 292 punched out to three hundred cubic inches, installed new pistons, a three-quarters-race camshaft, dual four-barrel carburetors, dual exhaust, an aluminum flywheel, and a three-speed manual transmission with a heavy-duty clutch.

I was seriously ready for San Fernando Boulevard in 1964. Within two years, I went through twenty-seven transmissions by dumping the clutch. I could get used transmissions at the junkyard for about twenty dollars. It got to the point where I could change out the transmission in that car in less than thirty minutes, and I never missed a Saturday night. I eventually went to a Muncie four-speed with Hurst linkage, which resolved the transmission replacement problem.

The point here is that throughout all this I became aware that I had an uncanny ability with mechanical things. All I had to do was just think about or focus my attention on the car and I would be able to see inside it. The first time this happened was with the U-joint on the 1940 Chevy. I could see worn or broken parts, movement, oil flowing, etc. I began to believe that when people took their cars to a mechanic, the mechanic was skilled in doing what seemed to come natural to me. I soon learned this wasn't true at all. Most mechanics did not have this ability.

Ten years hence, scientists would come to call this process *remote viewing*, a perceptual technique based on an innate human ability to mentally perceive and describe things separated or blocked by distance, shielding, or even time. That brings me back to my visit with Bob Monroe and that point in my military career when I was involved with remote viewing. What spiritual forces had guided me to this point in time? Had this divine intercession been limited to my childhood or had it always been with me, hidden in the shadows of my everyday life?

Chapter Two

Special Agent

At the end of the first semester of my third year in college, the draft board discovered that I had not been attending classes. "Greetings," the first line of the draft notice read. I was ordered to appear for a physical exam to ensure my eligibility for military service.

What a load of crap! I had just been offered a promotion at work. Well, there was only one thing to do if I was going to avoid the draft. I needed to join the army. (Wait a minute! Who came up with that? Another expression of Guidance?)

That very day, I walked into the army recruiting office and asked about joining up. The sergeant, a tall Adonis in uniform, explained to me that there were a number of excellent jobs and outstanding opportunities within the army and that if I was qualified I could select a position for which I would be trained and eventually serve. The easiest positions to get were the ones with the most vacancies, the ones the army needed the most, e.g., medics and infantrymen—who would most certainly be sent immediately to Vietnam.

An incredible calmness came over me as I picked up one of the small booklets from the display rack. On the back cover in bold, blue letters, centered below an official-looking golden insignia were the words "Army Intelligence." Below these words, it simply said in small-font, black type, "for those who are qualified."

Without looking at the pages in the booklet, I showed the back cover to the recruiting sergeant and asked, "What about this?" The sergeant replied by asking me how old I was, had I been to college, and had I ever been in trouble with the law. I explained that I had two years of college and had never been arrested. He told me that, due to army regulations, he couldn't interview me for a position with Army Intelligence but that he could set up an appointment for me if I was interested.

Looking the poster-boy recruiting sergeant straight in the eye and pointing to the back cover of the booklet, I spoke softly, as if I were repeating words being whispered somehow directly into my mind about a course of action perhaps charted long ago, "This is what I am here for." And with that one utterance, my childhood was over, a youth that had been filled with "normal" experiences, psychic and spiritual realities I did not yet appreciate.

I joined the U.S. Army on the delayed-entry program, to delay my army training cycle so that I would be twenty-one when I graduated from Advanced Individual Training, or AIT. The minimum age requirement for training to become a counterintelligence special agent was twenty-one.

Before I left for basic training in February 1968, I had what was probably my first adult conversation with my mother. Sitting at the round, oak table in the kitchen, I told Mom that I was having second thoughts about joining the army because I didn't think I could actually shoot anyone. Without bringing up moral issues of killing, Mom told me that in life I would be presented with many circumstances that would temper my soul and that if shooting someone was not in my best interests such a circumstance would not emerge. It never did. Oh . . . she also reminded me once again that I would always be taken care of.

On a different note, the last thing the recruiting sergeant said to me before I left for basic training was helpful to me over the next two months and, as it turned out, over the rest of my entire military career. This veteran sergeant told me that basic training was all about learning what it was like to be a soldier and that I would never forget the experience. These were important words for me before I entered the elite intelligence community. Whatever I did in the intelligence field, it was important to remember the intensity, the devotion of the combat soldier. Perhaps this well-seasoned recruiting sergeant was divinely guided to touch base with me in this way just at this moment in my life.

Basic Training

On February 14, 1968, I became Private Frederick H. Atwater and I raised my right hand in an oath of allegiance to America and a promise to obey the orders of my military superiors. I boarded a bus in downtown Los Angeles bound for Fort Ord, California—and the next twenty years of my life.

This was the Vietnam era, and the drill sergeants at Fort Ord were hardened combat veterans. The lieutenants, on the other hand, had been in the army *all day long* and offered little leadership for the new recruits. They looked good though, in their starched uniforms and shiny black helmet liners. I quickly recognized basic training for what it was. My reaction (as in "perform an act that had served me well before") to the trials and tribulations of basic training was to become invisible, and the first confirmation of the advantages of invisibility happened within hours of arrival at Fort Ord.

A drill sergeant in a freshly starched uniform, highly polished boots, and wearing a Smokey-the-Bear hat strutted into the barracks and demanded to know if any of the new recruits had a license to drive. He said that he needed at least two privates for special duty. Several lanky kids raised their hands and were subsequently instructed to step forward. Standing with his hands on his hips, the drill sergeant looked over the group of recruits who, having just had all their hair cut off, were no longer seen by him as individuals but as soldiers. He picked out four qualified volunteers (they had raised their hands) and ordered them to get brooms out of the closet and drive them around the floor of the barracks.

From my invisible venue, basic training was relatively uneventful. Early-morning physical training, called PT, was accompanied by the compulsory dirge, "More PT, drill sergeant!" Each day's training became a simple routine—well, almost every day's training. It seemed Guidance was once again with me. But there were some trying times.

The visit to the gas chamber scared the shit out of everyone. Once your training company had "done the gas chamber," you were considered an authority on such life-and-death matters. There were always stories about the gas chamber shared by brave survivors. A couple of days before we went into the gas chamber, a soldier in the company in the barracks next door yelled out his window that they had just done the gas chamber and that only three people in the whole company had died. Keep in mind that nobody really dies in the gas chamber; they only wish they could to escape the misery. But naïve kids becoming soldiers don't find this out until they too have done the gas chamber. There is nothing like an experience of CS gas to convince everyone to treasure a gas mask.

For me, the most meaningful part of the whole basic training experience actually happened after I graduated. Shortly before graduation, I was hospitalized with a URI, the ERMA (Easily Remembered Military Acronym) for an upper respiratory infection, otherwise known as pneumonia (a rather pejorative medical expression the army didn't like to use). Because of this, I was unable to proceed on my travel orders to AIT at Fort Holibird, Maryland, the army's intelligence training center.

I was placed in what was known as holdover status for several weeks. During this time, I was an asset of the same training company—B Company, First Battalion, First Brigade—that had been the home of my fellow basic trainees. Except for me, all of my compatriots had moved on to their respective AIT schools.

This proved to be a beneficial experience, which I now see as having been *guided*. A new group of recruits arrived in the company and I became an assistant to the drill instructor. I was no longer addressed like the other recruits as "trainee" but as "Private Atwater." The new recruits looked to me for assistance and some assurance that they would survive basic training. I showed them how to roll their socks, set up their footlockers, and make their beds compliant with the drill sergeant's standards (so tight that a quarter would bounce off the wool blanket).

As the days of my holdover status at Fort Ord turned into weeks, I occasionally visited with the clerks, soldiers like myself, who worked in the orderly room and asked if there was any word on my reassignment orders. There never was. I eventually requested to speak to the first sergeant, a pock-faced Vietnam veteran with a know-it-all attitude when it came to privates. I asked him what had been done to find out about my orders. He said, without the slightest lilt in his voice, "Nothing, nothing at all."

He went on to tell me that his office's only responsibility was the earlier paperwork associated with my being in the hospital. I asked him if there was anything I could do to find out about my orders. He told me the only thing I was supposed to do was to wait . . . to wait for the army. Although he didn't laugh out loud, I suspect that I was the brunt of his NCO-Club jokes over a beer or two later that evening.

When the first sergeant dismissed me, I realized that my questioning the first sergeant had been prompted by divine Guidance. Being who he was, the first sergeant didn't recognize this and thought he was just talking to Private Atwater. Respecting his perspective, I could see he was right. There was little that Private Atwater could do in this situation. But deep inside, beyond the limitations of my lowly military rank, I knew there was much that could be done.

One Thursday morning, I was instructed to escort a newly assigned recruit to an office in another area of Fort Ord for a scheduled appointment of some kind. I was to wait for the recruit and escort him back to the company area when he was through.

When I was assigned this duty, I remembered that before I left home for basic training, the army intelligence people in Los Angeles gave me their office telephone number to call should I have any questions. So while the recruit was busy with his appointment, I found a payphone and called that number. I explained that I had been in the hospital when my class graduated from basic training and that my assignment orders to Fort Holibird had been canceled or "returned," as the clerk in the orderly room had said.

The army intelligence people seemed to feel that my orders shouldn't have been canceled and that the basic training company should have sent me on my way when I got out of the hospital. They gave me a telephone number in the Pentagon and told me to ask for the sergeant major (I forget his name) who was in charge of assignments for all enlisted personnel in Army Intelligence. I was to explain what had happened and ask what I should do.

The minute I hung up the phone, I placed a call to the Pentagon number and asked to speak to the sergeant major. Very politely, knowing that he probably didn't get many calls from privates, I introduced myself as Private Atwater calling from Fort Ord, California. The sergeant major replied, "Yes, Private Atwater, what can I do for you?"

A bit startled by the seemingly warm response, I described my situation and told him that the Los Angeles office had suggested that I call. He said, "You did the right thing, Private." He asked me to confirm that I had completed basic training and I assured him that I had, reiterating that my present job was an assistant drill instructor. He then asked me to spell my name for him and tell him my service number. I complied. He put me on hold for three or four minutes, then came back on the line.

"I have your file here, Private Atwater," he said. "We'd better get you on to Fort Holibird as soon as possible." He told me to return to my company as instructed; he would see what he could do from his end. He ended by saying, "Thank you for calling me, Private Atwater."

Well, that put a smile on my face. I found the recruit I had been escorting and marched him back to the company area. By the time we got back to the company, the morning was gone. Drill sergeants in their starched fatigues were outside the mess hall, harassing the usual line of haggard and hungry trainees before lunch. I delivered the recruit to his platoon and went into the mess hall to get some chow.

I had just finished eating when the company clerk came through the door and said loudly, "Private Atwater, the company commander wants to see you right now!" I asked if he knew why and he said, "You know why. Just get into the orderly room right now." Everybody around me turned and gave me one of those you're-in-trouble-now kind of looks. Confident that Guidance had been working in my favor, I headed for the commander's office.

As I walked into the orderly room, the nervous clerks looked up from their desks. Their eyes followed me as I approached the first sergeant. The first sergeant's eyes met mine and before I could utter an official-sounding "Reporting as ordered, First Sergeant," he told me to take a seat and that the company commander would see me in a minute.

Just as I sat down, the commander came out of his office and headed directly for the first sergeant's desk. Before the captain could speak, the first sergeant gestured toward me and I stood to attention just as the captain's eyes met mine. "Oh, Private Atwater, come into my office," he said as he executed a military about-face and walked quickly back through his door and stepped behind his desk. Remembering my best military etiquette, I glanced at the first sergeant and marched courteously into the captain's office.

Just as he sat in his chair and glanced up at me, I stood at attention in front of his desk, saluted, and said, "Private Atwater reporting, Sir." He returned the salute, ordered me to stand at ease, and said (I think in one big breath), "Atwater, I just got a call from battalion headquarters. They said someone in the Pentagon wants you on an airplane to Fort Holibird tomorrow. You will be on that plane, Atwater. It is my job to see that happens. Pack your things and the first sergeant will drive you to the airport at 0530 hours tomorrow morning. Do you understand, Private?"

"Yes, Sir."

"Dismissed," he barked. I came to attention, saluted, executed an about-face, and marched out of his office. With each step I knew that I was not alone in moving into the next adventure of life. As my mom had said, I would always be taken care of. There was something more to all this than was apparent to my so-called five senses at the time. Bob Monroe would ask me years later, "Surely, you have a sense of self that is greater than your physical body?"

Becoming a Special Agent

I flew into Washington National Airport and checked with the military liaison there about getting to Fort Holibird. As it turned out, there was an army shuttle bus that went directly from the airport to the base. I arrived at my new post late on Friday afternoon. The staff was very well organized, and I was assigned a barracks based on a class cycle. Because this was 1968 in the midst of the Vietnam War, the intelligence school ran classes through as fast as they could, and I joined a class group starting the following Monday.

Many, if not all, experiences at Fort Holibird must have been the result of divine Guidance. Such experiences were to have a profound effect on my course in life. I was, unknowingly, being equipped to deal with future situations in life from a perspective of confidence and knowledge.

Classes at Fort Holibird consisted of about thirty soldiers, most of whom were privates. Some specialists and sergeants who were transferring into intelligence from another military occupational specialty were sometimes included. The ranking soldier became class leader. I immediately noticed the caliber of my classmates. People from all walks of life went through basic training. But at the Army Intelligence School, the general population was carefully screened. I learned later that, for the most part, loyalty, integrity, discretion, morals, and character were apt descriptors for all of us who aspired to be U.S. Army Counterintelligence Special Agents.

Back in that era, a special agent was trained in several aspects of physical security, document security (techniques for the protection of classified material), and personnel security, which amounted to controlling who had access to sensitive material. The duties of the special agent included a wide range of counter-intelligence activities, including the conduct of personnel background investigations, security inspections and surveys, counterespionage and counter-sabotage investigations and activities—and, in Vietnam, battlefield counterintelligence measures.

The intelligence school had three months to prepare us for entry into this elite world of intelligence operatives. I thought the school did a great job, considering the demands of Vietnam for qualified soldiers of all specialties. I especially appreciated the methods used to teach us how to interview character references for those requiring background checks for security clearances. I never guessed, though, that these techniques would become useful years in the future when I would be working with remote viewers, and later with out-of-body voyagers at The Monroe Institute.

The Fort Holibird intelligence school employed actors to play various characters typified over the years as the usual kind of people one may encounter during the conduct of background investigations. On stage in front of our classmates, we interviewed "Mr. Jones" about "Johnny Smith" who had recently joined the army. Mr. Jones played a neighbor, ex-employer, or perhaps a high school teacher or college professor who had some knowledge of the supposed subject of a background investigation.

The actors helped the students along when they needed it and gave them a hard time when a point was to be made. As this was done on stage in front of our classmates, it provided some performance anxiety but also allowed classmates to learn along with the one on stage.

As an example of a learning point, one of the last items to be covered in a background interview is to obtain a recommendation from the interviewee. If we asked the actor, "Would you recommend Johnny Smith for a position of trust and responsibility with the army?" the actor would reply, "Well, if anybody asked me, I might." As a student, the first time we heard this rejoinder we were puzzled. But we all soon learned that there was one, and only one, correct way to ask the original question. The special agent must ask, "Do you recommend Johnny Smith for a position of trust and responsibility with the army?"

Another questioning technique the actors taught was not to ask multiple-choice or double questions that would suggest an answer. For example, asking something like, "Did Johnny ever get into trouble with the police, or was he a pretty good kid?" would be inappropriate. The actors would simply answer back, "Yes."

Sitting there red-faced on stage in front of our classmates, we suddenly realized that either Johnny had been in trouble with the police or perhaps not. We didn't know from the actor's answer. If this was the first time in the hot seat, we were likely to get ourselves in more trouble by asking, "What kind of trouble did he have with the police?" to which the actor would reply, "I don't know. I didn't say that he did."

Confident that we'd figured out the situation, we would continue, "Well, would you say then that he was a pretty good kid?" "I might," the actor would retort, "if anybody would ask me." So there we were, special agents in training, embarrassed in front of our classmates and reduced once again to asking what we should have in the first place, "Did Johnny ever get into trouble with the police?" "No." "Do you consider Johnny to be a pretty good kid?" "Yes." And so on . . .

I admit that I played these games with my kids as they were growing up. I hope they learned to think before opening their mouths as I did back so many years ago. These same skills would prove valuable to me far beyond the confines of my job as a counterintelligence special agent.

One particular event, in retrospect, revealed that I was indeed on the right course, following Guidance. We were about two weeks from graduation and we had begun to review what we had learned. We now had an overall picture in our minds of the scope and duties of the counterintelligence special agent of the late 1960s, which included physical security, document security, and personnel security.

From this perspective, I stood up in class one day and asked about the television pictures taken from space of the surface of the moon, pictures that I had seen on the nightly news broadcast.

Specifically, I asked if such cameras were in Earth orbit taking pictures of the surface of the Earth, and if they were, what were we as counterintelligence specialists to do to guard against hostile exploitation of such pictures? It seemed obvious to me that information from such pictures would be of immense intelligence value, and nothing had been said in class so far about this threat.

A hush filled the classroom as I finished my question. The instructor that day, a young captain, looked me square in the eyes and said in a stern voice, "Private Atwater, sit down. Do not discuss or ask such questions ever again. The purpose of this class is to review the material covered in this course. Do you understand?" "Yes, Sir," I answered, and sat down.

When the class was dismissed, the instructor told me to remain in the classroom for a few minutes. I thought that I was in trouble for insubordination because I had asked a question not covered in his lesson plan. Once he and I were alone in the classroom, he told me that the subject I had asked about was a form of special intelligence so highly classified that it was actually illegal to discuss it in the school building. I was told that since I didn't have the necessary security clearances or an appropriate need to know, I should avoid discussing the subject.

I asked when such discussions might be appropriate, and he told me that conceivably during my career as a special agent I would get an assignment where I would be involved with this kind of work. He reminded me not to discuss "the subject" again and dismissed me. But this same inquisitive nature concerning extraordinary intelligence-collection methods would lead me later in life into the world of military remote viewing.

First Assignment

As young privates, and some seasoned sergeants, about ready to graduate from AIT, we wondered if we too would be sent to Vietnam when we became special agents for what was then called the U.S. Army Intelligence Agency. Classes graduated every week and it seemed to us that about half the classes were sent directly to

Vietnam and the other half got assigned various places around the world. One good friend was assigned to Pasadena, California, his hometown. I envied him and his assignment. I too would have liked to have been assigned back to my hometown for the duration of my enlistment. After all, the only thing I thought I knew was that I had joined the army to avoid getting drafted and sent to Vietnam.

Wrapped up in the intensity of the moment, I forgot (lost consciousness of the fact) that, as my mother had said so long ago, I would always be taken care of. When my assignment orders came through, they were not for Vietnam but another exotic land called Alabama.

Alabama in 1968 was a strange place for a boy raised in the 1950s and 1960s in white, upper-middle-class Glendale, California. This was the land of the burgeoning civil rights movement and marches on Washington, D.C., and some guy named Martin Luther King, Jr. On the brighter side, it wasn't Vietnam.

Fort McClellan—and Anniston, Alabama—turned out to be a blessing. I was on course. Guidance was with me. I met my first wife, Joan, a clerk in the Women's Army Corp. (Women had not yet been integrated into the "regular" army.) Joan grew up in a military family, her father being in the Air Force, and had three brothers who were also in the service. My beautiful bride and I wed in the post chapel in a small ceremony attended by our friends from Fort McClellan but without our families. Our loving marriage thrived for twenty years and was blessed with three wonderful children. Sometimes, very little beyond my wife and family seemed important, but in the larger scheme of things I knew there was more.

As a counterintelligence special agent in Alabama, I discovered through experience how to conduct investigations, research and cite army security regulations, participate in a bureaucracy, talk to and elicit information from people, and work in an office environment with others. But I soon found I was being ever so gently compelled by a spiritual wisdom from within to proceed on course.

I was involved in two fender-bender car accidents in my assigned government vehicle at Fort McClellan. Perhaps they were not accidents as such but incidents manifested by spirit for a greater cause. My administrative punishment for being involved in these accidents in a government vehicle was office duty for two weeks.

For several days, I worked the Teletype machine, which was high-class rapid electronic communications for the late 1960s, in the headquarters building. One day, a notice came in requesting names of special agents interested in training to be electronic-surveillance technicians. I immediately returned the message, pressing the Send key and providing the name Corporal Frederick H. Atwater.

Several days later, a similar request for names of special agents came over the Teletype. This time they wanted volunteers for language school. Acceptance for language training would require worldwide reassignment based on "the needs of the army" for foreign-language-speaking counterintelligence agents. I pressed the Send key again and volunteered for Spanish language training. Within a month, I got orders to begin training on my first request as an electronic-surveillance technician. Language training would follow.

Back to School

Right after getting married, I left Fort McClellan for Redstone Arsenal, Alabama, for training in basic electronics, the first phase of my training in electronic surveillance. Joan left the service and joined me at Redstone Arsenal about a month after the wedding. (In the 1960s, women could be released from military service when they married.) While at Redstone, I got my first real promotion, that is, based on work performance and not just on length of service or attendance at school. I was now Sergeant Atwater.

Before we were to leave Redstone Arsenal to continue my training in electronic surveillance, I received orders to attend Spanish language school in Washington, D.C., upon completion of my training in electronic surveillance. After language school, I was to be assigned to the 470th Military Intelligence Group in the Panama Canal Zone.

We left Redstone Arsenal for Fort Holibird, Maryland, for technical intelligence training in electronic surveillance, and Joan found a job at a corner eatery near the fort. We lived in the rented upstairs rooms of a house near a steel mill in Sparrows Point, Maryland. Joan was soon pregnant with my first son. Somewhere around this same time, I saw man's first walk on the moon on a ten-inch, black-and-white portable television that had been a high-school graduation present from my parents. When I finished my electronic surveillance courses, we moved to Alexandria, Virginia, for six months of Spanish language training.

So for six hours a day, two other special agents and Joan and I attended language school in Alexandria. (Spouses of service members were encouraged to attend, for free, to support the learning environment.) This was a very difficult time for me. It was very hard for me to learn a foreign language. Military and government language schools immersed students in a foreign language environment six hours a day. In this case, the Spanish instructor didn't speak any English. Joan learned her nightly dialogs easily, but it took me hours and hours. Additionally, Washington, D.C., is a horribly expensive place to assign a junior enlisted service member. There was a year-long waiting list for housing, and the Spanish language school only lasted a little over six months, so I had to get an extra job at night as a checkout clerk at the local pharmacy so we could pay the rent on the small apartment.

As difficult a period as this was, the Spanish that I did learn stayed with me for life. My ability to speak Spanish has been essential to a number of my life experiences. I think there was a bigger plan all along. When we graduated from language school, Joan's pregnancy was nearly to term and I had to go on ahead to Panama while she stayed with her parents in Topeka, Kansas.

Second Assignment

When the plane door opened in Panama, it seemed like I had landed in a sauna. This was seriously different from the snowy winter I had just experienced in Washington, D.C. The personnel officer at the 470th MI Group, Fort Amador, Canal Zone, was happy to see that I was not only a Spanish linguist but also an electronic-surveillance technician. They were in need of a tech specialist in their lab, and I was immediately sent to see the warrant officer in charge. I really liked the lab environment, the people who worked there, and the work involved. I didn't know, consciously anyway, that nearly twenty years later I would wind up in an interestingly similar lab environment at The Monroe Institute.

Because there was a six-month wait for housing in the Canal Zone, I decided to rent an apartment in Panama City so that Joan and my new son, Fred Jr., could join me. (I first saw my son at age three months when Joan brought him to Panama.) At night, we could hear gunfire in the neighborhood, and one afternoon I saw somebody staggering down the street with a knife in his stomach. Fortunately, we didn't have to stay in Panama City too long. About two months after Joan and Fred Jr. arrived, we were assigned government housing on Fort Amador. I could easily walk to work, and from our living room windows there was a great view of Panama Bay. Special Agent Atwater had it made.

Life on Fort Amador with Joan, Fred, and eventually Michelle (born in the Canal Zone) was wonderful. I had regular work hours with a challenging and interesting job. The cost of living was reasonable for an enlisted service member. When Michelle was a little older, we hired a housekeeper, and Joan took some college classes and eventually was hired by U.S. Navy Intelligence. We made lots of friends and socialized with other couples weekly. I traveled occasionally to other Central American and South American countries to check for bugging devices in various military assistance groups or to teach, in Spanish, for the School of the Americas. While working in the lab at the 470th, I was able to learn intelligence photography in addition to my electronic-surveillance certification and was awarded a notation of that specialty in my 201 File (my official personnel record).

The counterintelligence side of technical surveillance involves guessing how a hostile intelligence service would bug or wiretap or photograph classified discussions or material. Much of the work has to do with physically searching, either by visual or instrumented inspection. However, the agents' concepts of where to search and what to look for depend on their experience, their knowledge of the enemy's capabilities, and a great deal of intuitive insight.

I found that intuitive insight was my forte. My out-of-body experiences as a young child and remote viewing or intuitive insights as a teenager taught me to trust other ways of knowing. When searching a building for a bugging device, I simply expanded my awareness to include the entirety of the structure and look for—remote view?—such a device within my very self or the awareness of myself as the structure. I would then focus the technical resources at my disposal toward suspicious areas. If I was concerned about photographic penetration of an office area, I would simply visualize angles that extended beyond the confines of target area. (Good architects can do something similar by imagining a structure from many angles, both inside and out.)

This is not as strange or difficult as it may seem. For example, when you are walking you are aware of the sense of you as being your physical body. When you get into a car to drive, your awareness automatically expands until what you think of as you extends from bumper to bumper. You become aware, to some extent, of this new you quite naturally. As you move down the street with some speed, you become aware of a zone beyond the limits of the front bumper of the car, a sort of an out-of-car experience. Whether around a car or a building (or ostensibly the universe) this expanded awareness of you provides cognitive access to data within the specified environs. I define this investigative form of intuitive insight, therefore, as a simple act of self-examination. All one has to do is expand one's awareness beyond the confines of the physical body and extend it throughout the structure under inspection.

I have also used this concept of intuitive insight as a special agent working outside the world of technical intelligence. During interviews and interrogations, I expanded my awareness to include the persona of the other individual. This simple act of intimacy makes deception very difficult because an awareness of my own intuitive insight reveals the thoughts and feelings within the unity. Presumably, such unity always exists. This is what we do when we make love to one another.

The words "expand awareness" are semantically burdensome here. It is less a matter of a verb like "expand" than akin to purposefully—consciously?—taking up a perspective encompassing a greater wholeness. Once this viewpoint is realized ("real-ized," as in made real through personal experience), knowledge of this greater wholeness becomes available. I guess some who knew me back then thought my ideas were weird, but I thought of myself as a very special agent. I had a sense of myself, a spiritual identity, that was greater than my physical body.

When my enlistment contract was up, and I had to decide whether to leave the army, an assessment of my situation revealed that I was married with two children, I didn't have a college degree, and I didn't have a skill that would be marketable in the civilian world, as far as I knew. The Army Recruiting Command was telling me that if I reenlisted for six years, they would give me a nine-thousand-dollar bonus. In 1971, nine thousand dollars sounded like a lot of money. My marriage, my family, my work—my whole life—seemed to be going okay, so I reenlisted for six years. It was smooth, easy, unfettered by confusion or stress; I was on course.

As my assignment in Panama neared an end, the quiet voice from within began to whisper of the adventures to come. This was important, because one part of me (Sergeant Atwater) had the urge to maintain the status quo, to say to God, "Hey, stop right here; this is great; I'll stay with this for the rest of my life." I had a good marriage, wonderful children, good friends, and financial security. I was even driving a red convertible with white-leather seats and a white top—and it was paid for.

Life in Panama was so pleasant. But the impulse from within to move on was greater.

Back to College

A few months after I reenlisted, the U.S. Congress passed a new military-appropriations bill allocating funds to pay for the higher education of military personnel. In their thinking, the various problems of the conscription military were due to insufficient numbers of college-educated service members. (Somehow the insanity of Vietnam didn't compute. Never mind.) I applied to have the army pay my tuition and full salary for a year while I finished a baccalaureate degree. "Sure," the army said, "Congress gave us lots of money for that." So I received reassignment orders that gave me nine days to get out of Panama, take some holiday leave, and matriculate at the University of Nebraska at Omaha. I could hardly believe it. The army was all right. Of course, I was in the intelligence community, wearing civilian clothes, and not in Vietnam shooting at people who shoot back. The war, by the way, was winding down by this time (1972), and it looked like I had successfully avoided the Vietnam fiasco.

Joan, the kids, and I celebrated Thanksgiving in California with my family and Christmas in Kansas with Joan's. We bought a split-level, three-bedroom house in a nice neighborhood in Omaha, and I started school at the university in January 1973. The year in Nebraska went by quickly and effortlessly. I was on course. I received my college diploma before I could settle down and think of myself as living in the Midwest. The year passed so swiftly that it truly was just a "ticket punch" as they say. You need a college degree? You got one.

Third Assignment

A couple of months before graduation, I received notification that after completing the program, I was to be reassigned to South Korea for an unaccompanied short-tour of duty.

The house we had bought for $24,000 sold for $27,500, and I moved the family out to California and set them up in an apartment near my parents. After many sorrowful good-byes and with some trepidation, I boarded a plane and headed for Asia shortly after Christmas. I trusted my internal wisdom. I knew I would always be taken care of, and this was surely just another reach to sail on the course of my life.

When I got to South Korea, I was taken to the headquarters of the Military Intelligence Group. The first question put to me when

I arrived was, "Do you plan to bring your family over?" This was the first time such a possibility had ever been presented. Without understanding the ramifications of my answer, I said that I didn't think so. "In that case," said the personnel NCO (noncommissioned officer), "we'll send you up to the demilitarized zone with the Second Infantry Division. They have the highest priority for available personnel right now." (Translated, that means that the first sergeant of the intelligence unit there had been in his office all day bugging him.)

Within minutes, I was sitting in a jeep with the first sergeant of the Second Military Intelligence Detachment (MID) on my way to Camp Casey, South Korea. There was no consideration of my technical qualifications, previous assignments, or experience as a special agent. I was simply the next warm body in country and destined by circumstances (so I thought at the time) to go north to the demilitarized zone.

As we drove northward through the countryside and countless villages, the first sergeant, an overweight, worn-out soldier, spoke very little. He did explain that the Second MID had its own fenced compound on Camp Casey apart from the rest of the Second Infantry Division, which was headquartered there. He spoke in a gravely voice and told me that he had only two months left on his short-tour and was looking forward to getting back to "the world" and his family. He hoped to retire soon.

We finally approached Camp Casey. Driving north, a wall on the right side of the road separated the military post from the adjacent village on the left. There were several gates in the wall guarded by military police, both U.S. Army and South Korean. Passing by a couple of gates, the first sergeant indicated that ours was farther up the road.

Within a couple of minutes, he slowed the jeep and beeped the horn as we turned into an opening in the wall. Dutifully, a South Korean guard quickly opened the gate and motioned us into the compound of pale-green Quonset huts. We parked in a line of jeeps, and the first sergeant told me that I would be assigned my own jeep to use while I was in country.

South Korea has been an "occupied country" since the '50s. The overbearing presence of the U.S. military has taken its toll on the indigenous people and their culture. Nearly all the people alive in South Korea today as we move into the twenty-first century know their homeland only in its Americanized form. The attitude of U.S. soldiers is not so much a dedication to duty but a desire to simply survive the year so that they can get back to "the world" and their lives.

This attitude mirrors feelings related by Vietnam veterans. There is a plastic sense of camaraderie amongst the soldiers, an ever-present odor of "we are not really here in this place," or "this is not the real world," as if they are saying that their hearts and minds are elsewhere. Are these ambassadors of Americanism seen then as zombies by the South Korean people?

This attitude of unreality gives many U.S. soldiers the freedom to abandon cultural values and behaviors that would otherwise be precious to them. In South Korea, prostitution has been legalized and is monitored by the local government. "Working girls" are given regular medical exams and treatment when necessary. Drunkenness and debauchery in the village next to Camp Casey provide an off-duty escape for the infantry soldiers of the Second Infantry Division.

During the day, the bars are quiet and merchants bid welcome and offer bargains for the American dollar. Some soldiers have made arrangements to live within the community and "rent" a wife for the length of their tour. Such practices have become commonplace after fifty years of U.S. military occupation.

When I was introduced to the commander of the Second MID, he asked me to tell him about my previous military assignments. He had my 201 File in front of him but said that he wanted me to describe my impressions, my likes and dislikes about my previous assignments, and what I wanted to do while I was in South Korea. I liked his casual yet genuine approach. Unlike the administration in Seoul, he was genuinely interested in his soldiers.

Since I had a great deal of experience with security inspections of various types, I emphasized those special-agent abilities in my review of military assignments. He noted that I had a college degree and suggested that I talk with the staff at the Army Education Center. When he was finished interviewing me, he called the operations NCO, a disgruntled sergeant in crumpled clothes, into his office and told him quite matter-of-factly, "This is Special Agent Atwater. Put him in charge of security surveys and inspections. Get in touch with the inspector general (IG) and tell him that we have a security specialist for his team whenever he is needed. See that Atwater gets to the Army Education Center, as they will need him." And with that, both the operations NCO and I were dismissed. I found an empty bunk in one of the Quonset huts, and I was home for the next twelve months.

The commander's insistence that I visit the education center led to a part-time job. They were in need of teachers to support university extension programs offered to military personnel. I was hired to teach after-duty for the Los Angeles City College extension program. I taught psychology, abnormal psychology, and criminology. So, by day I was Special Agent Atwater, and after duty I was a college teacher at the education center. I was able to make enough extra money that my entire military salary went back home to Joan and the kids in California.

My special agent duties required me to visit various military posts in the northern part of South Korea to conduct counterintelligence security inspections and surveys, background investigations, counterespionage investigations, and participate in Broken Arrow (lost nuclear weapon) exercises and provide support to the IG Team.

I wasn't sure why, exactly, Guidance arranged for me to be in Korea, but I had a lot of fun between my Second MID security inspection duties and being a member of the IG Team.

When I visited an army unit as a member of the Second MID for a courtesy inspection, no formal report was filed through command channels, and I would tell them that I was there to help them prepare for their annual inspection by the IG. In Korea, nobody usually stays in a unit more than one year, so no one knows what to expect from an annual IG visit.

Special Agent Atwater in Korea

During my courtesy inspection, I stressed how much their "passing the IG" depended on my guidelines. Later, when the IG Team arrived, there I would be, wearing an official Inspector General armband designating me as the team's Counterintelligence and Security Specialist. I would just smile and ask them if they had done everything that I had suggested during my Second MID courtesy visit. Then we would all sit down and have a big laugh.

After eight months in South Korea, I took thirty days' leave to move Joan and the kids from California to Arizona in preparation for my next assignment at the Army Intelligence School, which had been moved from Fort Holibird, Maryland, to Fort Huachuca, Arizona. This leave was a tough call because it meant returning to South Korea to finish my tour and separating from my family again after the move. Tougher still was the fact that my kids did not recognize me when I met up with them in California.

I was a stranger to my own children after having not seen them for eight months. Talk about heart-wrenching emotional pain. But, it all worked out. I got the family moved and they were waiting for me at Fort Huachuca when I returned from South Korea nearly four months later. As it turned out, getting the assignment to Fort

Huachuca at that exact point in time seemed to be the reason behind the Korea assignment.

Fourth Assignment

At Fort Huachuca, I came off "civilian clothes status" and wore a regular military uniform for the first time since language school in 1970. Special Agent Atwater became Staff Sergeant Atwater. The assignment turned out to be a pivotal point in my military career and my life. It was as though I was somehow destined or guided to this a long time before I consciously realized what was happening. The assignment got started with the inevitable "what should we do with the new guy" interview that I had with a short, balding man wearing glasses, who was named Mr. Spaeth.

Mr. Spaeth was an experienced intelligence operative from the days of the Cuban missile crisis who, after military retirement, became a civilian instructor at the Army Intelligence School. He had been around a while and had worked his way up to a supervisory position in the section dedicated to teaching document control and accountability and personnel security investigations. I was sent to talk to him about working in his section.

When I sat down to talk to him, he had my 201 File in front of him on a desk in a very small office. He looked up at me over his glasses and asked, "What are you doing here, Sergeant Atwater?" He looked back down at my file and casually flipped through several pages as I began to think about my answer.

Quite unexpectedly, an answer to his question emerged from deep within me. "I have two college degrees. I have taught college classes. I have had eight years of experience conducting counterintelligence security inspections and surveys, including technical surveillance types, and I have worked on an inspector general team doing the same. I know all the army and Department of Defense security regulations and can quote from them verbatim. In your language, Mr. Spaeth, my shit doesn't stink. I am here to teach document control and accountability for you."

This spontaneous utterance from within had been seemingly

pent-up for some time waiting for this particular moment. I began to think about the possible consequences of what I had said and what Mr. Spaeth might do.

Without the slightest hesitation, gasp, glance, or gesture, he closed my 201 File, looked over his glasses at me again, and said, "Report to Lieutenant Ray in Room 201 down the hall. Tell him you're his new document control and accountability instructor."

Just then, the phone rang and Mr. Spaeth turned away from me and began to talk. Feeling uncomfortable in the room while he was on the phone, I got up and left. Over the next two years, I got to know Mr. Spaeth and we became great friends. As it turns out, he might have been one of my instructors back at Fort Holibird.

Before I met Lieutenant Ray, I was introduced to the Section Chief, Captain Allard. I sized up Allard as a noncareer officer. I told him that I had spoken to Mr. Spaeth and had been instructed to inform a Lieutenant Ray that I would be teaching document control and accountability. "Fine," Allard said as he began to introduce me to the other NCOs in the section.

Allard left us to chat. I asked about this Lieutenant Ray who I was supposed to meet. I was concerned about working for a lieutenant who had been in the army *all day long* whereas I had several years of experience as a counterintelligence special agent and was up for promotion to sergeant first class, a senior NCO. All of my fellow NCOs smiled and assured me that everything would be all right.

They said that Lieutenant Ray had served previously as special agent for a number of years and then gone to Officer Candidate School (OCS) to get his commission. This was his first assignment since OCS and they were all impressed with his professionalism. They showed me to an office cubicle that was to be mine and told me to go home for the day. They said that I should come back around 0900 the next day so I could meet with Lieutenant Ray, who would be busy teaching classes until then.

The next day, I returned to the office and found Lieutenant Ray in the cubicle next to mine. He looked very distinguished sitting there smoking a pipe and looking through some documents on his desk. Before I could say anything, he stood up, stuck out his hand, gesturing for a handshake, and said, "Sergeant Atwater, I'm Lieutenant Ray. I've been looking over your personnel file and have been wondering what you're doing here. You have a fine military record, a good deal of experience as a special agent, and two college degrees. Why are you here? Why haven't you gone to OCS?"

"Well, Sir," I said. "I wanted to teach, to share what I have experienced with those just entering the field."

"All right. But you really should go to OCS. We'll talk about it later." He excused himself and went off to teach another class.

I was impressed. Ray spoke his mind, didn't dilly-dally around with any small talk, and took his military duty seriously. He was my kind of guy, and I hoped I would do well working for him. I didn't know then that we would become life-long friends and he would play a major role in my future in remote viewing.

As a next step, I attended a how-to-be-a-teacher course, where I learned to develop and write lesson plans, to use multimedia training aids, and to give presentations, all of which has paid off in my present position some thirty years hence. As soon as I was qualified as a military instructor, I began to teach document control and accountability classes, trading off with Lieutenant Ray.

As time passed, we became friends within the limitations of the military fraternization rules. Nearly every day, at least three or four times a week, whenever I saw Lieutenant Ray, he would say, "Sergeant Atwater, what are you doing here? I thought I told you to go to OCS." I would courteously reply, "Sir, I haven't gone yet. I'm still teaching classes for you."

About the same time that Lieutenant Ray got promoted and started calling himself First Lieutenant Ray, I met Staff Sergeant Cowart, who had also been assigned as an instructor to our section. We had kids of similar ages and quickly became friends. It was then that I first was introduced to a scientific perspective of psychic ability—remote viewing.

Rob Cowart and I discovered a book, *Mind-Reach, Scientists Look at Psychic Ability*, by Russell Targ and Harold Puthoff (1977). We both read this book through the eyes of counterintelligence specialists concerned about hostile intelligence collection abilities.

We saw the psychic ability to remote view as documented in this book as a possible threat to national security. Tactical and strategic military advantage could be compromised through this process. The perceptual phenomenon or experience of remote viewing was not strange to me, but this nomenclature "remote viewing" was. I was somewhat startled to find that two scientists had written about something that I had taken for granted all my life.

Rob and I talked about remote viewing for hours and wondered if anybody in our own military intelligence community was interested. I thought back to my early Fort Holibird days when I had hinted at the idea of satellite photography and was told never to discuss such highly classified subjects outside specially designated secure areas. Was this remote viewing the same sort of thing? Rob and I wondered and wondered. On the other hand, how could it be classified if this book by these two scientists was available to the public? We wondered some more. Neither Rob nor I had stumbled across anything like this in our work as special agents.

During the Fort Huachuca assignment, family life was great. Joan blessed me with a second son, James. I was able to be in the delivery room and see him come into our world. Birth—what a wonderful event!

Housing on Fort Huachuca was great and, all things being good, we soon settled in as a family after the Korea separation. As an instructor at the school, I worked regular hours and was able to be with the family a great deal.

I attended graduate school in the evenings and studied Counseling Psychology, a master's program offered by the extension campus of the University of Northern Colorado. The course of my life slowly emerged from the foggy future with each day that passed. I was once again being taken care of.

At First Lieutenant Ray's continued insistence, I finally put in my application to go to OCS. Lieutenant Colonel Webb, a senior officer at the school, informed me of my acceptance to the program. Webb and I had met several times. He came into my classes several times, as he did with all instructors to monitor their performance. I had also visited with him at several office and school social occasions.

When I reported to Lieutenant Colonel Webb in his office, we exchanged salutes and he invited me to sit down. He told me that my application to attend OCS had been approved by "the brass" and he wanted to talk to me personally before I left Fort Huachuca for OSC at Fort Benning, Georgia. He told me that his last job had been in the Pentagon in the assignments branch for intelligence personnel.

Webb said that he had been watching me and admired my professionalism during my assignment to the Army Intelligence School. Finally he said, "Sergeant Atwater, keep your nose clean at OCS and if you're commissioned as an intelligence officer, I will see to it that you get whatever assignment you want." And with that he dismissed me.

This is what is known in the military as "grandfathering." It was important to get a senior officer to look after you and your assignments, to help you to be in the right place at the right time—maximizing your career potential. Lieutenant Colonel Webb had just adopted me.

Back to School Again

In the summer of 1976, we moved to Fort Benning. Joan and the kids were in post housing, but I lived in the barracks with more than two hundred other officer candidates. While I was away in training, my youngest child, James, got very sick and nearly died of meningitis, the first of many serious medical challenges he has had in his life. My father died in November of 1976, and I was granted a few days of compassionate leave to be with the family in Glendale, California. The traditional holiday season also came in the middle of my OCS training cycle, which provided for some leave time and a break in the training.

By this time in my life, I had been in the army nearly nine years and I knew the system in and out. Many of my fellow officer candidates spent hours studying army regulations and policies. An academic study, combined with the stresses imposed by our TAC officers, was trying for most. For me, OCS was a snap and I graduated tenth in a class of over two hundred.

Only two candidates received commissions into the Intelligence Corps. I was one of them, and I was on my way to the Officer Basic Course at Fort Huachuca with assignment orders in hand to eventually report to Fort Bliss, Texas. More importantly, I was on my way back to Lieutenant Colonel Webb, an angel from God, who had promised me my assignment of choice.

Having me attend the Officer Basic Course at Fort Huachuca was ridiculous. I could have taught nearly all the classes. But when I reported to Lieutenant Colonel Webb with a smile on my face, I was once again "being taken care of," as my mother had said so long ago.

"Well, Lieutenant Atwater," he said, with emphasis on the "Lieutenant." "Where do you want to go?" Handing him the book *Mind-Reach*, I said, "Sir, I don't know exactly, but I do know that what is presented in this book represents a threat to our national security and I would like to be assigned someplace where I can do something about that."

"Let me look at this book tonight. Check with my secretary and get an appointment with me tomorrow."

"Yes, Sir." We exchanged salutes and I left his office.

The next afternoon as I entered his office, he rose from behind his desk before I could report to him in the prescribed military manner. He handed me the book and said, "I've never heard of anything like this remote viewing stuff. But if what these scientists say is true, then you are exactly right. This is a threat to our national security."

"Yes, Sir," I replied.

"If anything like this is going on, it will be documented in the Pentagon. I'm going to have you assigned to the Pentagon Counterintelligence Force. As a lieutenant, you will be a team chief and will have access to all areas of the Pentagon. No door will be locked to you. You will have the highest security clearances. It will be up to you to find this project, if it exists."

"Thank you, Sir," I said. He walked me to his office door and we parted without exchanging salutes. I wish we had saluted. I think this may have been the last time I saw him. I heard some time later that he took ill and died. Anyway, a few days later, I received a change of orders. My Fort Bliss assignment was canceled, and I was to report to the Pentagon upon graduation from the Officer's Basic Course at Fort Huachuca.

Joan and I talked about the assignment to the Pentagon. On the surface, an assignment to Washington, D.C., seemed better than Fort Bliss, Texas. But we had lived in the D.C. area when we went to language school. The cost of living was very high and there was no military housing. As a young lieutenant with three children, I was going to have trouble making ends meet.

We talked about looking for a place to live in Manassas, Virginia, several miles west of Washington, D.C., where the cost of housing was more reasonable. I would have long commutes every day but at least we might be able to afford living there. On the very day we were to leave for Washington, serendipity, divine Guidance, or whatever, intervened. I was "taken care of" once again.

A Change of Assignment

As we were packing our VW bus and pop-up trailer for the trip from Arizona to Washington, D.C., I got a phone message telling me to call the 902nd Military Intelligence Group of the newly formed U.S. Army Intelligence and Security Command (INSCOM) at Fort Meade, Maryland, about my assignment. I left Joan with the kids and the packing job and went back on post (Fort Huachuca) to call Fort Meade.

INSCOM informed me that my assignment orders had been changed again (not through Lieutenant Colonel Webb's influence) and that I was now to report to Fort Meade for duty to the Systems Exploitation Detachment (SED). They were in need of experienced intelligence officers, and when the personnel officer at headquarters of INSCOM reviewed my personnel file she felt I, as an experienced counterintelligence special agent, would be better suited to an assignment with SED at Fort Meade than the Pentagon Counterintelligence Force in Washington, D.C. I was assured that there would be written orders waiting for me when I arrived. I acknowledged the verbal change in my orders and told them that I would report as soon as I could move my family across the country.

When I hung up the phone, my mind began to race. Fort Meade would be great. We would have family housing. No longer were we facing financial ruin. I couldn't wait to tell Joan and the kids the good news.

As we drove across country, camping every night at a KOA with our pop-up, we talked about our new life, schools for the kids, on-post housing, family medical care at a military hospital, and the post exchange and commissary, all of which were military benefits we would have missed if we had had to live in Manassas. We also had friends—the Compton family, who we knew from Panama—who were assigned to Fort Meade.

Overcome with gratitude, I forgot about my assignment request and my desire to find out about any remote-viewing projects documented in the secret corridors of the Pentagon. We were on our way to a new life. But I was on course, as I always had been all along. I was going to be able to personally experience the reality of remote viewing in a way I would have never guessed. Later, I would come to understand the true spiritual implications of remote viewing beyond its use as an intelligence surveillance tool.

Chapter Three

Igniting Grill Flame

Fort Meade lies about halfway between Washington, D.C., and Baltimore, Maryland, just off the Baltimore-Washington Parkway. We found ourselves in the middle of rush-hour traffic on the I-495 Capital Beltway north of Washington, D.C., late on a Friday afternoon. Joan and I and the three kids had been on the road a couple of weeks in our VW bus pulling our pop-up trailer. We were all tired, stressed by the day's drive and the cacophony of the beltway traffic. But less than thirty minutes away was Fort Meade and what would be our home for the next ten years (although we didn't know that at the time).

Captain Atwater

Our first stop on post was the quarters of Chief Warrant Officer Grover Compton, who had been my military supervisor in the lab in Panama. We had kids in the same age range and our families had become friends. When he had returned from Panama en route to Fort Meade, he and his family had stopped by to visit us in Fort Huachuca. Now we were assigned to Fort Meade and our old friends were there to meet us.

Grover told me there was an abundance of three-bedroom, company-grade housing and there probably wouldn't be a long waiting list. We spent the weekend at the guest house on post, and on Monday Grover showed me where the 902nd Headquarters, Intelligence and Security Command (INSCOM), building was located. My orders were waiting, just as had been promised. (To get military housing for my family, I needed written orders officially assigning me to Fort Meade.) I was told to take as much time as I needed to get my family settled and then report to Major Keenan, Commander of the Systems Exploitation Detachment or SED.

I went over to Post Housing immediately. Grover was right. I was offered a choice of two different neighborhoods and three different sets of quarters. I selected a townhouse on Buckner Avenue because it had more square footage of living space, was close to work, and was nearest to all the usual military facilities like the commissary, the post Exchange, the bank, etc. The townhouse had an unfinished basement, which I completed and, at first, became a playroom for the kids. Later, as the kids grew, it became our master bedroom and the kids each had their own bedroom upstairs.

By the end of the week, the family was beginning to get settled and I sought out Major Keenan, who turned out to be a gruff, battlefield-commissioned officer, proud to have been from the era of the old brown-shoe army. I found that the SED worked "behind the green door" and I would need a special identification badge depicting my Top Secret code-word security clearance to gain access. This work area was one of those "special places" the instructor back at Fort Holibird some ten years ago had talked about.

Highly classified information drove the work product here. Keenan told me that I was to become a member of a SAVE Team.

The acronym SAVE meant Sensitive Activity Vulnerability Estimate. I'll explain a little bit about all this so that you will understand later how the remote-viewing surveillance issue fits.

This was the day and age of OPSEC—Operations Security—when commanders were expected to do more than just safeguard their classified material. Due to the increased sophistication of intelligence collection methods, military commanders were required to take measures to protect all critical aspects of their operational capabilities. (Remember my interesting questions about satellite photography back in the Fort Holibird days!)

An inspection by a SAVE Team was the ultimate survey of a command's OPSEC status. Once a verifiable threat (a proven hostile-intelligence effort against an installation or organization) was identified, a SAVE Team targeted the installation or organization using sophisticated U.S. intelligence assets, thereby testing the vulnerability of the surveyed facility to hostile intelligence methods. The entire array of photo intelligence (PHOTINT), signal intelligence (SIGINT), and human intelligence (HUMINT) was employed against a designated army facility or command to give a complete OPSEC profile.

Getting back to the story, I spent a couple of weeks meeting and visiting with people around the office. I wasn't assigned a desk or cubicle, so I just shuffled around from place to place. My peers were sizing me up to see how I might be best utilized within the unit. Because of my teaching background and the fact that I was a brand-new lieutenant, one of my first jobs was to brief visitors on the overall mission and functions of SED. For me, it was just a typical lieutenant-type duty.

Finally, one day Major Keenan ceremoniously told me that it was about time that I got my own desk. The open floor space in this area of the building had been divided into individual work areas, or cubicles, with movable partitions. He walked me over to a cubicle with a typical, gray office desk, a safe, a typewriter (this was in the days before office workers had desktop computers), and a couple of chairs. Keenan said that this had been Lieutenant Colonel Skotzko's desk back in the days when the unit worked directly for General Thompson, the army's Assistant Chief of Staff for Intelligence (ACSI), and I would need to clean it out and make it my own.

This gesture, giving me my own workspace, was symbolic of my acceptance within the office. Keenan could have found me unsuitable for the SED job and had me reassigned elsewhere with INSCOM. The SED personnel were an elite assemblage of army intelligence professionals, and I had been accepted by them in less than a month.

The Discovery

I looked through the drawers of the desk in my new work area and found old pens and pencils, rubber stamps for marking classified documents, dated memos, old notebooks, and assorted leftover paraphernalia.

Next, I turned my attention to the safe and began to look through the drawers. As I pulled open each heavy drawer, I found empty folders and file hangers. The file folders were still labeled and marked with security classifications, but the documents they once contained, Lieutenant Colonel Skotzko's work, had since been moved or destroyed. There were four essentially empty drawers until I came to the fifth, the bottom drawer.

There, in the bottom drawer, were three Department of Defense classified documents. Two of the reports detailed various aspects of Soviet interest in parapsychology, and the third was about remote viewing at SRI-International.

I had put the whole remote-viewing thing out of my mind back in Fort Huachuca when my orders to the Pentagon were changed. And yet, here I was thumbing through two classified documents about Soviet parapsychology research and another prepared by Puthoff and Targ, the authors of that book I had read back at Fort Huachuca!

The two classified documents about Soviet parapsychology came from the Medical Intelligence Office of the Army Surgeon General. Apparently, in the early 1970s somebody considered the Office of the Surgeon General a competent authority in the area of parapsychology and assigned their intelligence resources as the lead agency on this issue.

One of the classified documents was published in 1972 and was called *Controlled Offensive Behavior—U.S.S.R.* The document focused on the concept that the Soviets were interested in modifying human behavior through the use of telepathy or telekinesis. This wasn't exactly the same as remote viewing as described by Puthoff and Targ, but it was in the ballpark.

What got my attention was that the document said that parapsychology research in the Soviet Union was probably being conducted at more than twenty separate institutions with an operating budget of more than twenty-one million dollars per year.

In 1972, twenty-one million dollars was a lot of money and the principal source of their funding was from the KGB, what was then the Soviet equivalent of our CIA. If the Soviet KGB was spending this kind of cash, they were either being very foolish or they were having some promising results from their research efforts.

The other classified document from the same Medical Intelligence Office, published in 1975, detailed Soviet and Czechoslovakian parapsychology research. The report was divided into two sections. The *Bioinformation* section concerned things like telepathy, precognition, and clairvoyance (all of which sounded a lot like remote viewing to me). The *Bioenergetics* section talked about psychokinesis and telekinesis.[3]

The third classified document from the safe drawer was called *Project* SCANATE. It told about classified U.S. Government remote-viewing research, conducted mostly by the Stanford Research Institute (SRI) in Menlo Park, California. This convincing report demonstrated the ability of remote-viewing surveillance to acquire and report information of interest to the intelligence community.

The *Project* SCANATE report has not been declassified as have the Medical Intelligence Office documents, but for years I have had

[3] Both of these Medical Intelligence Office documents have been redacted and declassified and are available under the Freedom of Information Act. Copies are included on the CD-ROM accompanying this book.

an unclassified draft of the report and I have included a copy of it on the CD-ROM accompanying this book.

The authors of the *Project SCANATE* report were the same researchers, Puthoff and Targ, who had written the book *Mind-Reach,* which had earlier fascinated Rob Cowart and myself. Without any conscious effort on my part, I had been guided to this moment of discovery all along, even when I felt as though only "earthly" forces were controlling my military career.

I told Major Keenan that I had found three classified documents in the safe in my cubicle and described their subject matter. He said that Lieutenant Colonel Skotzko had been looking into remote viewing for General Thompson. Keenan said that General Thompson thought that there might be something to this phenomenon of remote viewing and took the subject quite seriously.

Keenan asked if I knew anything about remote viewing and I told him that I did. He instructed me to keep the documents in my safe since I was familiar with the concept. He also told me that Staff Sergeant Riley, a photo interpreter assigned to SED, had an interest in this area as well. I had met Sergeant Riley before but until this moment didn't know of his interest in remote viewing. Riley impressed me as a professional soldier who was an expert in his field and who took great pride in his accomplishments.

So, for the next couple of weeks, I read and reread the documents I had found in the bottom drawer. I thought back to the days at Fort Huachuca when Rob Cowart and I talked about the counterintelligence implications of remote viewing. In my mind, I replayed the scenario with Lieutenant Colonel Webb and how I had showed him the remote-viewing book written by the researchers Puthoff and Targ.

I wondered how and why my orders had been changed from the Pentagon assignment to the SED at Fort Meade. I couldn't tell my wife about finding these documents because of my security oath, and I didn't know Sergeant Riley well enough yet. So there was no one with whom I could discuss this twist of fate, this serendipitous happenstance. Most interestingly, the loop wasn't quite closed yet.

The Request

The U.S. Army Missile Command at Redstone Arsenal, Alabama, had formally requested OPSEC support, and several members of SED were selected to go to Alabama to answer the request. Since I was the junior officer in the unit, it was decided that this would be a good opportunity for me to learn, hands-on, about OPSEC support. I was invited go along to observe and play a small role.

The missile command was concerned about security because much of their testing involved ground-to-air missile telemetry, the radio signals that guide a ground-fired missile to an airborne target. They wanted to know the actual hostile-intelligence threat posed and what OPSEC measures should be taken to counter this threat.

Much of the data supporting our recommendations was assembled prior to visiting Redstone Arsenal. The on-site visit to the missile command was to better understand ground operations, interview personnel about security procedures, and occasionally challenge those security procedures.

For example, if we were told during the official tour inspection that only personnel wearing a certain type of security badge could enter into an area, we might come back (uninvited) that night or the next day and see if we could penetrate their security without a badge or with an obviously bogus one.

When we completed the on-site phase of the survey, we sat down to provide the command with an exit briefing, to be followed later by a formal, written report. I sat quietly as the senior members of our SED entourage talked of the threat posed by Soviet satellites, which passed over Redstone Arsenal at regular intervals. The OPSEC solution was to schedule critical telemetry tests during periods of time when the satellites were in orbit over a different part of the planet.

We also discussed the threat posed by Soviet ships in the Gulf of Mexico that could intercept telemetry signals. We told them that the missile command's OPSEC office could be provided with information about Soviet ships and which ones were known hostile-intelligence assets.

Human agents presented an additional threat, because Redstone Arsenal offered a NASA display for tourists. We informed the missile command that U.S. Immigration could provide the declared travel plans of foreign visitors. By matching this information with a list of names provided by classified sources of known hostile-intelligence agents, their OPSEC officer could develop a system to alert personnel when known hostile agents were in the immediate area.

The exit briefing contained many more details and several suggestions for OPSEC, counterintelligence, and physical security measures common to nearly every survey. Just before we all got up from the conference table, one of the project managers sitting directly across from me said, "I appreciate all that you have told us, but how are we supposed to protect ourselves from *this?*" He pulled a book out of his briefcase and slid it across the table to me. I reached out for the book, wondering what he could be asking about. It was *Mind-Reach*!

As I held the book in my hand, staring at the title, the missile command OPSEC officer at the head of the table abruptly asked, "What's this all about?" The project manager had surprised him, and I could tell from the sound of his voice that he was befuddled.

A hush fell over the room; I turned to address the OPSEC officer's question and spoke slowly and deliberately, the words coming from somewhere deep inside me, "He is worried about the threat posed by remote viewing, a human perceptual ability being investigated under classified government contracts at the prestigious Stanford Research Institute. He wants to know what OPSEC measures we recommend to counter this threat. This subject is beyond the scope of this survey and today's briefing. I will have to get back to you later on this, Sir."

For those few, brief moments, I commanded the attention of everyone in the room. I handed the book back to the project manager and he put it back in his briefcase. I glanced over to the SED team leader and nodded. "Well," he said, as he turned to the OPSEC officer and offered a departing handshake, "I guess we'll be in touch with you later."

Dumbfounded, the OPSEC officer smiled and thanked us for our time and effort. We departed Redstone Arsenal without any further mention of remote viewing or the curious incident during the exit briefing.

On the trip back to Fort Meade, I couldn't stop thinking about all that had been happening. Less than three months prior to this Alabama trip, I had been asking Lieutenant Colonel Webb, back at Fort Huachuca, for an assignment involving the security threat posed by remote viewing. Even when he had arranged for me to be assigned to the Pentagon, I was unexplainably redirected to Fort Meade and the SED. Just a couple of weeks prior to this OPSEC survey, I had discovered the secret remote-viewing documents in my safe. This was amazing. A warm smile filled my face. I was on course.

I didn't want to offend the senior member of the SED team that had gone to Alabama by going over his head, so I first asked him if I should tell Major Keenan about the remote-viewing question that had come up in the exit briefing. He told me he was glad to have me do it because he didn't know what to say.

The following week, I asked for a meeting with Keenan to tell him about the exit briefing at Redstone Arsenal. Since Keenan was familiar with the secret remote-viewing documents that I held in my safe, I felt comfortable bringing up the subject with him.

I had been in Major Keenan's office before, and his desk abutted a small conference table so that he could have several staff members in his office at the same time. As I entered his office carrying an armful of documents and a yellow legal pad, he said cordially, "What can I do for you, Lieutenant?" I set the papers on the small conference table and began to explain that during the exit briefing at Redstone Arsenal an unusual OPSEC request was made.

Keenan invited me to sit down and tell him more. And, rather than sitting behind his desk, he joined me at the conference table. This gesture indicated a willingness to talk as peers. Had he gone around behind his desk as "the boss," the discussion that followed might have had a different flavor altogether.

I started off slowly, explaining how well things had gone in Alabama and that I was sure the U.S. Army Missile Command would be very appreciative of INSCOM and the efforts of SED. I also thanked him for sending me along so that I could learn the "how to" of OPSEC support provided by SED. I casually told him that at the end of the exit briefing one of the project managers had asked for OPSEC recommendations to protect themselves from hostile surveillance by remote viewing.

As I was talking, I leafed through the documents I had set on the small conference table, and with perfect timing, just as I finished speaking, I fanned out the secret remote-viewing documents from my safe on the table in front of us.

"What did you tell him?" asked Major Keenan as he glanced at the documents ("evidence") on the table before him. I explained that I told the missile command OPSEC officer that the concerns of his project manager about remote viewing were genuine but that his query was beyond the scope of the present survey.

"Good," said Keenan. "But how are you going to answer his question, Lieutenant?"

"Yes, Sir," I said. "I know his question needs to be answered, and that's why I asked to meet with you."

The Plan

I explained that first we needed to determine if hostile exploitation of the remote-viewing phenomenon posed a probable threat. It was obvious from open-source material (newspapers, magazines, books, etc.) and published classified documents that remote viewing constituted a *possible* threat but that until we could demonstrate its *probable* exploitation by hostile intelligence, there was no need to address the concept of countermeasures.

Keenan smiled and said, "You've been thinking about this, haven't you, Lieutenant?" He asked what I planned to do next. I told him that I needed to see if there were more, or more up-to-date, classified documents on remote viewing, and that I needed to check to see if there were any outstanding Intelligence Collection Requirements (ICRs) for the hostile exploitation of remote viewing. (The CIA compiled a list of ICRs, as they were called back then, to address the identified needs of the intelligence community. This list sometimes chartered specific agencies to obtain the information, but many ICRs invited contributions from any appropriate organization.)

I explained that if I could demonstrate the probable exploitation of this unique, human perceptual ability by hostile intelligence services, we had an obligation to address countermeasures with our OPSEC expertise and policy. Keenan brought our short meeting to a close by saying, "You're probably right, Lieutenant. Find out what you can and get back to me when you've got something substantial."

"Yes, Sir." I picked up my papers and left his office.

My course had been set—in more ways than I was aware. The classified documents that I had listed the publishing offices, and it took little effort to query those offices for updated material.

In my search, I found another secret document prepared by the Air Force Systems Command, Foreign Technology Division, Wright-Patterson Air Force Base in Ohio, and published by the Defense Intelligence Agency (DIA). This document was called *Paraphysics R & D—Warsaw Pact.*[4] This was a very comprehensive review on the state of the parapsychology research in the Soviet Union and Warsaw-Pact countries. It detailed personnel involved in the research, institutions, and funding.

I reviewed the classified ICRs and found that the air force was responding to a list of requirements for information on remote-viewing and psychic phenomena. I discovered that there was a civilian employee at DIA by the name of Jim Salyer who was the point of contact with DIA on this subject, among other things. Jim was a somewhat standoffish fellow, but he had been involved with DIA's remote-viewing interests for some time. He was the first government official that I met who knew what was going on in this field.

When I asked about the work at SRI by Puthoff and Targ, Mr. Salyer explained that in response to outstanding ICRs published by

---

4 This document has also been redacted and declassified and is available under the Freedom of Information Act. A copy is included on the CD-ROM accompanying this book.

the CIA, information about Soviet remote-viewing experiments, and those of other nations as well, had been collected. He said that in the case of intelligence information about foreign remote-viewing experiments, one way to determine the probable truth of the information was to replicate the reported experiments.

Salyer said that this was the basis for the government-funded remote-viewing research at SRI. They were reproducing the experiments to see if the reported successes in remote viewing by Soviet and other foreign research facilities were valid. From time to time, the CIA itself would task SRI's remote viewers against the CIA's own foreign targets of interest. Some of those "test" results have been published elsewhere.

I learned from Mr. Salyer that an air force civilian employee by the name of Dale Graff was the point of contact at Air Force Systems Command, Foreign Technology Division. Dale was the principal author of *Paraphysics R & D—Warsaw Pact*. Before leaving DIA, I asked Mr. Salyer how to get in touch with Dale and he provided the necessary contact information.

I took a trip out to Wright-Patterson Air Force Base in Ohio to meet Dale Graff. Dale was a soft-spoken, mid-level civilian employee whose intellect far exceeded his job assignment. He had been investigating remote viewing on his own for years. He was genuinely interested in my inquiry and candidly reviewed the material about foreign research on remote viewing and other psychic phenomena with me without holding anything back.

It was clear from what Dale showed me that, as far as the Soviet Union was concerned, the principlal-funding source for this research was the KGB. The presumption was that the KGB was investigating remote-viewing surveillance as a possible source of intelligence information.

Coupling this hypothesis with the remote-viewing success in the government-funded SRI research, it looked to me as though I had found evidence to demonstrate the *probable* exploitation of remote viewing by hostile intelligence services.

As I made inquiries around the intelligence community, I found others who agreed with me. But how was I going to explain all this to Major Keenan? If he understood the OPSEC implications of what I had discovered, then what would he have me do next? I decided the best course of action would be to ask the authoritative Mr. Salyer from the DIA if he would come to Fort Meade and brief Keenan.

Within in a week, Mr. Salyer, Major Keenan, and I were sitting around that small conference table in Keenan's office. Salyer explained that the U.S. Government had been following remote-viewing research for some time but only recently had taken an increased interest when evidence of KGB funding of the Soviet effort came to light.

He reviewed the efforts of SRI to replicate Soviet experiments and showed us some results. I confirmed, for discussion purposes, that researchers Puthoff and Targ, the authors of *Mind-Reach*, were the ones under government contract. Salyer showed several startling examples in which SRI's remote viewers had correctly described strategic military facilities in the Soviet Union. The implication for OPSEC was vividly clear. If KGB remote viewers were targeted against U.S. facilities, similar results could be expected.

The DIA briefing lasted about forty-five minutes and after courteous handshakes all around, Mr. Salyer and I left Major Keenan's office. I walked Salyer to the door and thanked him for the briefing. Watching him descend the stairs on his way out of the building, I wasn't sure if this would be the end of my involvement with military remote viewing or perhaps the beginning of an even deeper participation. As I was returning to my desk, Keenan leaned out of his office doorway and said, "Lieutenant Atwater, be in my office at 0900 hours tomorrow morning."

The next morning, I woke up earlier than usual. I thought the briefing had gone well. Rather than me, Lieutenant Atwater, the junior officer, telling my commander that I had found evidence that remote viewing constituted a probable threat to national security, an official representative of the DIA had presented the argument for me.

In pursuit of this evidence, I had made several contacts within the Department of Defense (DOD) and in turn revealed to them that INSCOM had an interest in the security implications of remote viewing. At the same time, my fellow officers and co-workers in SED saw that not only was I busy with some "special project" but that I was getting an unexpected amount of attention from the boss: This junior lieutenant, this new guy on board, seemed to be moving pretty fast. Why did Keenan want to see me? Why did he announce from his doorway, in a voice that everyone in the office could hear, I was to meet with him the next morning?

From my office cubicle, I kept a watchful eye on the coat rack outside Major Keenan's office until I saw that his braided, field-grade officer's hat sat on the shelf above the hangars. Once I could see his hat, I knew he was in his office. At 0900, I showed up at the doorway outside Keenan's office with a yellow legal pad in hand, looking as much as I could like I was interested but not anxious to hear what he had to say to me. "Lieutenant Atwater," he said, "come in and have a seat." As I sat down at the small conference table, he went around behind his desk and assumed a commanding position.

"Would you like some coffee?"

"No, thank you," I replied. In this dance, the junior officer was not expected to accept the coffee. The offer was just setting the social dynamics for the meeting.

"I want to thank you for the meeting with Mr. Salyer yesterday. I was impressed."

"Yes, Sir," I replied cautiously.

"But you still haven't answered my question."

"Sir?"

In a rather stern voice, he said, "I asked you what you were going to tell the missile command down at Redstone Arsenal. They asked what they could do to protect themselves, their military operations, from remote-viewing surveillance."

"Yes, Sir, that's correct," I continued, "and as I told you before, it seemed to me that in keeping with the SED mission, our first step was to determine if remote viewing presented a probable threat."

"And with yesterday's DIA briefing it would appear that it is."

"Yes, Sir," I went on. "In keeping with SED's way of providing OPSEC support, our next step would be to use remote-viewing surveillance on the missile command ourselves to demonstrate its vulnerability to this form of hostile-intelligence collection to the commander, U.S. Army Missile Command, Redstone Arsenal, Alabama."

"And how do you propose we do that, Lieutenant?"

"Well, Sir, at SRI they have some remote viewers who would seem to be capable of performing such a task, but there is a problem with using them."

"What do you mean? What problem?"

"It would seem to me, Sir, that for us here at SED the issue is larger than just the missile command in Alabama. If remote viewing is in fact a hostile-intelligence threat, then the OPSEC posture of all army installations, operations, and assorted facilities are vulnerable."

"What are you saying, Lieutenant?"

"Sir, the remote viewers at SRI are basically research subjects, and they work as independent consultants or subcontractors to SRI. They do not have the appropriate security clearances or the proverbial need-to-know for much of the sensitive classified information at the missile command or other army facilities. And if we genuinely see remote viewing as a probable threat, we will need to include it in our OPSEC vulnerability estimates for many of the army commands for which we provide service."

"Yes. I see what you mean, Lieutenant," he said slowly. "The SRI remote viewers wouldn't have security clearances for any of that." Coming out from behind his desk, he sat down at the small conference table across from me and asked, "So what are we going to do now?" I leaned back in my chair and glanced down at the blank, yellow legal pad on the table in front of me. As my eyes slowly rose to meet his, my mind raced for an answer to his question.

"Major Keenan," I said carefully, "we need to train some of our own people—intelligence professionals with appropriate security clearances—to be remote viewers." In the back of my mind, I thought this sounded pretty good. I continued, "Once trained, these assets could be used repeatedly to provide remote viewing in support of SED's OPSEC-support mission. Just as we use other intelligence-surveillance assets such as satellites, communications intercepts, and facility penetration agents to demonstrate OPSEC vulnerabilities to army commanders, we could use these trained remote viewers to demonstrate vulnerabilities to this unique form of surveillance."

A pensive stillness filled the room as Keenan gathered his thoughts. "Lieutenant Atwater," he announced, "you're right!" And then he asked, "How do we train our people to be remote viewers?"

I didn't know exactly how to answer his question. How do you train someone to do something that to me seemed a natural aptitude? And yet, that's what training was all about, bringing out or developing natural aptitudes. You can't train people to play the piano, for example, unless they have some inherent aptitude. Maybe remote viewing worked the same way. But how could I identify people with this natural aptitude? I would want to select people for training who had some chance of being successful. I would want to have several people trained so I would have backup and multiple sources. As my thoughts raced on, very little objective time passed back at the small conference table. The wisdom from within that was always with me emerged and I answered Keenan's question.

"Sir," I said with authority, "I'll need to check with the researchers at SRI in Menlo Park and several other organizations about available training programs. We may be able to train personnel with these organizations initially with an eventual goal of in-house training. But first, we need to decide or determine our responsibility and commitment to remote-viewing surveillance as an issue of national security."

"That," Major Keenan said, "will be a decision for General Smith, Deputy Commander, INSCOM." Keenan spoke slowly as he thought it through, "This area of inquiry is beyond the scope of our planned budget, and the deputy commander must approve any expenditures on new projects. If he were to approve our looking into this, it would, in turn, be setting policy—official authority for INSCOM to consider the OPSEC ramifications of remote-viewing surveillance."

He stood up. "Lieutenant, prepare a briefing for General Smith during his visit next week. Work up a travel budget for yourself covering the rest of the fiscal year. Prepare a document for General Smith's signature, providing us the authority to train our personnel in remote viewing. Make sure you review with General Smith the threat information covered in Mr. Salyer's visit."

I rose from my chair and stood across the table from Keenan and obediently responded, "Yes, Sir." He smiled and extended his arm, inviting a handshake, a gentleman's agreement that we were taking the appropriate action. I took his hand and smiled back. He gestured, tossing his head toward the door and said, "Now get out of here, Lieutenant, and get to work." I picked up my yellow legal pad and headed out of his office and back to my own cubicle.

I spent the next several days preparing to brief General Smith. When the briefing schedule for the office was posted, my fellow intelligence officers in SED began to come around my work area, curious about the posted subject "Remote Viewing" and teasing me about briefing the deputy commander.

General Smith was a short, skinny, feisty old man with what was left of his silver hair cut very short. The only thing commanding about his appearance were the stars on his shoulders, which looked a little too big for him to be carrying around.

It seemed the general had a reputation. Officers and NCOs would spend day after day collecting backup documentation, preparing lecture notes and graphics, and rehearsing their presentations. When the day and the hour would finally arrive for them to stand in front of General Smith—we called him Snuffy Smith in honor of the cartoon character—they would march smartly into the conference room ready to dazzle him. More often than not, as soon as they announced the subject of their briefing, the general would say something along the lines of, "I know all about that. Don't waste my time. Get out of here."

I had witnessed this myself several times. My peers were teasing me about General Smith's eccentricities and were sure that I would be immediately and summarily dismissed when my time came.

It appeared to me that the general, because of his position, did in fact get briefings from a number of different offices, and many times subjects would overlap. He also did not want to appear as uninformed or ignorant to his junior officers. The rumor was that General Smith had been passed over for promotion and was on his way out and had been assigned the deputy commander position as a way of easing him into retirement.

The Approval

I knew that when my time finally came, if I was on course with my spiritual journey through life, my briefing the deputy commander would best serve those interests. As the moment approached, I stood in the hall outside the conference room with my fellow intelligence officers, and one by one we were called in turn to brief the general on a variety of subjects.

My name came up early on the list, so I didn't have to wait very long. I didn't bring any graphics or briefing notes, but I did carry the classified remote-viewing documents in case the general asked for them.

In an attempt to bolster my professional deportment and knowledge of the subject matter, I made sure that those in the conference room saw that I was carrying several officially published classified documents. (I was fighting the all-day-in-the-army-lieutenant factor here.) I set the documents on the conference table next to the podium and when my eyes met the general's, I smiled and attempted to establish some rapport by asking, "Are you enjoying your briefings this morning, General?"

"Get on with it, Lieutenant," he barked.

"Yes, Sir," I said. "This briefing concerns a subject about which you have not been kept fully informed."

Major Keenan glanced at the general to see his reaction. Snuffy (whoops, I mean General Smith) didn't bark again, so I continued. "More importantly, Sir, this is a decision briefing. We here at SED are soliciting a policy decision from you as deputy commander affecting the future of Army OPSEC procedures,

INSCOM's support responsibilities, and, from a larger perspective, a broad range of national defense issues."

He held up his hand, motioning me to stop, and turned to Keenan, "What's this all about, Major?"

Keenan replied, "Lieutenant Atwater has had ten years of experience as a counterintelligence special agent and has unique knowledge of this particular topic. I have asked him to bring you up to speed on this subject so you can sign off on our action plan."

As I stood there waiting, General Smith shuffled through the papers on the heavy, mahogany conference table in front of him. When he finally found the briefing schedule, he took a moment to peruse it and then looked up at me and said, "Lieutenant Atwater, tell me about remote viewing. This sounds like it's going to be interesting."

Well, there I was. I hadn't been thrown out. I stood there in a secure conference room before General Smith, the Deputy Commander of INSCOM, prepared to tell him about remote viewing. It had only been a few months since I had mentioned to Lieutenant Colonel Webb, back at Fort Huachuca, that I wanted to be involved with remote viewing and its obvious impact on national intelligence and security issues. It had been less than a year since Staff Sergeant Rob Cowart and I had last discussed and mused over the counterintelligence ramifications of remote viewing.

Somehow I knew this was another one of those pivotal times in my life. There was a sense, an overwhelming feeling, that all my previous life focused on this one moment and that in the future this briefing would be thought of as crucial in tracing the history of army remote-viewing operations.

Deep inside, I knew somehow that years into the future there was to be a history of army remote-viewing operations. This experience, this outside-of-time knowingness, filled me with self-confidence. So without trepidation or even the slightest inkling of a doubt about my future, I told General Smith about remote viewing.

"Remote viewing," I began, "is a natural, perceptual faculty defined as the human ability to describe locations, activities, or objects using the power of the mind without the use of our conventional senses."

"What do you mean, Lieutenant? Give me an example."

"Yes, Sir. If Major Keenan, for example, were asked as an intelligence officer to describe the current activities at a particular Soviet weapons depot, he would probably want to review current intercept traffic and look at any overhead satellite surveillance that might be on file. If activity at the depot was considered a particularly critical target, perhaps having been identified as an indicator of hostile intentions, there might even be some HUMINT (informants or agents paid by U.S. intelligence) available as well.

"Still another way for him to find out about the current activities at this supposed Soviet weapons depot would be through remote viewing. An experienced remote viewer might be able to accurately describe, by mental means alone, elements or goings-on at this Soviet depot. These descriptions could provide corroborative or additional information to intelligence analysts."

"Is this remote viewing some sort of mental telepathy sort of thing?"

I went on, adjusting my comments to address his question. "The concept of telepathy implies some sort of mind-to-mind exchange of information. Remote viewing, as presently understood, would appear to be different. If, by way of example here, we were able to contact a Soviet soldier at this supposed weapons depot by means of telepathy, any intelligence provided through such contact would be limited to that soldier's knowledge of the site. It would seem that remote viewing does not have this limitation. An experienced, reliable remote viewer could describe aspects of the depot, perspectives and activities beyond the confines or perceptions of personnel located there."

"But, Lieutenant, is such a thing possible?" he asked as he leaned forward in his chair.

"Yes, Sir, it is," Keenan interrupted and then pointed at me. "You only have a few minutes with the general, so move along, Atwater."

"Yes, Sir," I replied. Structuring my remaining time, I continued, "General, I will be discussing four topics of interest to you.

First, scientific evaluation and proof of remote viewing; second, KGB funding of Soviet research, which implies hostile intelligence exploitation of the phenomenon; third, INSCOM's OPSEC responsibilities; and finally, Major Keenan's proposed course of action for SED. Our purpose here is to get your approval for this proposed course of action."

"I don't have time for all that, Lieutenant. Do those documents there on the table in front of you cover all that stuff, the scientific proof, and the Soviet activities and all that?" he asked bluntly.

"Yes, Sir, with the exception of our proposed course of action," I said slowly and pensively.

"Well," he barked, "what do you propose to do about all this?"

Cautiously, I continued, "During a recent survey at the missile command at Redstone Arsenal, Alabama . . ."

"Yes," he snarled, "I know where the U.S. Army Missile Command is."

"Sir," I raised my voice and looked directly at him, "the missile command has officially asked us here at INSCOM what OPSEC measures should be taken to counter the threat of Soviet remote-viewing surveillance."

"Oh." He turned toward Major Keenan. "What are we going to do about this, Major?"

Keenan gestured toward me with a nod and said with a go-get-'em wink, "Tell him, Lieutenant. Tell him what we are going to do, and get the general's signature on that budget document you brought with you."

General Smith turned and looked me right in the eye as I told him what we would do. "SED will train professional intelligence personnel with high-level security clearances, people like those here in the conference room right now, in this remote-viewing skill. Once trained, these trusted personnel will be able to provide remote-viewing descriptions of U.S. Army installations and commands. These descriptions will provide us with an accurate means to assess OPSEC vulnerabilities to hostile remote-viewing surveillance of these same organizations.

"It is our opinion, General Smith, that this issue is of vital importance to national security and that INSCOM has a responsibility to provide the appropriate OPSEC support to U.S. Army activities. Further, because Major Keenan's detachment, SED, is the lead element in INSCOM's OPSEC effort, it is the logical and appropriate national-level organization to head this operation."

"This sounds like a good idea," the general said, "but how are you going to train these folks?"

With that, I picked up the budget request I brought with me and, avoiding his direct question, replied, "Since this training clearly falls outside the parameters of this fiscal year's budget, you as deputy commander need to approve this course of action."

"How much are we talking about?" he asked, as I walked out from behind the podium to hand him the SED remote-viewing action plan, cloaked as a budget request.

"Just a couple of thousand to cover travel expenses until the end of the fiscal year," I said casually.

Having handed him the budget request, I returned to the podium, turned, and began to speak, "If we . . ." and he cut me off midsentence. "Here's your approval, Lieutenant," he said, while handing the budget request to Keenan. The general had apparently signed it while I was returning to the podium. Looking at Keenan, he asked, "What's next, Major?" Keenan looked up at me and gruffly ordered, "Atwater, tell Captain Cole out in the hall he's next with his briefing on personnel security issues."

"Yes, Sir," I replied and without another word picked up my documents. As I headed out of the conference room, Keenan passed me the remote-viewing action plan that the general had signed.

As I left the conference room, I could see Captain Cole waiting patiently in the hall. I smiled at him and told him that Major Keenan said he was up next. After Cole went into the conference room, everyone else waiting wanted to know how it went for me. I just smiled and waved the signed budget authorization and action plan in the air.

As I walked back to my cubicle, I began to realize how fast things were moving and how far I had come in just the several weeks since I got assigned to Fort Meade. My plan was to use the funds the general had just authorized to visit SRI and other organizations and come up with a training plan to teach professional intelligence personnel remote viewing. Working with the DIA, I arranged a visit with Hal Puthoff and Russell Targ at SRI in Menlo Park.

Meeting the Scientists

As the airplane sped its way to California, my thoughts meandered through the many official business trips I had taken over the years. I looked around the plane, eavesdropping on my fellow passengers. I wondered how we all came together on this flight.

A business man; a college student returning home; a family on vacation; the stewardess with the tired feet—did they have any idea that right next to them was an intelligence officer developing a psychic-training program for government personnel? What would they think if they knew? Would they be proud that their government was acting quite responsibly to defend their constitutionally guaranteed freedoms?

These were rhetorical questions for, to reduce the probability that hostile intelligence services would find out about our OPSEC activities and implement countermeasures, what I was doing had been classified Secret and designated as an official Special Access Program (SAP) with a code-word caveat. (The first code name was Grill Flame. Over the years, it changed several times, and when it was declassified in 1995, the project was called Star Gate.)

During the flight, I amused myself by reading the Jane Roberts book *The Further Education of Oversoul Seven*. I could never completely understand the original Seth books but the series of *Oversoul Seven* books were in a story format and I really liked them. Much of *Further Education* describes adventures in nonphysical realms and how malleable these worlds are based on our preconceived expectations. According to the book, even other entities are robbed of their own true form and show themselves to us based on our expectations of how they should appear.

This understanding made me feel ashamed. How disrespectful and impertinent! In the middle of Chapter Nineteen, I put the book down on my lap and bowed my head in silent prayer. "God, when I die, please let me have the wisdom to allow others to be who they really are and not lay my expectations upon them."

Suddenly Guidance spoke with a voice in my head, a loud, booming voice, like when the voice of God is portrayed in the movies. "What do you think is happening now?"

I opened my eyes and looked around the cabin to see if anybody else had heard. It was cool. Everything was okay. I was the only one who had heard the voice. And then my embarrassment returned. Apparently, I didn't have to die to begin working on this. How many beings had I encountered throughout my life, seeing them only through the eyes of my own expectations, not allowing them to be who they really were? Divine expressions of God I Am, angels all! And I was on my way to meet two more.

I signed in at the security-control desk at SRI, and the receptionist called upstairs with notification of my arrival. Tall, lanky Russell Targ, with his bushy hair and thick glasses, came downstairs to meet me. He looked every bit like the mad scientist one might expect to be involved in psychic research. Over the years, we were to become friends, but this first encounter, my first impression of him, would not be described in my official trip report to Major Keenan.

Upstairs, I met Dr. Hal Puthoff, a soft-spoken man filled with wisdom too great to be confined in his small stature. Dr. Puthoff introduced me to other members of the office staff. With perfect timing, an SRI vice president happened by the office to meet me. To him, I was the new government guy with money and he wanted to make sure he met me. After the formalities, Puthoff, Targ, and I adjourned to a small conference room and I began to explain what I was doing there.

The idea of training someone to do remote viewing interested both Puthoff and Targ. Most of their work had been done with "naturals," people who brought their inherent psychic talent into the laboratory environment. They said, however, that in their experience almost everyone could do remote viewing. They knew this because Targ would routinely guide visitors to the lab through a remote-viewing exercise as the ultimate demonstration of what they were studying. I was not to be subject to such an illustration, as I didn't need convincing that remote viewing was a real phenomenon.

Hoping to discover some sort of screening mechanism that I could use with intelligence personnel to identify remote-viewing candidates, I asked if they had identified any personality traits or temperament types that seemed to take to remote viewing.

Puthoff and Targ were reluctant at first to approach the issue in this way. They were physicists, not psychologists. They insisted that the best screening mechanism would be a performance test and evaluation through the use of the established, tried-and-true remote-viewing protocol documented in their book.

I asked how many people they could test in a few months. They guessed that they could test three people over a period of four to six months. So I asked if they had identified any personality traits that I might use to find candidates for such testing. Having put the question to them in this manner, they told me that there were perhaps six traits that seemed to be characteristic of good remote viewers.

1. They felt that candidates should be at least open to the idea of remote viewing.

2. Candidates should have an artistic talent and be capable of using this talent to describe their remote-viewing impressions.

3. People who were highly regarded by their coworkers and supervisors did better at remote viewing than those who were not. The implication was that "office outcasts" or "weird guys" did not make good remote viewers.

4. Individuals who had the ability to in-flow data, or absorb a great deal of information without being compelled to form tentative or spurious conclusions, scored higher within the strict confines of scientific remote-viewing protocols.

5. Candidates should be highly motivated volunteers rather than be "ordered" or "assigned" to do remote viewing.

6. Potential remote viewers should be able to quiet their minds and focus their attention on the task at hand, setting aside the mental noise of daily trials and tribulations.

They insisted that even if I was able to identify soldiers with these traits, they would want to interview the candidates, and even under these conditions, there was no guarantee that these people would be able to do remote viewing or be trained. I found this comment amusing in light of Targ's previous claims that almost everybody who tries remote viewing has some success.

Thinking back, I imagine they thought I would select as remote viewers some highly skilled, snake-eating special forces types who had been kept away in some secret guerrilla-training camp because they could no longer function in society. Whatever they were thinking, their bottom line was that the only way to determine someone's remote-viewing ability (or trainability) was through some sort of performance test to identify particular aptitudes.

On the flight back from California, I began to develop a plan of action to present to Major Keenan. It seemed to me that SED would have to interview several dozen people to find a few that fit the criteria outlined by SRI, and the candidates would need to be available for special duty with SED. The greater Washington, D.C., area contained hundreds, perhaps thousands, of military and civilian intelligence professionals within INSCOM. With the endorsement of the INSCOM commander, there would definitely be sufficient resources from which to draw.

Puthoff and Targ had tentatively agreed to accept a contract to train (they preferred the term "evaluate") a few selected army personnel in remote viewing. I decided that I would recommend to Major Keenan that SED screen a number of INSCOM personnel and establish a contractual relationship with SRI to train them.

I also thought that because SRI's "evaluation" method was fully documented in *Mind-Reach*, SED could, with a little effort, complement the SRI contract and do our own remote-viewing skills testing and evaluation.[5]

As the plane sped eastward, I took out a yellow legal pad from my briefcase and drafted a trip report and a list of recommended actions.

---

[5] This process is detailed in the article, "Remote-Viewing Replication: Evaluated by Concept Analysis," by Russell Targ, published in *The Journal of Parapsychology*, vol. 58, September 1994.

Further Approval

When I returned to my office at Fort Meade, I typed up my report and routed it to Major Keenan. I didn't hear anything from him for more than two weeks, so I busied myself with other duties.

Unknown to me, Keenan had been told by the INSCOM commander to brief General Thompson at the Pentagon about SED's remote-viewing endeavor. General Thompson, the ACSI, had a personal interest in remote viewing and was the one who had originally interested Lieutenant Colonel Skotzko (the guy whose desk I took over).

General Thompson agreed with the recommendations in my report and encouraged Major Keenan to continue SED's efforts within INSCOM. At some point in the chain of command (I don't know where), the decision was made to consolidate the INSCOM remote-viewing program under one office. When Keenan finally called me into his office, he told me that my recommendations had been approved and informed me that I was to work with a Major Watt, a veteran intelligence officer, to carry out this project.

The remote-viewing effort would operate as a separate unit called Detachment G, with its own operating budget. From this budget, we would fund travel expenses, contracts with SRI, and whatever else became necessary. Major Watt would be my direct supervisor, and together we would conduct INSCOM's remote-viewing program. At the time, being unaware of all that had gone on up the chain-of-command, I thought this was all Major Keenan's idea.

Major Murray Watt—Scotty to his friends—was an extremely professional military officer. He had a great deal of experience in intelligence work but didn't know anything about remote viewing. So I was to be the remote-viewing "expert" and Watt the one who knew his way around the bureaucracy of the intelligence community and could ensure we stayed on track with the military counterintelligence focus of our mission.

Major Watt handled the administration of Detachment G and represented the unit to the brass and numerous other intelligence agencies and offices. He was perfect for the job. I was responsible for the remote-viewing activities of the unit. We were assigned our own office down the hall from SED, and as the weeks passed, Watt worked on formalizing a contract with SRI.

Together we came up with a plan to screen INSCOM personnel assigned throughout southern Maryland, northern Virginia, and Washington, D.C. Since we didn't want to reveal our plans to train a cadre of remote viewers, we decided to use a ruse.

Our plan was to tell those we questioned, as well as their supervisors and commanders, that we were conducting a survey for the commander, INSCOM, asking INSCOM personnel for their opinions on the idea of police using psychics to help in criminal investigations and whether they thought psychically derived information might be of assistance to the military-intelligence community. We collected several newspaper clippings about the police use of psychics and took the articles with us to the interviews.

Recruiting

Our first step was to contact INSCOM unit commanders and office supervisors. We told them about our survey and asked them to suggest personnel for us to interview. We told them we were looking for opinions from those who were most respected by their coworkers and were likely to speak openly to us about our survey.

Based on their recommendations, we began our interviews. As we spoke with INSCOM personnel, we gently elicited information regarding the six criteria provided by Puthoff and Targ. At first, Major Watt and I conducted the interviews together, and when we gained some confidence that we knew what we were doing, we interviewed separately then met later to discuss our findings. Altogether we interviewed between one hundred and one hundred twenty-five INSCOM personnel.

When one of us felt favorably about someone that we had interviewed, we reviewed his personnel file, and then the other would reinterview that person to double-check the finding. By comparing notes and accepting each other's recommendations, we decided that between twenty and thirty of the people we interviewed seemed to meet the criteria outlined by Puthoff and Targ.

We went back to the supervisors and commanders of the qualified interviewees to determine which of these personnel would be available for special duty with Detachment G. We were able to identify twelve military and civilian INSCOM personnel who could be freed up for extra duty.

We then contacted each of these individuals and asked them to meet us in the secure conference room at Fort Meade. We did not tell them individually that there would be others at the meeting. We only told them that we wanted to do a follow-up interview. On the day they arrived, they all sat around the conference table before the meeting started, sort of wondering what they were doing there.

The job fell to me to tell them what was going on. As I rose from my seat to address them, I looked thoughtfully at each. I told them we hadn't been completely truthful when Major Watt and I had spoken with them before. I held up a copy of Mind-Reach and told them about visiting SRI and talking with Puthoff and Targ. I showed them the classified remote-viewing documents I had and reviewed the hostile threat perspective published by the air force. I went on to explain that Detachment G was forming a cadre of remote viewers and that we were recruiting volunteers to be trained as remote viewers. I told them that, based on our initial interviews with them, we felt they might be interested.

Several of them asked questions about the materials I presented and what I meant by "volunteers to be trained as remote viewers." I answered the questions about SRI and the classified studies but sidestepped the training questions. When the discussion settled down, I asked, "Based on what I have told you up to this point, do any of you want to volunteer for special duty with Detachment G?" All twelve answered in the affirmative. It was time for Major Watt to take over.

"Before we can continue," he began, "I must ask you all to sign a security oath regarding this program." Major Watt explained that the Special Access Program had been given an official code name and that only those read-on to the program were allowed to discuss the project. By signing the Special Access Program security oath as we others had, the volunteers agreed to these conditions.

All of the volunteers were professional intelligence personnel and were familiar with code-named projects, so this process was not entirely new for them. Major Watt and I answered various questions that came up concerning Detachment G while they were signing their security oaths. After all the paperwork was completed, we took a coffee break, and during the break the volunteers talked among themselves, finding out where each other worked and sharing stories about what they had told Watt or myself during their interviews.

When we resumed, Major Watt turned the agenda back over to me. I told the group that Detachment G had a contractual relationship with SRI and that Puthoff and Targ would be coming to Fort Meade to select several of them to go to Menlo Park for training. I explained that others were to be trained at Fort Meade using the methods that had been developed at SRI. I showed them some examples from Mind-Reach and the classified documents I had. Then I described a typical SRI remote-viewing scenario as follows:

> A remote viewer and an interviewer sit alone in a room at a prearranged time. The interviewer prompts the remote viewer to describe a remote site unknown to either of them while a third person is visiting the site. The third person is assigned a random target location selected from a list of nearby targets. While the interviewer and the remote viewer are not told the target location, the remote viewer is nevertheless asked to draw and describe impressions of the target being visited by the third party. Because both the viewer and interviewer are unwitting, the interviewer can ask questions about the viewer's mental perceptions and help clarify descriptive elements. After the remote-viewing period is over, all the descriptive data are collected and both the viewer and interviewer are taken to the target site. While visiting the site, the viewer's descriptions are compared with apparent surroundings and the activities of the third person during the viewing

> period. Similarities, differences, and missing or distorted perceptions are discussed. During this post-viewing visit to the target site, the viewer presumably learns to improve descriptions of the remote-viewing experience.

At this point, I reminded the Detachment G volunteers that what was of interest to INSCOM was the degree to which the remote-viewing process could be used by hostile intelligence agencies as a surveillance method to compromise our own security.

In the classified documents I had shown to them were examples of SRI remote viewers describing Soviet military sites. So the question wasn't so much if remote viewing could compromise our security, but the severity and depth of such a compromise. Our mission was not to replicate the scientific work of SRI but to assess the strategic and tactical impact of remote-viewing surveillance on the operational security of the army.

Major Watt ended the meeting by welcoming the volunteers to their special duty with Detachment G. He told them that they would be notified when the SRI scientists were coming to Fort Meade. He provided them with our Detachment G office phone number, recommended they buy themselves their own copy of Mind-Reach, and sent them back to their respective "regular" jobs in INSCOM.

It had been less than a year since I had reported for duty to Fort Meade and I seemed to be floating downstream, effortlessly drifting toward a future that I had envisioned in my discussions with Rob Cowart not so very long ago. It seemed that everything that had happened in my life up to this point had been preparing me for what was happening now.

This concept that there was some plan or purpose to my life was not new to me. But, in the days in the Panama Canal Zone, when life seemed so complete, I had never thought I would someday be training a cadre of military remote viewers. So perhaps foreknowledge of my course through life was meant to remain below my threshold of awareness. I wondered if some greater part of me, my true spiritual identity, had known all along what was happening.

Several weeks passed before Puthoff and Targ came to Fort Meade. As Major Watt had been negotiating a contract with them to train our volunteers, he had been discussing the concept of training three. When we told them we had identified twelve people for them to meet, they were a bit overwhelmed. They thought that we wanted them to train all twelve, and everybody sort of panicked, but they agreed to come to Fort Meade without resolving this "numbers" issue.

Our twelve volunteers met as a group with Puthoff and Targ early in 1979. After a group introduction and discussion, the scientists interviewed each of the volunteers individually. As each completed their interview, Major Watt and I thanked them and sent them back to their respective INSCOM jobs with an assuring "We'll be in touch."

After Puthoff and Targ had finished interviewing all the candidates, Major Watt suggested that we go to lunch. During lunch, we avoided talking about the remote-viewing project and took advantage of the time to get to know each other better. We learned, for example, that Dr. Puthoff had been in the navy and had been assigned to Fort Meade for a short time. He even pointed out the neighborhood where he had lived. This getting to know one another was just what was needed to further our after-lunch discussions.

When we returned to the office, Major Watt and I wanted to know what Puthoff and Targ thought of our volunteers. They, on the other hand, were somewhat focused on generating a lucrative contract to support their work. I say somewhat focused because they started the afternoon discussion rather sheepishly by explaining that in their opinion all the candidates looked fine and they were hard-pressed to pick only three out of the twelve. I think this must have been Watt's strategy all along . . . if they became enamored with our people they would be more flexible on their contract terms.

It was understood by all of us that, while Watt and I used the words "training remote viewers," the SRI scientists felt that what they offered was more akin to an ability or talent assessment. They weren't so sure anyone could be trained to do remote viewing.

The contract would, most assuredly, say training, as this was a palatable concept—government personnel were trained to do many things—but none had ever been evaluated for a psychic talent. Watt and I always told our volunteers they were being trained to be remote viewers, even though that might not have been the case in fact.

So impossible was it for Puthoff and Targ to reduce our twelve candidates to three, they proposed that the contract include two phases. The first phase would involve working with six candidates to determine the best three performers of those six. The second phase would involve in-depth work with those three candidates who showed the most promise.

Major Watt asked about costs and they said that there would be no increase in amounts previously discussed. I asked if they had six candidates in mind. They said that they did. Watt glanced over at me to see if I thought their proposal was okay, and I inconspicuously nodded my approval.

Watt stood up, extended his hand, and announced, "Gentlemen, your proposal is acceptable. We have a deal." Puthoff took his hand and smiled. Contracts would have to be signed later, of course, but at this point we were essentially on our way to SRI and remote-viewing history. (At some point, Stanford Research Institute changed its name to SRI International to distance itself from Stanford University. The name change didn't have anything to do with its involvement in remote viewing, and I continue to refer to the institution as SRI when in fact at some point its proper name became SRI International.)

The Training

Military duty is a balance between operations and training. If you are a tank driver and there isn't an ongoing military battle, you occupy your time training for that eventuality. When there isn't an ongoing ground war, the foot soldier trains for one. Besides physical training to keep their bodies in shape and personal weapons training, military personnel spend hours rehearsing tactics, practicing maneuvers, and planning operations.

Detachment G was no different. As the unit's operations and training officer, I was responsible for . . . well, here it is copied from my official Officer Efficiency Report, DA Form 68-7:

> Operations Officer for an INSCOM special access, sensitive intelligence collection program. Responsible to plan, schedule and implement individual collection requirements and prepare intelligence reports based upon information obtained. Training Officer for division personnel. Responsible to organize and execute the division training program; conduct specialized training to enhance individual capabilities and integrate new collection techniques into the current program; maintain an expertise in state-of-the-art technology. Member of the Military Intelligence Excepted Career Program [nickname: Great Skills].

It was my responsibility, then, to develop and implement a remote-viewing training program for Detachment G. Through the months, I had been reading up on different remote-viewing programs at various organizations. When I talked with Puthoff and Targ about specific remote-viewing techniques, as opposed to scientific remote-viewing protocols, they told me that they pretty much let the individual remote viewers do whatever they wanted to during the perceptual process. If viewers wanted to lie down or meditate, that was perfectly acceptable. One of their viewers had some "lucky socks" that she liked to wear while remote viewing.

The Puthoff and Targ perspective was basically this: viewers should be encouraged to sketch or draw elements of the target site and provide short, perhaps one- to three-word, descriptions of their perceptions. Their personal habits or ceremonies were of little relevance. Stated another way, based on their observations of performance verses results, they didn't feel there was any behavior, special state of consciousness, or physical or mental preparedness particularly conducive or enhancing to remote viewing.

Another highly respected researcher, William G. Braud from the University of Houston, Texas, theorized a "PSI-conducive syndrome," or set of circumstances that seemed to be related to increased psychic performance. These circumstances involved such things as percipients being physically relaxed, receptive, and attuned to internal perceptual processes, an environment of reduced raucous sensory stimulus, and a psychic task of some relevant importance. These concepts seemed to "fill in the blanks" not addressed by the physicists at SRI.[6]

Charles Honorton and his colleagues at the Psychophysical Research Laboratories in Princeton, New Jersey, offered another point of view. Operating within the concept that psychic or remote-viewing information presents itself below the threshold of conscious awareness and is therefore overwhelmed by physical sensation, they postulated that neutralizing the physical senses would help this lower-amplitude mental information bubble up into awareness.

Further, remote-viewing experiments had shown that spurious sensory data often contaminated remote-viewing descriptions. For instance, elements within decorative pictures on the walls of the remote-viewing room sometimes showed up in the viewer's target descriptions. By neutralizing such sensory data, valid remote-viewing information was expected to increase—an improved signal-to-noise ratio, so to speak.

Honorton's neutralization process was called the Ganzfeld (German for "whole field") technique. Translucent acetate hemispheres (Ping-Pong ball halves) were put over the remote viewer's eyes, and headphones were placed over the ears. White noise was played through the headphones. Eyes remained open when wearing the translucent eye shields, and a bright red light was shown through the shields, which provided a homogeneous visual field. Tactile stimulation was reduced by having the remote viewer recline in a comfortable chair and do relaxation exercise to reduce muscular tension.

Operating within this Ganzfeld environment, the remote viewer was then cued to perceive the selected target, which of course was unknown to the viewer. The viewer remained in the Ganzfeld setting

---

[6] See the article, "PSI Conducive States," by William G. Braud, published in the *Journal of Communication* (1975).

for about thirty minutes, reporting via a microphone any perceptions of the target. According to my review of the literature, forty-two Ganzfeld studies conducted by investigators in ten laboratories reported average hit rates of about thirty-five percent with a chance expectation, based on judging criteria, of twenty-five percent. The statistical probability of getting a thirty-five percent hit rate across forty-two studies was highly significant, greater than a billion to one.[7]

The idea of quieting the mind to become aware of subtle cognitive processes was not limited to Honorton and the Ganzfeld researchers. This idea was the cornerstone of many traditional eastern meditation techniques. It seemed to me that the ability to quiet one's prosaic thoughts and focus one's attention might have a great deal to do with successful remote viewing.

My own "remote viewing" experience was more akin to an intuitive process—direct knowledge coupled with introspective observation. This stream of consciousness united two distinct experiences. In the first case, immersed within some task or curiosity, I moved through an adventure, seeking only to achieve a particular goal. In the second case, I became aware of my own mental content, noticing my own thoughts about what was happening to me.

The content of the second-case observation differed from that of the first-case adventure. In the first-case adventure, my goal-oriented intention aligned my perceptual venues. It was a form of pure knowing unencumbered by the need to conform the data perceived to conventional wisdom.

My intention in the second case was to make some sense out of what was happening and to validate or place my perceptions within an acceptable social framework. The content of the second-case experience became the "past-lived" pure experience colored by outside thoughts, memories, and emotional opinion.

Seemingly incorrect remote-viewing information may be the result of reporting the second-case experience along with its inher-

---

[7] The complete history of Ganzfeld research was summarized by Daryl J. Bem and Charles Honorton in the January 1994 issue of the *Psychological Bulletin of the American Psychological Association.*

ent overlay. (These inaccuracies can be reduced through the use of a mediator or coach to help the remote viewer objectify the direct knowledge of the first-case experience.)

Bringing together what I learned from Puthoff and Targ and other respected scientists, a review of the pertinent literature, and my own personal experience, a generic framework for training began to emerge. From this perspective, I began to develop what became the army's remote-viewing training program.

If successful, trained remote viewers would be able to assess the strategic and tactical impact of remote-viewing surveillance on the operational security of the army. But, as I would eventually realize, this whole episode in my life would generate waves of change throughout our culture for decades to come.

Chapter Four

Remote-Viewing Training and Operations

What follows is a somewhat cumbersome detailing of what became the army's remote-viewing training and operations program. If you are more interested in the overall meaning all this had and less interested in the specific details, then perhaps you should flip forward a few pages to the section called The Training Begins. Because of my personal involvement in this government-sanctioned project, I felt obligated to provide a complete and informative account. So, here goes.

Technical Background

Remote viewing can be divided into categories or *behaviors* (relaxing, connecting, listening, becoming aware, and reporting) that can be reinforced using conventional learning techniques.

Relaxing

The first behavior is *letting go and turning inward*. Remote viewing appears to be dependent on an "interior state" or perceptual viewpoint. In a sense, the remote viewer discovers information from within rather than from sensory sources.

This reorientation can sometimes be brought about deliberately by modifying body posture, or exhibiting certain physical gestures, or by regulating one's breathing. This state may also be accessed through deliberately modifying ongoing mental activity, like willfully visualizing a favorite tranquil scene. Conversely, this remote-viewing state may resist deliberate provocation. One can't *try* to release or use effort to "let go." It is something one simply and voluntarily allows to happen.

Once obtained, this letting go and turning inward state changes one's perception of the body space and produces certain alterations in thinking processes. While remote viewing, the viewer may have sensations of being unified or whole, while at the same time expanding to the point where the sense of body or personal space disappears.

In the letting go and turning inward state, mental calmness replaces cognitive activity and the mind seems to slow down. This transformation results in setting aside conceptual rambling and replacing it with bodily or kinesthetic experience. These characteristics of the letting go and turning inward remote-viewing state are common also to so-called borderline or twilight states of consciousness.

Some remote viewers seem to know when they have achieved this receptive state of consciousness and know how to maintain or perpetuate this state, perhaps by adjusting their body position or checking their breathing.

From a training perspective, then, teaching people to allow themselves access to this interior state of knowing should enhance the overall remote-viewing behavior. Such training is available in a number of disciplines. I simply needed to restructure existing formats and set up modeling and reinforcement scenarios, as a sports coach or music teacher might do. Some of this was evident in SRI's remote-viewing protocol, but their interest was in results-oriented testing and evaluation. They never thought about what they were doing from a teaching perspective.

So, for the initial training, I provided the remote-viewing recruits with reading materials and practical exercises designed to enhance their ability to relax their minds and bodies and focus their attention on internal perceptual processes. When they reported appropriate feelings, sensations, and perceptions, I reinforced this behavior with verbal appreciation, a smile, and gestures of praise.

Connecting

The second behavior characteristic of remote viewing is a *resonance phase,* during which the viewer contacts the "information of interest," which may be a physical object, a particular activity, or a location. Sometimes remote viewers seem to be able to align themselves with personal questions, the emotional or mental states of others, health issues, or even scientific and technical dilemmas.

The actual nature of the information, the space/time relation to the viewer, and the sensorial vocabulary available define the connection. For the most part, the process of connecting appears to emerge from the unconscious, and different viewers experience variations of the connection process. Some bring the information into the interior mental space freed during the opening preparation process. Other viewers extend their perceptual windows across the "distance" between them and the information of interest until a unity is achieved. Still other remote viewers perceive themselves harmonizing or synchronizing with the information of interest.

Teaching the connection behavior is simply a matter of attending to the preferences of each individual trainee and coaching them along until they begin to trust in themselves and their own process. Imagine for a moment teaching (coaching) children how to "connect" with the soccer ball during play. First, you just place the ball at their feet and tell them to kick it. The better they do, the more you reward and praise them for their performance. You might suggest a pointed toe or a bent knee, but for the most part you simply give them the opportunity to practice "connecting" with the ball. Next, you gently roll the ball to them and again ask them to kick it. Then you get them to approach the ball as it is rolling toward them and kick it again. So the coach's job here is to present a variety of opportunities for them to "connect" with the ball.

Their first-person experience of "connecting" will be based on both what you suggest to them and on previous experiences. You might tell them as a matter of course to visualize their foot striking the ball. Some players will take well to this internal process. Others may prefer to see themselves becoming one with the ball and rocketing off to a distant field position.

In remote-viewing training, it is appropriate to teach this connecting process by starting off with a number of very tangible experiences similar to the original SRI protocol. The remote viewer meets an individual and later is asked to "resonate" with and describe that person's location. This is a very tangible concept, easily imagined by the trainee. The remote viewer can imagine being one with the person at the designated site of interest, think about observing the person's activities at the site, or even expand awareness to the point of becoming the site—its description therefore becomes a matter of self-discovery.

The teacher or coach praises evidence of strong connections with the target and the trainee internalizes the processes that are successful. Another tangible connecting experience that can be offered is to have a remote viewer describe a picture concealed in an envelope. As the viewer develops confidence, less tangible connecting experiences are offered.

Geographic coordinates representing global positions can be provided to the viewer with the expectation that the viewer access and describe relevant information about that location. The teacher/coach similarly reinforces behavior-evidencing resonance with the site of interest. When the viewer further internalizes those processes that yield accurate target descriptions, even more abstract cueing can be used to initiate the connection process.

Listening

The third behavior characteristic of remote viewing is a *listening stage,* during which remote viewers find themselves in a state of interior calm, listening very closely to their own sensations. This stage of the process may involve different sensory modes and attention states.

The information desired by a remote viewer appears at first to express its essence within the habit-limited sensory process of the physical body. Initially, the remote viewer may experience only sensory elements. Different viewers characteristically perceive and respond to information differently. Some of us operate in a visual context ("I see what you mean"), some with an auditory codicil ("I hear what you are saying"), and still others perceive and respond kinesthetically ("I feel you are right"). There are interpersonal-communications schools based on these principles; one can learn to interrelate on all three dimensions.

The remote viewer's focus of attention may be internal or external or even panoramic, not focused on any special aspect. Unlike focused attention that attends to a particular element and is narrow and rigid, the remote viewer's attention is open, ambient, without any precise intention. It is more a waiting patiently without expectation, a receptive state without looking for or grasping at anything. During the listening stage, the viewer peacefully welcomes the arrival—the awareness—of information about the site of interest, which launches the fourth behavior characteristic of remote viewing.

In teaching this listening stage, it is important to remember that at this point the viewer is not expected to report perceptions, a "second-case" experience which occurs sometime later. So in coaching the listening stage, we told viewers to experience without describing or reporting, to simply observe the experience they have in response to cueing. After a few minutes of silence, trainees were asked to describe not their perceptions of the cued information but their experience of observing. At first they might have had a tendency to describe the cued information, but through gentle coaching they could be guided to explain and identify with the experience of "listening" with an open mind to their own perceptual processes.

Becoming Aware

The fourth behavior characteristic of remote viewing is actually *becoming aware of information*. This phase includes the moment just before the awareness, the awareness itself, and the brief period following the awareness.

There comes a moment, just preceding the emergence of informational awareness, during which remote viewers experience an emptiness or disorienting moment of confusion, as though the mind was released from the confines of the physical dimension. Following this void of *physicalness*, information appears in awareness. This can be internal images, feelings, sounds, words, tastes and smells, thoughts without words, etc. A feeling of surety and a sense of meaning usually accompany the emergence of this information into consciousness.

At the moment of awareness, the remote viewer's internal state is passive. Preconceived concepts, rules, learned knowledge, memory, and premeditation are suspended. The sensation of being an individual separate from what is perceived vanishes.

Because research has shown that psychic perceptions can influence our behavior before reaching the threshold of awareness, it is assumed that remote-viewing information is always available, even if not realized. Many perceptions are on the boundaries of awareness and do not always emerge in a complete or understandable form. One's first awareness may be an indistinct image or a vague sensation. As one practices bringing on internal calmness and listening with an open mind, remote-viewing awareness will develop, and one will be better able to discriminate among the sensations perceived.

In the brief period after awareness, remote viewers can adopt several interior attitudes. They can repress the sensation or grasp the sensation by attaching it to emotions or by binding it to interior dialogue that will distort it and disturb "listening," or, worse, they could seek to recognize the sensation, understand it, and interpret it. All these cognitive processes have the effect of "fixing up" these possibly indistinct or vague impressions and putting an end to the flow of information awareness. Optimally, the remote viewer quietly accepts the awareness and confidently and patiently lets it blossom and take form without analyzing or interpreting it.

Teaching this unique awareness phase involves monitoring the cognitive processes of trainees and reinforcing those that support accurate recovery of information of interest (site data). Viewers must be coached to maintain an open mind, and their reactions to their perceptions must be measured, to ensure that they do not adopt an attitude that distorts or terminates the information flow.

Students should be encouraged to write down in essay form their cognitive content during this awareness phase. These writings should not be about the site of interest—the cued information—but about the internal mentation processes of the viewer while becoming aware of these data. The teacher/coach can use these written accounts to assess and reinforce appropriate behavior.

Remote viewers should be encouraged to let inklings become stable, and then gently deepen the "contact" (see the connection phase above) *without forcing,* until the inkling takes form. When objectified (see below), correct descriptions will tend to further resolve the impression and further involve the viewer with the information of interest.

Reporting

The fifth behavior characteristic of remote viewing is *describing or reporting* information perceived while "connected." This behavior constitutes a second-case experience of the actual awareness phase of remote viewing and is sometimes called objectifying. It involves skillfully conveying potentially valid intersubjective perceptions from the mental realm of awareness into the physical, objective world. The remote viewer trainee must learn precise strategies to translate impressions into communicable form without engaging habitual interpretation, analysis, or blocking behavior. Ideally, remote-viewing data represent direct knowledge, unfiltered by an intermediary reasoning process.

When remote viewers set aside their representations, beliefs, judgments, and preconceived notions about the information of interest,[8] and begin speaking slowly from a quiet place inside, where they become more and more connected with the first-case experience of the information of interest, site descriptions become precious insights.

An experienced interviewer can be very helpful during the process of objectifying. The interviewer's job requires sensitivity to the remote viewer's phrasing, body language, and subtle, sometimes unconscious, behaviors. The most effective interviewers are themselves experienced intuitives capable of empathetic appreciation of the remote viewer's perspective.

The role of the teacher/coach and interviewer intertwine during this process. So teaching remote viewers to objectify their impressions necessarily involves mastery of appropriate interviewing techniques.[9] The teacher/interviewer/coach (monitor) helps the remote viewers unfold their first-case act, through verbalization and drawing, by posing questions that elicit more information than the viewers realize or suppose that they know. The monitor attends to their phrasing, body language, and subtle behaviors—above and beyond what is being said—and then uses this information to refocus or redirect the remote viewer.

Becoming aware (the fourth behavior discussed above) and being able to objectify (as in verbalize and/or draw) are distinctly different behaviors. The intent to *objectify* information subordinates, to some degree, the intent to *acquire* information. Viewers must be taught to maintain a delicate balance between the first-case experience of awareness and the second-case experience of objectifying.

During objectification, there are indications, certain micro behaviors exhibited by the remote viewers, which indicate to the interviewer that they are accessing first-case experience information.

---

[8] My somewhat redundant use of "information of interest" rather than "designated target" or "remote-viewing site" is meant to convey that, whatever a remote viewer is asked to describe or engage, it would seem that the viewer connects with data in a non-space/time pool of information.

[9] A detailed account of the interviewing skills necessary is beyond the scope of this writing. Suffice it to say that my previous special agent training at Fort Holibird, Maryland, came in very handy.

A loss of eye-to-eye contact, with the viewer looking off into emptiness, a break in the speech pattern of the viewer, or even the use of present-tense instead of past-tense verbs can all be indications of first-case experience reporting rather than interpretation or analysis.

A slowing down of the rhythm of verbalization can be an indication that the remote viewers are not simply reciting previous knowledge in *reaction to* perception but are accurately reporting aspects of their first-case experiences.

Remote viewers often resort to the use of abstract descriptions (metaphors, similes, conditional judgments, etc.) rather than sticking to a precise description of the perceived information. Such use of abstracts indicates cognitive interpretation, analysis, and/or integration rather than direct experiential knowledge gained as a result of the first-case remote-viewing experience.

The interview provides, firstly, a sequence of *moments* during which remote viewers silently relive an aspect of their first-case experience. Secondly, the interview provides subsequent time periods during which remote viewers objectify these moments (describing them verbally and/or with drawings) while at the same time maintaining a mental connection to the information of interest.

The monitor encourages the remote viewers to describe their experiences using an Ericksonian style of questioning—referring to the American psychotherapist Milton Erickson, whose technique is characterized by indirect suggestion instead of the more traditional, authoritarian approach. This allows the remote viewer to clarify first-case experience without inducing content or influencing the choice of words or descriptions used by the viewer. It is difficult, if not impossible, for some remote viewers to remain within their first-case experience and simultaneously objectify this as a second-case experience.

If remote viewers lose this connection—this psychic link—to the site, they can be reimmersed into the first-case experience through the use of auto-cueing techniques or through monitor cueing. A productive interview can then resume.

In the end, learning remote viewing involves the trainees not in learning progressively accumulating knowledge but in giving up old habits of representation, categorization, abstraction, and identification. They soon realize that their awareness extends beyond their physical bodies and/or the sum of their sensory neural activity.

The Training Begins

Focusing on the above-outlined remote-viewing behaviors (relaxing, connecting, listening, becoming aware, and reporting), I began training our recruits at Fort Meade months before they went out to SRI. All recruit remote viewers experienced several of these initial remote-viewing exercises, as we felt that the remote viewers who had been selected to go to SRI would benefit from the practice, while those recruits who had not been selected would have an opportunity to demonstrate their ability and be part of the project.

This effort also gave me a chance to hone my skills as a remote-viewing interviewer/coach. Major Watt was able to see firsthand that professional intelligence personnel were able to remote view if placed in a conducive environment.

Using the initial "out-bounder" protocol common to the remote viewing done at SRI, Major Watt would randomly select a target envelope from a target pool of sites within a thirty-minute drive of Fort Meade. When one of the remote viewers and I would enter the viewing room, Watt would drive away, opening the sealed envelope only when he was some distance from the office. In the envelope was the name of the designated target site and driving instructions to get there. Back in the office, sequestered in the viewing room, I would stay with the remote viewer while preparing for the exercise.

In these first months of the project, remote viewers usually used the time while Watt was driving to the target site to practice getting into a state of consciousness conducive to remote viewing. Each of them had a slightly different method for doing this. I coached and encouraged their various physical relaxation and mental clearing techniques. At the appropriate, designated time, I would prompt the remote viewer to focus attention on Watt's location. This was the cue for the remote viewer to "connect" with the information of interest.

The room usually fell silent for a few moments while the remote viewer turned inward and listened intently for some emerging perception. If after a few minutes the remote viewer didn't seem to be connected with the information of interest, I would prompt the viewer again to focus attention on Watt's location.

Once the remote viewer became aware of data emerging into consciousness as evidenced by micro behaviors (eye movements, spontaneous gestures, etc.) and verbal utterances, I changed my prompting slightly and directed the viewer to "describe" Watt's location. This was the cue for the remote viewer to enter the second-case objectification experience. I coached and encouraged short, nonanalytic comments concerning the information of interest. If the viewers lost contact with the site, I would simply prompt them to focus once again on Watt's location.

Some remote viewers liked to draw while describing Watt's location; others preferred to complete the verbal interview first. Viewers who waited until after the interview to draw seemed to have a more defined second-case experience. When viewers waited to draw until after the interview, I simply went over my notes with them, directing their objectification by saying something like, "You described a brick wall at the site. Draw that wall for me, showing where it is located." Although this drawing activity seemed to me to be an experience "here" (in the office) rather than "there" (at the target site), remote viewers seemed able to describe more information of interest during this drawing experience. (SRI, too, encouraged drawing as a valuable component of the remote-viewing process.) This advantage seemed to have two dimensions.

In the first place, raw remote-viewing impressions may be "right-brain," or nonverbal, perceptions emerging more easily into awareness as a gestalt and easily objectified through drawing and autonomic involvement. Second, once completed, a drawing could be used to cue the remote viewer to describe in more detail selected aspects of the site.

For example, in the notional wall drawing in the illustration above, I could point to one side of the wall and direct the remote viewer to describe that specific area. Such direction would prompt the viewer to once again connect with the target and the newly designated information of interest, listen for some emerging perception, become aware of site data, and then objectify those insights.

After the viewing session, the viewer and the interviewer were taken to the designated site to compare the remote-viewing descriptions with the "ground-truth" perceptions of the site (information of interest).

SRI Training

In May 1979, we started sending remote-viewing candidates out to Menlo Park. They were told that they were being sent for remote-viewing training. They were not told that this was to be an evaluation and that only three of them would return to SRI for in-depth work. (We didn't want to add to any performance anxiety they might already be experiencing.)

Each candidate spent one week in Menlo Park conducting remote-viewing trials, and an independent analyst judged the trials using a complexly structured evaluation method called "blind differential discrimination."

As the weeks went by and each candidate returned from Menlo Park, Major Watt and I debriefed them, curious about how well they had done and what they thought of the experience.

The article, "Remote-Viewing Replication: Evaluated By Concept Analysis," by Russell Targ, published in *The Journal of Parapsychology*, Vol. 58, September 1994, is a detailed reporting of the performance of the six Detachment G remote-viewing recruits. Their identities were not provided in the article so as to protect their anonymity.

Targ's article, and SRI's 1979 report, stated that four of the six candidates evidenced superb remote-viewing abilities, producing independently significant remote-viewing results. The two other candidates showed some evidence for good remote-viewing skills, even though their individual series of target-site descriptions did not reach statistical significance.

While the six volunteers cycled through the first SRI evaluation, we continued training practice at Fort Meade. During this time, natural attrition reduced the numbers of volunteers. Some volunteers had taken well to the remote-viewing process, while others were less successful or were attracted to other professional pursuits. I don't think any were particularly disillusioned about their own remote-viewing abilities. The higher-performing recruits were culled from the original volunteer list, and a core cadre of army remote viewers began to form.

We stayed focused on our mission. We had been charged with training professional intelligence personnel to do remote viewing. Once trained, they were to provide remote-viewing descriptions of U.S. Army installations and commands all over the world, in an attempt to assess OPSEC vulnerabilities to hostile remote-viewing surveillance. SED and Detachment G felt that this effort was of vital importance to national security.

Major Watt and I, in consult with Puthoff and Targ, needed to decide which of the six original recruits would return to SRI for further testing and evaluation (training). Watt and I wanted SRI input on which recruits they thought would develop dependable remote-viewing skills. We also wanted to get the three permanently reassigned to Detachment G at Fort Meade. As it turned out, there was overwhelming agreement among all parties, and the three best recruits were selected.

The official report of results of this second-phase training/evaluation at SRI has not been declassified. However, SRI's efforts at that time moved beyond the basic out-bounder protocol into alternate cueing methodologies, different types or styles of targets, and the evaluation of enhanced remote-viewing skills.

The basic out-bounder protocol involved sending a person known to the remote viewer to a randomly selected nearby location. Alternate cueing methodologies included, but were not limited to, cueing by geographic coordinates[10] and sealed-envelope exercises.

---

[10] It is said that Ingo Swann first introduced the idea of cueing a remote viewer by using latitude and longitude geographic coordinates. The expression CRV or "coordinate remote viewing" emerged when Ingo was working with SRI. I was recently informed that Ingo prefers the expression "controlled remote viewing."

The out-bounder protocol was used as an initial screening tool and training methodology to enhance viewer confidence. It had little applications potential, however. Coordinate remote viewing (CRV) could be applied directly to our OPSEC mission. To initiate connection with the information of interest in CRV, the interviewer simply cued the remote viewer by reciting the latitude and longitude in degrees, minutes, and seconds of the designated site.

In the early days before Ingo Swann's specialized training, some remote viewers would write the coordinates down, while others seemed to pay little or no attention to the enumeration. It was occasionally necessary to read the coordinates again at some point during the session if the viewer lost contact with the site.

We assembled a target pool of interesting and distinguishable sites (mountains, lakes, cities, factories, bridges, etc.) and determined the latitude and longitude coordinates. We prepared folders containing pictures or other information about the site and wrote the geographic coordinates of the site on the folder. When time came to conduct a remote-viewing session, one of the target folders was selected at random.

Within the SRI protocol, the interviewer/monitor was then provided with only the designated geographic coordinates. Once the remote-viewing session began, the viewer was cued with those coordinates as described above. The session progressed in much the same manner as before, with some viewers reporting verbally, others sketching or drawing, and still others combining these two methods of objectifying their perceptions.

Since it was impractical to take the viewer to the designated location after the viewing session, as had been done under the out-bounder protocol, the contents of the target folder—pictures, verbal descriptions, etc.—were provided as a learning-feedback instrument.

If the latitude and longitude coordinates designated an island or something like the Grand Canyon, or even the Eiffel Tower, this form of feedback worked well. But suppose, for example, the coordinates designated a volcano. The feedback folder might contain pictures from National Geographic magazine showing the volcano erupting some twenty years ago. Although the assumed intent of the session would be to have the remote viewers access and describe information of interest on the day of the viewing—i.e., the present, an inactive volcano—everything about the feedback folder encouraged (rewarded) the remote viewing description of an erupting volcano.

So, if during the remote-viewing session the viewer describes an erupting volcano, what data are being accessed and objectified? What information packet has the viewer connected to? Do remote viewers subconsciously realize that the mountain they are describing is a volcano? And do they embellish descriptions with the eruption scenario in an ill-fated attempt to accurately convey their impressions?

Rather than remote viewing the coordinate-cued volcano itself, do the viewers time-displace into their imminent feedback event only a few minutes away, and thereby describe the pictures in the folder? Or, has the eruption of the volcano "imprinted" or "signatured" in some way the very nature of the volcano and caused a retrocognitive remote-viewing time-displacement to the past?

Such a meaningful past event may attract (displace) the attention of the remote viewer across time. And if time displacements are possible with remote viewing, perhaps the eruption objectified by the remote viewer describes a future eruption.

Obviously, cueing must include a time dimension, a time stamp (so to speak) resonant with the information of interest which one intends the remote viewer describe. Rather than seeing these issues as problematic, I thought of them as supportive and helpful in moving toward operational use of remote viewing.

We used a learning-feedback instrument to encourage self-confidence. (However, it is important to note that decades of scientific remote-viewing research suggest that even the most skilled remote viewers are generally unable to consciously distinguish "good" sessions from "bad" ones.)

But in the operational use of remote viewing, feedback was not always available. So training that led remote viewers to remote view their own (future) feedback would have been of little value in operational remote viewing. When I worked with the remote viewers, I carefully controlled their learning-feedback using the usual behaviorist techniques to reduce their dependence on it and encourage remote-viewing contact with the information of interest in the operational setting.

For those viewers who couldn't move beyond remote viewing their own feedback, I slowly extended the time interval between the session and the feedback. If they could maintain their proficiency when feedback was delayed a week or two or even a month or more, they became excellent candidates for associative remote viewing or forecasting operations for which feedback could be provided. From an OPSEC perspective, a forecasting operation might be structured something like the following:

> The remote-viewing task is to describe the surface-to-air missile test being conducted on Tuesday of next week. A complete report that will detail the results of the test will be made available one week following the test. The viewer is given as cueing only the appropriate geographic coordinates. The viewer is not told anything about the test or the nature of the task at hand and after the session is informed that feedback will be provided on [some specified date].
>
> In this case, a "time stamp" is omitted, as the actual target expected to be described by the viewer is her own future feedback. So, composing the feedback folder becomes critical to the success of the operation. Good pictures, accurate descriptions, etc., all contribute to —and become—the information of interest in the mission.
>
> There are three probable test results: (1) The test may be canceled or postponed, (2) the test may be a mishap, with the missile failing to hit the airborne target, and (3) the test may be successful, with the missile hitting and destroying the airborne target. The details of any of these possible results need to be included in the feedback envelope for the remote viewer.
>
> It is implicitly understood that conventional space/time does not bind the remote-viewing process. But this scenario is not so much a demonstration that remote viewing can collect information from the future, or can predict future events, as it is an operationally engineered method for obtaining the most information about the event.

During this second-phase training/evaluation at SRI, another form of cueing was used that is best described under the generic concept of "sealed-envelope exercises." We constructed a target pool similar to the CRV target pool, except that we omitted geographic coordinate designations from the folders. Then the interviewer randomly selected a sealed envelope from the target pool and cued the viewer by saying, "Describe the target specified in this envelope."

As you might imagine, this could lead to issues similar to the ones discussed above. What is the intent of the session? Is the intent to remote view the contents of the envelope or the place or event suggested by the contents of the envelope? Does the viewer's intent differ from that of the interviewer? Is the viewer's unconscious intent to "do well" so he remote views his future feedback—the opening of the envelope moments after the session?

Some sealed-envelope exercises obviously described the contents of the envelope. I remember one case where the viewer described a motorcycle on a bed. In the envelope was a page torn from a magazine and folded in half. On one side of the page was an advertisement and picture of a bedroom suite and on the other side of the page an advertisement and picture of a motorcycle.

In other cases, it was obvious that the picture in the envelope directed the remote viewer to describe something else. For example, the picture in the sealed envelope might be of a marketplace in a village in a third-world country. During the remote-viewing session, the viewer describes a lake. When the envelope is opened for feedback, both the interviewer and the remote viewer initially assess the session as a miss.

Weeks later, it is discovered that the picture in the envelope was taken from National Geographic and is over twenty-five years old. Further investigation reveals that the article published (but not included in the folder) along with the picture was about a dam that was being built that would eventually flood the village. Recent pictures of the area reveal that the whole area is now a lake, with the population long since relocated. So what happened here? The possibilities are numerous.

Back at Fort Meade, I found training the remote viewers with the sealed-envelope protocol to be a valuable technique directly applicable to later operational implementation. From an OPSEC perspective, I could put a picture of a weapons system—a tank, for example—in a sealed envelope and ask the remote viewer to describe the object shown in the sealed envelope.

If I wanted to, I could add a date stamp to my cueing or wait to see what the viewer described. If the viewer accurately described the tank in the photographic setting, I had a pretty good idea that he was describing the contents of the sealed envelope rather than being directed by the picture and the intent of the session. If this happened, I would tell the remote viewer that he was doing well and would then ask him to describe the object not at the time of the photograph but at some other designated date (like maybe during a critical test of the tank's armor). Once the viewer had connected well with the information of interest, this slight detour in time prompted by my date cueing was of little consequence and was easily achieved.

I kept track of which viewers did well with this sealed-envelope cueing. Eventually, I put pictures of people in the sealed envelopes and cued the remote viewers by saying, "In the envelope is a picture of a person. Describe their location to me."

For those remote viewers who did well with this, I went even further. I found it was sometimes possible to write specific instructions on a three-by-five index card and then put that card in a sealed envelope. The instructions on the card were straightforward, e.g., describe the location of Army Aircraft Number 31TY on 4 July 1979. All I would have to do is cue the remote viewer at the beginning of the session by saying, "Describe target specified in the envelope."

The viewer, of course, had no idea what was in the envelope. It could have been a picture of a missile, an island in the ocean, a float in the Pasadena Rose Parade, or one of my three-by-five index cards. This methodology prevented front loading (telling the viewer something about the target before the session) when there was no other way to approach a problem. In my experience, only a select few remote viewers ever reached this level of confidence and expertise.

During the second-phase training/evaluation at SRI, our remote viewers were tested for their ability to access other types of targets. Most of the work to this point was concerned with remote viewing ground locations like mountains, lakes, bridges, skyscrapers, factories, airports, etc. As part of their assessment process, SRI wanted to find out if the viewers who seemed to be doing so well could do as well with other types of targets.

The Ganzfeld research used slide photographs as targets, and SRI wanted to try something similar with army remote viewers. A number of pictures (the target pool) were mounted on a slide carousel projector located in a locked room some distance from the remote-viewing room. Before a session, a random number designated which slide was to be the target. (It's important to say that it doesn't really matter if you randomly pick the target before or after the viewing session. The target is the target, and time is not relevant to the remote viewing process.)

Several types of cueing phrases were tried. The interviewer might say to the viewer, "Tell me about the slide you will see when we go downstairs after the session." This particular phrasing tended to encourage the viewer to connect with his own feedback (which can be operationally advantageous or not, depending on what one is trying to find out). An alternative might be to say, "Describe the picture being projected on the screen right now."

Another type of target of interest to SRI involved letters and words. If the remote viewers could describe objects and activities, could they "read" information blocked by time, distance, or shielding? In this type of session, words were randomly selected though a complex, multilevel system.

In an office in another building, the letters making up these words were inscribed on cards and prominently displayed. The viewers knew they were attempting to read a word displayed in a designated place. They were cued to try to connect with the designated area and describe the prominently displayed words.

This provided some intriguing information about remote viewing. When words were accurately reported, it was easy to assume that the viewer had connected with individual letters and put them together to form the words. (I won't even get into a possible telepathic explanation here.) To test this concept, the SRI researchers mixed up the letters of the word when they put it up for display. For example, if the randomly selected word was "cattle," the scientist put the letters T-E-L-C-T-A written on cards on display in the room. But the remote viewers still reported the correct word, cattle, not the jumbled letters.

So can a remote viewer read? Maybe. But I find it easier to say that a remote viewer can "describe" information about written material.

The other thing done during the second-phase training/evaluation at SRI was a sort of skill evaluation. Why did some remote viewers do better than others at some tasks? Were specific talents related to previous experiences in life? This was of immense operational interest to us at Fort Meade. If we were going to remote view a nuclear weapons facility, would it be beneficial to train a nuclear physicist to do the remote viewing?

One of our remote viewers, by way of example, seemed to have a superb ability to orient perceptions with relation to the compass directions. (Perhaps this was because he had worked as a radio direction-finding specialist during the Vietnam era, or perhaps this was an innate talent.) This talent carried over into his remote viewing to a degree I have never seen in another remote viewer.

Once he connected with a target, he could describe what was to the north, south, east, and west of the site. I could even instruct him to move by distance and direction: "Move three miles southeast of your location and describe." We eventually worked so well together that all I had to say to him was, "Work the compass." He would proceed to accurately describe what was around him (his perceptual remote-viewing perspective) in all directions.

The official report of the second-phase training/evaluation at SRI detailing the results of the research remains classified under code-word caveat. But I hope I have provided some explanation of the SRI work without disclosing classified information.

Back at Fort Meade, we too moved beyond the basic out-bounder protocol into alternate cueing methods and different types of targets. Part of my job became to determine the operational capabilities and limitations of remote viewing, to identify and develop individual skills, and to evaluate the accuracy of remote viewing on *unique* targets.

As the weeks turned into months, and into years, I began to establish a knowledge base. I knew what kinds of intelligence tasks could be accomplished by remote viewing and which remote viewers could best accomplish them. Some remote viewers were better with technical sites like nuclear facilities, munitions factories, or specific pieces of equipment. Others seemed to have a better track record with sites like train stations or a missile firing, where the detection of movement was important. And still others did very well with "people targets"—describing human activity at a site or making *telepathic* contact with people at designated locations.

Operational Remote Viewing

The Fort Meade remote viewers' first operational mission, which took place on September 4, 1979, was not an OPSEC mission. Instead, the Office of the Assistant Chief of Staff for Intelligence for the Army requested that we help locate a downed U.S. aircraft. Of course, neither the interviewer (myself) nor the remote viewer had any idea where in the world the plane might have gone missing. But in just one remote-viewing session we were able to provide the name of a major terrain feature later identified as the name of a mountain into which the aircraft had crashed, and we provided a map location "guess" that proved to be within fifteen miles of the actual site of the crash.

I remain bound by my original secrecy oath and cannot disclose much about operational missions. (For interesting insights, I would suggest Jim Schnabel's book *Remote Viewers: The Secret History of America's Psychic Spies*, published by Dell.) Because of security restrictions, I am unable to provide the names of the various agencies that requested remote-viewing information or the nature of the requests themselves. But as I examine the official logbook of all the operational missions conducted while I was with the Fort Meade remote-viewing unit, I see that in 1979 we completed seven operational missions, which required a number of remote-viewing sessions, and during my tour of duty with the unit I conducted 122 operational missions consisting of many hundreds of separate remote-viewing sessions with a number of individual remote viewers.

SRI used a standard of *blind differential discrimination* to judge remote-viewing efforts. We at Fort Meade simply asked the tasking agencies to tell us if the information provided was of intelligence value. But by the nature of intelligence work, this sometimes involved difficulties. Many times, remote viewers provided accurate descriptions of areas of interest, but those descriptions were not necessarily of value.

For example, if a tasking agency wanted to determine if a certain type of aircraft was located at a designated airfield, we would cue the remote viewer with the geographic coordinates of that airfield. Since the viewer had no overt idea that she was targeted against an airfield, a remote viewing session that described an airfield provided some evidence that the viewer had "connected" with the target area. But if the session provided no information that could confirm or refute the presence of the suspected aircraft, the session would be rated by the tasking agency as having no intelligence value, the viewer not having connected with the information of interest.

Let's look a little more closely at the issue. Imagine that you're given a camera and a roll of film and told to take pictures of a certain building. You go out to the neighborhood, taking a few snapshots along the way. You find the address, and you begin to photograph the building. The person who told you to take the pictures actually wants to know if there is a red car parked in front of the building but didn't want you to know this. Not knowing the client's special interest, you take some nice pictures of the building from as many angles as you think appropriate. After you're through, you take some more pictures of the neighborhood, including the cars in front of the building.

Now, when you take the pictures back, your client thumbs

through them rapidly, tossing most of them aside. Some are good pictures of the building but of no intelligence value. Some are not of the building at all. A few pictures, however, clearly show the red car parked in front of the building and, as luck would have it, one of your extra pictures is of the car itself.

In the same manner, certain remote-viewing missions provided information of intelligence value. Some were quite spectacular, and special military commendations were awarded to the remote viewers. Others were great examples of remote viewing but provided little or no information of direct intelligence value. Still other sessions were complete misses, demonstrating that remote viewing is, among other things, constrained by individual differences. Even the best baseball sluggers only get a hit about thirty percent of the time they are at bat. That's what "batting 300" means.

This idea of *intelligence value* went to the core of our OPSEC evaluation of the remote-viewing surveillance technique. In fact, we had been chartered to determine if hostile exploitation of remote-viewing surveillance was a threat to national security. According to the official logbook, during my tour of duty as the operations and training officer, forty-seven percent of the operational projects I conducted were rated by the tasking agency as being of intelligence value. (Again, due to continued security restrictions, I cannot describe the detailed results of specific operations.)

Special Considerations

The use of remote viewing as an intelligence surveillance tool carries with it some special considerations. In working with human sources over the years, the intelligence community has established a rating system to attest to the bona fides of an individual human source and the authenticity of the information provided.

The bona fides of the source is rated by letter from A to F, with A meaning that the source is absolutely reliable (has always been correct in the past). The relatively low rating of E signifies that the source is nearly always unreliable (has always or nearly always been wrong in the past, though even an unreliable source may occasionally provide accurate information). The lowest source rating of F signifies that the source is of unknown reliability (e.g., perhaps a first-time or unevaluated source).

The authenticity of the information provided is rated by a number from 1 to 6, with 1 indicating that the information provided is almost certainly true because it has been corroborated by other significant or reliable information. A 5 signifies that the information is almost certainly wrong, often because other, certifiably correct information contradicts it. The lowest level of authenticity rating is a 6, indicating that the probable veracity of the information provided by the source is unknown or unconfirmed by any other source but that no information discrediting it is known, either. Information obtained from a U.S. intelligence agent who has always been accurate in the past, reporting something that is substantiated by other sources would be rated A-1, whereas information reported by a known liar that the moon is made of green cheese would be rated E-5.

It's entirely possible to have source/information ratings of A-5, E-1, C-2, etc. A rating of F-6 would mean essentially that a source of unknown veracity has provided information that can, at this point, neither be confirmed nor denied. An analyst would take a wait-and-see attitude with this sort of information, with hopes that further intelligence from other sources would either corroborate or reject the F-6 information.

The human-source rating system long used by the intelligence community is of little value when dealing with remote viewers. Throughout history, all of the serious scientific inquiry into remote viewing has demonstrated its veracity. These same investigations have, however, repeatedly indicated that the human behavioral mechanism behind remote viewing is neither understood nor reliable and, therefore, that the information reported by a remote viewer is characteristically undependable.

The information stream objectified by a remote viewer can be erroneous or valid or a mixture of both. The remote viewers themselves are of little help in determining which. From the perspective of a behavioral model, remote viewing would seem to have two principal dimensions. First, can the remote viewer acquire the target, and second, how well can the remote viewer become aware of the target and describe information of interest about the target?

Ken Kress of the CIA developed an operational protocol with two characterization methods to deal with these dimensions. Before the remote-viewing session, Ken would select a few obvious features, which, if described by the remote viewer, would show that he or she had at least some contact with the designated site. For example, if the intelligence mission was to describe the construction of a new ballistic missile and the remote viewer began by objectifying factory buildings and smokestacks known to be at the site, there was some level of confidence that the remote viewer was able to establish contact.

During the session, a quality characterization was accomplished by periodically asking the remote viewer to describe specific known features of the site. The accuracy of these "audit" descriptions would be used to estimate the quality of the unverifiable remote-viewing information. Through application of this operational protocol, remote-viewing data became intelligence information.

Some time later, SRI became sensitive to the operational reliability issue and developed a simple, straightforward calibration system. Their view was that remote viewers were either "on" or "off" and that they had good days and bad days like anyone else.

To provide the intelligence customer with some level of confidence about the remote-viewing information, viewers were given a randomly selected training target both before and after the operational target. If they did well with both the verifiable training targets, the assumption was that the information provided about the operational target was probably accurate to some degree. This calibration system was also helpful in building a sense of surety for the remote viewer. If the viewers did well on the training targets, they could, in effect, walk away from the operational mission with a sense of contributing even if they could not be given feedback on the operational site.

I always felt that remote viewing was modulated by many of

the same factors that affect other human abilities. An individual's expertise, based on previous practice, contributes to the ability to remote view. Psychological and sociological factors as well as meteorological and solar/geophysical conditions all affect the performance of remote viewers. Simply stated, one's focus of attention, a headache, lack of sleep, mood, personality traits, motivation, expectation, state of consciousness, etc., all affect the ability to remote view. With so many variables at work, it would be inappropriate to depend on a single factor such as mood or even previous experience to estimate the reliability of a remote viewer's information when reporting to a consumer.

Remote viewing is multifaceted, interactive, nonlinear, and dynamic. A complex systems approach is the only way to understand remote-viewing performance. By observing a number of conditions (psychological, physical, physiological, and environmental data) during training sessions and then matching these up with successful performance, I was eventually able to establish profiles which could be used to rate the dependability of remote-viewing sessions. (An excellent article by Dean I. Radin, Ph.D., "Towards a Complex Systems Model of PSI Performance," *Subtle Energies and Energy Medicine Journal*, vol. 7, no. 1 [1996]: 35–69, describes the use of 149 relevant variables divided into eight categories—mood, personality, beliefs, meteorology, solar/geophysical, abnormal behavior, PSI performance, and composite factors—used in an artificial neural network to successfully predict PSI performance.)

I also found that we could increase the probability that we could respond to intelligence requirements with information of value by using multiple remote viewers. Knowing that the best remote viewers don't always provide accurate information, I developed operational scenarios employing several remote viewers against the same requirements.

Working as a team, we were able to produce results more frequently than if we had used just one remote viewer. If a baseball team had to depend on just one player to get all the runs in a game, it would be hard-pressed, especially since the best sluggers only get a hit thirty percent of the time. Working as a team, however, it has a much better chance of getting a number of scoring runs and winning the game.

Earlier in this chapter, I explained that military duty is a balance between operations and training. When there isn't an ongoing military operation, the troops train for one. When the remote viewers weren't involved in an operational tasking, they were rehearsing—practicing with dozens and, in some cases, hundreds of training sessions.

Training More Personnel

The number of operational activities slowed down from time to time as the unit began to experience the normal attrition of any military organization. Military personnel began to move on to other assignments. Unit commanders changed several times. Efforts were made to retain the most qualified remote viewers, but some wanted to move on because they felt that their careers would stagnate and they would not be able to compete with their contemporaries for promotions if they stayed. We were only able to keep one of the original remote viewers with the unit over the years, and one other returned to the unit after a European tour of duty.

We needed to recruit and train new remote viewers and continue operational missions. We went out to the Army Intelligence School at Fort Huachuca, Arizona, and recruited two graduates of the Officer's Advanced Course. These new recruits were scheduled to attend an external training program developed under contract with SRI. This training program was based, for the most part, on theoretical concepts set forth by Ingo Swann, a renowned remote viewer.

Ingo's training program was somewhat different from previous efforts. Although it had been thoroughly evaluated and was theoretically sound, it was widely criticized. Even SRI had a number of detractors of Ingo's training program. I thought that Ingo's program held promise, and I looked forward to seeing how our new recruits would perform. Ingo called his technique Coordinate Remote Viewing, as this cueing technique somewhat represented his calling card. It was intended for individuals who had little or no prior experience or understanding of the remote-viewing phenomena.

What follows is a somewhat cumbersome explanation of Ingo's training program. If you are uninterested in the specific details of this program, then perhaps you should flip forward a few pages to the section called "Training with Challenge Targets." Again, because of my personal involvement in this, I felt obligated to provide a comprehensive account.

Coordinate Remote Viewing

Ingo Swann defined Coordinate Remote Viewing (CRV) as the process of remote viewing using longitude and latitude geographic coordinates for cueing.[11] As I noted before, nowadays Ingo prefers the expression Controlled Remote Viewing, as the fundamental *structure* is not dependent on the use of geographic coordinates.

Paul H. Smith, who now teaches remote viewing professionally, and the other Ingo trainees in the unit put together the *Coordinate Remote Viewing Manual* which was published by the Defense Intelligence Agency on May 1, 1986. The manual adhered as closely as possible to what Ingo Swann delivered when working with trainees one-on-one. When Ingo reviewed the manual, he complimented Paul and his colleagues on producing "such a comprehensive and accurate document."

In Ingo's opinion, remote viewing is the process of detecting and decoding a "signal line" that provides information about what he called a "Matrix" of information about persons, places, things, or events. Note that this is somewhat different from the conventional concept that a remote viewer somehow "travels to" or "sees" the target location or information of interest. In Ingo's theory, the remote viewer contacts the signal line of the Matrix, not the physical site itself. He feels that the remote-viewing session consists of the remote viewer's contact with the signal line as well as the interaction between the viewer and the interviewer/monitor.

In this CRV technique, the monitor and remote viewer sit at

[11] On the companion CD-ROM included with this book there is an interactive file illustrating the CRV process.

Skip with Paul H. Smith (right)

opposite ends of a table. The monitor cues and guides the remote viewer through a carefully structured CRV process divided into discreet, progressive stages. Each stage deals with different and more detailed aspects of the designated target. Each stage builds on the information in the previous stage in a natural progression.

From the *CRV Manual*:

> The Matrix has been described as a huge, nonmaterial, highly structured, mentally accessible "framework" of information containing all data pertaining to everything in both the physical and nonphysical universe. . . . The Matrix is open to and comprises all conscious entities as well as information relating to everything else living or nonliving by accepted human definition. It is this informational framework from which the data encoded on the signal line originates. This Matrix can be envisioned as a vast, three-dimensional, geometric arrangement of dots, each dot representing a discrete information bit. Each geographic location on the Earth has a segment of the Matrix corresponding exactly to the nature of the physical location. When the viewer is prompted by coordinate or other targeting methodology, he accesses the signal line for data derived from the Matrix. By successfully acquiring (detecting) this information from the signal line, then coherently decoding it through his conscious awareness

> and faculties, he makes it available for analysis and further exploitation by himself or others.
>
> Remote viewing is made possible through the agency of a hypothetical "signal line." In a manner roughly analogous to standard radio propagation theory, this signal line is a carrier wave, which is inductively modulated by its intercourse with information, and may be detected and decoded by a remote viewer. The signal line radiates in many different frequencies, and its impact on the viewer's perceptive faculties is controlled through a phenomenon known as "aperture." Essentially, when the remote viewer first detects the signal line in Stage I, it manifests itself as a sharp, rapid influx of signal energy—representing large gestalts of information. In this situation, we therefore speak of a "narrow" aperture, since only a very narrow portion of the signal line is allowed to access the consciousness. In later stages involving longer, slower, more enduring waves, the aperture is spoken of as being "wider."

Under a subcontract to Ingo Swann, SRI agreed to train our two new recruits in the first four stages of Ingo's program. This "basic" training took place in Menlo Park and eventually in New York. The training lasted several months and consisted of two-week sessions with Ingo, followed by two weeks of practice at Fort Meade. Since practice continued at Fort Meade, the CRV methodology was effectively transferred to us. Our goal was to eventually be able to train this technique in-house. Before describing Ingo's stages, it is necessary to explain a little bit more about his remote-viewing theories.

Ingo felt that a remote viewer's first contact with the signal line is unconscious and stimulates the autonomic nervous system. The signal line is thus expressed as a reflexive nervous response of the muscles controlled by the autonomic nervous system. At the same time, the signal passes into the edges of awareness.

In Stage I, the remote viewer takes advantage of this initial contact by objectifying a spontaneous graphic expression of the target's major gestalt, called the ideogram. The remote viewer describes the ideogram in writing in terms of its "feeling/motion" and one's first analytic response to the signal line. This description represents the remote viewer's first elementary awareness of the target.

Ingo felt this process of emerging awareness carries with it certain inherent behaviors. So valuable were his thoughts on this that they are worth repeating here from the *CRV Manual*:

> . . . the normal waking consciousness poses certain problems for remote viewing, occasioned largely because of the linear, analytic thought processes which are societally enhanced and ingrained from our earliest stages of cognitive development. While extremely useful in a society relying heavily on quantitative data and technological development, such analytic thinking hampers remote viewing by the manufacture of what is known as "analytic overlay," or AOL. As the signal line surges up across the limen and into the threshold areas of consciousness, the mind's conscious analytic process feels duty-bound to assign coherence to what at first blush seems virtually incomprehensible data coming from an unaccustomed source. It must, in other words, make a "logical" assessment based on the impressions being received. Essentially, the mind jumps to one or a number of instantaneous conclusions about the incoming information without waiting for sufficient information to make an accurate judgment. This process is completely reflexive and happens even when not desired by the individual involved. Instead of allowing wholistic [sic] "right-brain" processes (through which the signal line apparently manifests itself) to assemble a complete and accurate concept, untrained "left-brain" based analytic processes seize upon whatever bit of information seems most familiar and forms an AOL construct based on it.

The manual continues with an example of what Ingo was describing:

> . . . a viewer has been given the coordinates to a large, steel girder bridge. A flash of a complex, metal, manmade structure may impinge on the liminary regions of the viewer's mind but so briefly that no coherent response can be made to it. The conscious mind, working at a much greater speed than the viewer expects, perceives bits and pieces such as angles, riveted girders, and a sense of being "roofed over" and paved, whereupon it suggests to the physical awareness of the viewer that the site

is the outside of a large sports stadium. The "image" is of course wrong but is at least composed of factual elements, though these have been combined by the viewer's overeager analytical processes to form an erroneous conclusion.

In his training, Ingo acted as monitor and knew the target to be described as he read the geographic coordinates, longitude and latitude, to the remote viewer. There are numerous objections to having the monitor knowledgeable, but Ingo felt that during training it was vital to guide the remote-viewing process during the early stages. He attempted to do this without leading the remote viewer's descriptions by providing very limited feedback. As the remote viewer scrawled the ideogram and described it, the monitor provided limited, very controlled feedback words indicating to the viewer that he was responding appropriately to the signal line. A remote viewer could take the coordinate cue several times until perceptions solidified. Once the Stage-I perception seemed complete, the remote viewer moved on sequentially within structure to Stage II, signal-line data relevant to physical sensory input.

Speaking of structure, here is what the manual says:

> Structure is the key to usable remote-viewing technology. It is through proper structure-discipline that mental noise is suppressed and signal line information allowed to emerge cleanly. As expressed by one early student, "Structure! Content be damned!" is the universal motto of the remote viewer. As long as proper structure is maintained, information obtained may be relied on. If the viewer starts speculating about content—wondering "what it is"—he will begin to depart from proper structure, and analytic overlay will inevitably result. One of the primary duties of both monitor and viewer is to ensure the viewer maintains proper structure, taking information in the correct sequence, at the correct stage, and in the proper manner.

Stage II, in Ingo Swann's CRV structure, is described as equivalent to the sensory experience remote viewers would have if they were physically present at the designated target site. This signal-line information, which centers on the five physical senses, usually rises into awareness as small groups of sensory-rich words: light color, rough, bumpy texture, pungent odor, etc.

The signal line is thought to come into awareness more slowly in Stage II and provides the remote viewer with a more intimate contact with the site. During training, the monitor provides positive, very specific feedback when the viewer correctly objectifies sensory aspects of the target.

For example:

Viewer: Green, cool. *Monitor*: Correct.
Viewer: Loud. *Monitor*: Correct.
Viewer: Feels funny. *Monitor*: Can't feedback.
Viewer: Tastes fresh. *Monitor*: Probably correct.
Viewer: Moving, flowing. *Monitor*: Correct.

As the Stage-II perceptions mature, dimensional elements begin to emerge from the unconscious into awareness. Remote viewers begin to objectify *in structure* dimensional words relating the concepts of vertical, horizontal, angularity, volume (space), and mass. They use words like big, long, high, etc.

As dimensional characteristics are objectified, a threshold is reached for the transition into Stage III. This further decoding of the signal line and awareness (Stage III) is usually accompanied by aesthetic impact. The concept of aesthetic impact is related to a plethora of information impacting the unconscious and provoking a subjective emotional response. Objectifying aesthetic impact is an important, if not critical, factor in reducing subsequent analytic overlay.

Drawings and sketches are the structure for Swann's Stage-III CRV. True dimensional aspects of the site are expressed in this stage. Stage-II dimensional elements, expressed as words, represent individual portions of the site whereas Stage-III sketches and drawings represent a composite of inherent site aspects.

Initially, remote viewers are not usually aware of their own perceptual perspective or relationship to the site. This suggests that during the initial objectification of Stage-III perceptions the remote viewers are not consciously aware of all the dimensional relationships of various site components. The viewers rely on various tools outlined in Swann's training to organize the increased information perceived in Stage III.

Again from the manual:

> With the expansion of the aperture and after dissipation of AI, the viewer is prepared to make representation of the site dimensional aspects with pen on paper. A sketch is a rapidly executed general idea of the site. In some cases it may be highly representational of the actual physical appearance of the site, yet in other cases only portions of the site appear. The observed accuracy of aesthetic qualities of a sketch are not particularly important. The main function of the sketch is to stimulate further intimate contact with the signal line while continuing to aid in the suppression of the viewer's subjective analytic mental functioning. Sketches are distinguished from drawings by the convention that drawings are more deliberate, detailed representations and are therefore subject to far greater analytic (and therefore AOL-producing) interpretation in their execution.

With the successful objectification of Stage-III perceptions, the remote viewer's contact with the site expands, and she becomes aware of an enormous amount of information. A Stage-IV objectification structure is implemented to facilitate and guide the viewer's focusing of perceptions on details of the site.

In Swann's view, this array is a more complete and detailed decoding of the signal line. The viewer objectifies Stage-IV responses, usually as single-word concepts, under designated headings or categories within columns in the structured array. These columns are labeled:

S2 for Stage-II sensory perceptions;
D for dimensional Stage-II perceptions;
AI for aesthetic impact;
EI for emotional impact (perceived emotions or feelings of people at the site or of the remote viewer);
T for tangible aspects of the site (solid or "touchable" objects or characteristics of the site, e.g., cars, foliage, buildings, odors, noises);

I for intangible site aspects (abstract qualities such as purposes, categorizations, e.g., "foreign," "medical," "church," "museum," "library," etc.);

AOL and *AOL/S* for analytical overlay that coincidentally matches site data.

As in Stage II, the viewer seems to become aware of this information in clusters. Within the discipline of Swann's CRV structure, these clusters are objectified in the Stage IV array generally left-to-right and top-to-bottom with some degree of vertical spacing between individual clusters. A complete understanding of the CRV structure is, therefore, critical in interpreting objectified site data.

In Stage-IV CRV, the remote viewer can exercise some degree of control over the order of information entering awareness and subsequently objectified. By placing his pen in a particular column in the array (S2–D–AI–EI–T–I–AOL–AOL/S), the viewer can effectively prompt or, in the words of the manual, "induce the signal line to provide information pertinent to the column selected."

In the Stage-IV process, awareness of site information expands rapidly and care must be taken to accurately objectify the data as they come. If the flow of information (awareness) slows, viewers can encourage further contact with—and awareness of—the site by placing their pen in the "EI" array column to further stimulate, in the words of the manual, "signal line activity and acquisition."

With the completion of Stage-IV CRV training with Ingo Swann, our new recruits had completed "basic" training and were integrated into operational missions. In between our operational jobs, we continued training practice with a variety of targets and cross-trained other remote viewers we had recruited using an in-house version of Swann's "basic" CRV technique. Four additional people were recruited and matriculated into "basic" training with Swann.

Training with Challenge Targets

As part of my responsibilities as operations and training officer, I was charged with determining the operational capabilities and limitations of remote viewing, identifying and developing individual remote-viewing skills, and testing and evaluating the accuracy of remote viewing on *unique* targets.

Completion of the formalized training was not the end of remote-viewing training for members of the unit. As with any other military training program, it was necessary to hone their skills and to stretch their capabilities. The viewers needed practice with complex targets rather than the lakes, islands, mountains, or bridges typical of "basic" training. They needed to be tasked with the responsibility of collecting specific information. So what if they could remote view a football field? From an intelligence perspective, we needed specific information—like, was there a terrorist bomb in the stadium?

The Natural History Museum in San Francisco is an example of a challenge target I used for such training. If viewers were skilled enough to acquire and describe the building and further classify the building as being open to the public or as a tourist attraction, they were then asked to explore the building further. Within the building, the challenge began.

The inside of the building was arranged as a spiral walking tour through historical panoramas. As viewers began to objectify their findings, many would become disoriented and begin to lose confidence in their contact with the site. With practice and in conjunction with careful interviewing techniques, remote viewers eventually learned to control their focus of attention to specific tasking and not become mired in the complexity of the overall site.

Some remote viewers became so skilled that, when viewing the Natural History Museum challenge target, I could task them to describe a specific display by cueing something like, "Describe #A-125," as though the display's designation was a *coordinate* within the museum. Such training paralleled operational tasks, as when remote viewers were directed to describe specific rooms within a foreign embassy or a designated area within a weapons factory.

Occasionally, during this challenge-target training, I used targets that had to do with extraterrestrials or unidentified flying objects (UFOs).[12] Since, by protocol, the remote viewers never knew when I would use one of these targets, they were blind as to what they were remote viewing. None of these controversial challenge targets were ever directed or approved by higher military authority. I was the operations and training officer and the sole authority on the use of these as training targets. The information resulting from these training sessions was never officially reported and, presumably, has been destroyed in the years since the project was closed.

The controversy surrounding the use of remote viewing for exploring these topics is worth mentioning. From some scientists' perspective, such targets are a detriment to acceptance of remote viewing. Their view seems to be that comparing a viewer's description with an observable object or location will eventually lead to an understanding of the phenomena and its acceptance as a valid human perceptual ability. With UFO targets there is hardly ever anything to compare with a remote viewer's description. Additionally, any association with the UFO phenomena may be seen by some as pejorative and, therefore, best avoided.

Alternatively, more adventuresome folks feel that, since remote-viewing surveillance is unbound by the constraints of time and space (as we understand them), it is the ideal technique for exploring the extraterrestrial and UFO realm. However, several of these people have become overzealous and have forgotten that the information stream objectified by a remote viewer can be erroneous or valid or a mixture of both. Remote viewers themselves are of little help in determining which. Therefore, without some sort of protocol to determine if the remote viewer acquired the target and, if so, how well she described information of interest about the target, such remote viewing sessions may amount to nothing but folly.

My feeling is that the use of remote-viewing surveillance as a corroborative information source concerning UFO reports is appropriate. If a thousand people in Phoenix, Arizona, report see-

[12] Included on the CD-ROM accompanying this book is an example of this type of challenge targeting.

ing a UFO on a certain date, as has happened, it seems logical to find out if local radar detected anything or if there is any photographic evidence of such a sighting (which there was). It also seems logical to me that remote-viewing surveillance of that particular space-time coordinate, carefully tasked with appropriate "blinding" protocols, would provide further information of interest. Enough said.

Advanced Training

As the weeks and months turned into years and our remote viewers continued to develop their own expertise, we wanted to provide our adept viewers with some form of advanced training. Ingo further developed his training methodology and offered two additional stages within his CRV technique. One of the two personnel who originally attended his "basic" training was sent off to New York for Stage-V and Stage-VI training with Ingo.

Stage-V CRV does not rely on a direct link to the "signal line" (what I would call further contact with the site) but access to information theoretically "in the brain and autonomic nervous system," available below the liminal threshold. Swann hypothesizes that this information is deposited in earlier stages when the signal line passes through the system and "imprints" data on the brain by causing cognitrons, or neural-cell assembly, to form through the rearrangement of the brain's neuronal clusters.

The remote viewer, through prompting, can access information "stored" in a cognitron. When properly prompted, the Stage V information emerging into awareness consists of the subelements that together form the complete cognitron objectified during earlier CRV Stages. From the *CRV Manual*:

> . . . the concept "religious" may be represented by one complete cognitron (cluster of neurons); each neuron would store a subelement of that cognitron. Hence, the cognitron for "religious" could have neurons storing data for the following elements: "quiet," "incense," "harmonious chanting," "bowed heads," "robes," "candles," "dimly lit," "reverence," "worship,"

"respect," etc. If attention is paid to what underlies the concept of "religious" as it is originally evoked in Stage IV, the subelements, which may themselves provide valuable information far beyond their collective meaning of "religious," may be broken out and assembled.

These Stage-V subelements of previously perceived data are called emanations, as Swann felt that these concepts literally issued from or flowed forth or were actually emitted by subliminally known aspects of the site. Training the remote viewer to bring this information above the liminal threshold and objectify it was again a matter of proper *structure*. Stage-V structure consists of dividing the possible types of emanations obtainable into four categories: Objects, Attributes, Subjects, and Topics.

The viewer prompts the release of subliminally held information by saying and writing the previously objectified lower-Stage concept, e.g., the "I" (Stage-IV Intangible) "religious," and under that writes the name of a Stage-V Category, e.g., "Objects," and below that writes the word "Emanations," followed by a simple question mark (?). Using the "religious" example from above, the Stage-V objectified structure might look something like the chart on the following page.

The word "Emanations" represents the subelements of the "religious" cognitron that emerged from below the liminal threshold (in Stage IV) as a collective concept for these subelements.

Swann theorized that the overall cognitron-concept possesses the combined neural energy of its components and therefore easily passes into the awareness of the remote viewer. This assumes that the individual subelements themselves do not have sufficient impetus to break through the liminal barrier into the consciousness of the viewer and must be invoked intentionally.

The operational value of Stage-V CRV is obvious. Once rendered to its subelements and details, earlier-stage perceptions produce a wealth of additional information of use to the intelligence analyst. In the above example, the "religious" perception might be enough to testify to the validity of remote viewing. But Stage V goes far beyond this simple proof, providing useful information of

STAGE V STRUCTURE (EXAMPLE)
Possible Types of Emanations for the Word "RELIGIOUS"

religious
Objects
Emanations?

robes
candles
incense

religious
Attributes
Emanations?

quiet
dimly lit
echoing
large

religious
Subjects
Emanations?

worship
reverence
respect
harmonious chanting

religious
Topics
Emanations?

mass
Catholic
priest
communion

---

potential intelligence value. It's easy to imagine how Stage-V CRV could be used in a strategic or tactical intelligence remote-viewing surveillance mission.

With Stage-VI CRV, three-dimensional modeling of the site is possible. Conceptually, Stage VI is a continuation of the objectification of the site's physical characteristics begun in Stage III. In practice, however, it is commonly implemented to objectify the interrelationship of

"T" (Stage-IV Tangibles) elements at the site. The kinesthetic interaction with the site in Stage VI both facilitates the assessment of relative temporal and spatial dimensional elements of the site and effectively focuses the remote viewer's attention to specific locales.

In training and practice, the remote viewer establishes a structured array identical to the one in Stage IV. The array sheet is labeled "Stage VI" for record keeping purposes and to indicate that the array pertains to a specific site locale in space/time rather than the entire site, which would be a Stage-IV array.

The remote viewer also has easy access to modeling material (usually clay). Cueing on Stage-IV "T" elements, the viewer constructs three-dimensional models and records information perceived from the "signal line" in the columns on the prepared Stage-VI array sheet. During the Stage-VI CRV process, the remote viewer must focus awareness on the "signal line," not the model. The model does not have to be an accurate rendering. The manual emphasizes, "It is the objectified information resulting from the modeling that is important."

Alternative Advanced Training

Rather than CRV, other members of the unit adopted a more meditative-based style of remote viewing. I coined the acronym ERV. (Army people love to make up acronyms.) ERV stood for Extended Remote Viewing, because the remote-viewing sessions took longer to conduct.

As good as these remote viewers were, they expressed an interest in receiving some form of "advanced" training. From a management position, I too wanted to see if their remote-viewing skills could be enhanced. Since the foundation of their remote-viewing behavior was based on the notion of achieving a special state of consciousness conducive to the detection and acquisition of site-relevant data—the proverbial information of interest—I recommend Hemi-Sync training from The Monroe Institute. Aside from any out-of-body expectations imbued by Robert Monroe's books, the Hemi-Sync training process offered a pragmatic, scientific-based method of teaching people to access levels of cortical arousal supportive of a variety of focus states of consciousness.

With practice, a graduate could willfully and reliably enter a propitious level of cortical arousal without the aid of the Hemi-Sync sound technology. I hoped that our remote viewers could be trained to access arousal levels conducive to the five behaviors I had outlined years earlier, based on what I had learned from Puthoff and Targ, other research labs, a review of the pertinent literature, and my own personal remote-viewing experiences.

As the years passed, I learned a great deal from the SRI scientists, their remote viewers, and Ingo Swann himself, and from working with our own cadre of army remote viewers. It all reinforced my original thoughts about the five basic behaviors of remote viewing: relaxing, connecting, listening, becoming aware, and reporting. If the viewers could develop their expertise in these behavior skills, chances were that their remote viewing would improve. Yes, they would have good days and bad days and a variety of factors would surely influence their performance, but any "advanced" training supportive of these basic behaviors seemed appropriate for the ERVers, and The Monroe Institute offered such training.

Hemi-Sync and Remote Viewing

We contracted privately with Robert Monroe to work with Joe McMoneagle, our best ERVer, for ten nonconsecutive weeks over a period of one year. Joe discussed his training with Monroe in his first book, *Mind Trek*.

Joe, a beefy man with hardly any neck, was a first-rate military officer when I recruited him for the unit and since then had established himself as our most accomplished remote viewer.

During these training sessions, Monroe worked one-on-one with Joe, experimenting with him and teaching him how to access different levels of arousal. The recipe for this training involved several identifiable processes.

First was learning how to physically relax.

Joe McMoneagle

Monroe coached a relaxation process directing Joe's focus of attention to various parts of his body, encouraging him to tell these areas of his body to "relax, let go, sleep." Next, Monroe coached him to attend to his breathing, to slow his respiration and to imagine that his breath represented the flow of life-energy. Monroe then suggested that he set his intent for this session through a process of affirmation.

Once these first three ingredients were solidified, Monroe coached Joe to focus his attention on his internal world or, stated another way, become aware of his own mental realm without the "noise" of the physical senses. The final ingredient in this training recipe was the addition of Hemi-Sync, an audio technology capable of altering one's state of consciousness or first-person experience by altering the brain's cortical level of arousal. Properly applied, this recipe would enable Joe to orally report and/or journal his perceptions. This Monroe formula seemed to me very similar in many aspects to the behaviors that I had identified as conducive to the remote-viewing process.

Each training week, I conducted an *audit* remote-viewing session to try to determine any improvement in Joe's remote-viewing performance. During these sessions, we were able to monitor physiological changes from electrodes placed on Joe's fingers. A couple of these "audit" sessions proved to be some of the most demonstrative training sessions I had the privilege of conducting with Joe. During one of these, I decided to use coordinates of some unusual structures on the planet Mars that Puthoff had provided. Joe reclined with headphones in a soundproofed room in the lab at

The Monroe Institute, and Bob Monroe and I sat in the adjacent control room.[13]

In preparation for this exercise, I had written, "The planet Mars, one million years B.C." on a standard three-by-five index card, sealed it in a small, opaque envelope, and asked Bob to put the envelope in his breast pocket. Bob (and, of course, Joe) did not know what I had written on the index card. I kept the list of specific coordinates (unseen by either Bob or Joe) provided by Puthoff with me. When Joe finished his cool-down period, I directed Joe to focus by saying, "Using the information in the envelope . . . " and then read him the first Martian coordinate. Bob adjusted Joe's Hemi-Sync patterns.

Joe seemed very deep (slowed respiration; slurred speech; incomplete sentences)—a good sign. He usually did well when he really got into the process. When he began to describe an "arid climate" in "some distant place," I knew he was probably on target. I reviewed the list of Martian coordinates provided by Puthoff and directed Joe to "move" from his present location to the next set of coordinates on the list.

Of course, if he had started off by describing an aircraft carrier, a factory, a person having coffee, or some other irrelevant locale, I would have figured that the session was a bust and would not have continued with the Martian coordinates.

When directed to focus on the time period designated in the sealed envelope, Joe reported the "aftereffect of a major geologic problem." When asked to move to a time before the geologic problem (perhaps thousands or tens or hundreds of thousands of years), he reported a "total difference" in the terrain. He also found a "shadow" of "very large" people. Joe went on to explain that by "shadow" he meant that they weren't there anymore. Once again I asked Joe to move back in time—to the period when the people were still there (again, perhaps thousands or tens or hundreds of

[13] I have included the unedited audio recording of this unique remote-viewing session on the CD-ROM accompanying this book. Martian reconnaissance imagery in the presentation shows the sites Joe described—at least in terms of the twentieth century.

thousands of years). Joe described "very large people" who were "wearing very strange clothes."

As it turned out, Joe described eight different coordinate-designated locations on Mars. When Joe began to describe the unusual structures on Mars, Bob did not know if Joe was on target; he asked me what was happening. As he continued to adjust the Hemi-Sync sound patterns, he asked repeatedly about Joe's descriptions. I gestured, "Wait," several times until I finally turned to Bob and winked while saying simply, "Joe is on Mars."

Bob listened carefully to Joe's intriguing descriptions of an ancient race of "very large people" and a cataclysmic disaster that caused them to abandon their home. At one point, Joe was in telepathic contact with one of the Martians. During this deep-contact period, Joe's skin-potential voltage (measured from finger electrodes) reversed polarity—crossing the zero or null point—indicating a discrete shift in perception.

After the session, Bob and I debriefed Joe before revealing the contents of the sealed envelope. Joe reiterated his feelings of having been "a long way off" and that this session was very different than his previous remote-viewing experiences. Joe did a great job during this audit session. Again, his comments on this unique remote viewing are in his book *Mind Trek*.

The importance of this remote viewing for Joe McMoneagle (and the rest of us) extends far beyond the implications it may have for the exploration of the planet Mars in the twenty-first century. What I'm iterating here relates to what this session did for Joe back in 1984. He was able to extend his consciousness across millions of miles and millions of years (in terms of space/time reality). This must have had a tremendous impact on Joe's concept of self. He not only experienced his consciousness extending beyond the confines of his physical body but also reaching across our solar system, spanning millennia, and bonding (telepathically?) with another being. Who is this guy named Joe McMoneagle? And if he is an example of our true nature, who are we?

The final results of this Hemi-Sync training cannot be explained in terms of better or higher-resolution remote viewing.

Hemi-Sync training did not necessarily improve the overall remote-viewing quality but rather the reliability of the remote viewer. The training provided remote viewers with a dependable tool that they could use to access beneficial states of cortical arousal, states conducive to relaxing physically and mentally, to connecting with the target, to listening quietly to internal perceptual processes, to becoming aware of the information of interest, and to accurately reporting (objectifying) such information. (When asked, Joe simply says that the process helps him relax or prepare himself.)

Joe McMoneagle retired from military service shortly after completing the Hemi-Sync training. No other remote viewers were ever trained personally by Robert Monroe. I felt that the Gateway Voyage, a Hemi-Sync training program for the public, offered a sufficient orientation to the Hemi-Sync process at a greatly reduced cost. But of the several remote viewers with an affinity for the ERV process that were selected and attended the Gateway Voyage program, none ever did quite as well as Joe, who admittedly was a superb remote viewer even without the Hemi-Sync training. In terms of reliability or dependability, perhaps the prolonged ten weeks of Hemi-Sync training was better after all.

Closing the Remote-Viewing Chapter of My Life

In June 1987, I relinquished my position as operations and training officer of the Star Gate remote-viewing program. It had been some ten years since I had shown Lieutenant Colonel Webb the book *Mind-Reach* and had asked for a military assignment in remote viewing. I stayed on with the unit as an advisor until December, when I went on terminal leave and moved to Virginia.

I retired from military service in February of 1988. My personal experience with military remote-viewing surveillance had objectively demonstrated the validity of a process I had been experiencing throughout my life. There was a greater cultural impact too.

Through Star Gate, two presidents, members of the National Security Council, CIA, FBI, etc., and numerous military and civilian government personnel discovered that what we know and experience is not bound by the confines of our physical perceptions. Our very being extends beyond the physical body in a very real way. The impact of this realization continues to grow as more and more people are uncovering the details of the government-sponsored work in remote viewing.

Today, hundreds of people are learning how to do remote viewing through a variety of techniques. The International Remote Viewing Association (see website at IRVA.org), organized by selected scientists and practitioners, encourages scientifically sound research, provides ethical standards, and offers overview educational information to the public. This widespread interest in a consciousness-expanding discipline reflects a basic realization by individuals of their own true spiritual identity and a cultural desire for reconnecting with the spiritual foundation of humanity.

These implications have not gone unnoticed by me. In retirement, I headed to The Monroe Institute, where I would once again adventure "through the Flavor Straw" to my own awareness as I had done so many years before. I was on course.

Looking Back, an Epilogue

My experiences with remote viewing have become *past-life* experiences, a part of life rapidly becoming "remember-when" stories imprinted in the retreating memories of my mind.

Over the years, as I have talked with people about remote viewing, some have reacted with indignant disapproval, others with skepticism, and others with enthusiasm. Some are seriously interested and wish to get to the bottom of it (whatever that means). These varying reactions seem to be the result of differing educational backgrounds, of spiritual or peak experiences in their own lives, of their level of openness to new information, etc.

In the course of their lives, people don't necessarily maintain one certain concept of the world (or opinion about remote viewing). Experience changes and shapes ways of thinking, our very concept of reality. Over the years, some with whom I have spoken have changed.

Those with a *materialistic* perspective disregard the notion of remote viewing because of the incapacity of proving objective mechanisms responsible for the observed effects. Those representing this perspective deem remote viewing impossible from the start. They therefore search for causes that might explain the phenomena. They suppose deceit, sleight of hand, or mistakes by the experimenter.

A *physicalist* perspective holds remote viewing to be possible as either conscious or unconscious mental processes in the living human being. Extra-dimensional considerations of the phenomena are discarded as being speculative. Numerous protocols are invoked to demonstrate the efficacy of remote viewing. Statistical models, behavioral profiles, double-blind cueing, analytical techniques, etc., are the calling cards of these "true believers."

The *spiritualistic* (not meaning holy) approach is open to the possibility that remote viewing represents our own multidimensional nature and that reality is more than our physical senses tell us. I have found that many who publicly avow a physicalist perspective are closet spiritualists, especially the ones who are psychically experiential themselves. This group endeavors to improve remote-viewing methods and techniques with the aim of getting better and more frequent "hits" demonstrating their abilities.

Additionally, these particular "true believers" want to develop different applications for remote viewing, i.e., remote medical diagnosis and healing or early warning of imminent danger of future events. In their enthusiasm, this group is easily seduced into putting aside due caution and a critical view of themselves. They neglect to test the validity of individual remote-viewing sessions and run the risk of getting tangled in dependence and an irrational belief in their own remote-viewing skills. Some consider trivialities or contradictory absurdities to be the "ultimate truth" and may even announce the said "truths" as doctrine. In so doing, the legitimate endeavors for responsible remote viewing may be discredited.

An ethical or conscientious approach to all this takes into account the reasonable aspects of all the above approaches. The materialistic perspective advocates guarding against deceit and trickery by unscrupulous practitioners. (Of course, some would say that any government involvement is unscrupulous by definition.)

The physicalist approach points out that our unconscious minds may be a repository for remote-viewing information and that careful scientific investigation of the phenomenon may help us understand our boundless perceptual abilities.

The spiritualistic viewpoint suggests that reality itself is greater than we know and that we truly are more than our physical bodies.

Is remote viewing real? Those who research the field may come to convince themselves of its veracity based on the accumulating scientific evidence of the psychic phenomena. Psychologically, however, these well-meaning truth seekers remain protected by a defense mechanism. They can always escape back into their old belief systems under the guise that all the research is bogus and that it couldn't possibly be true.

I, however, do not have the luxury of this psychological safe haven. I was the operations officer for the Star Gate remote-viewing unit. I controlled the protocols and information overtly available to the remote viewers. I *know*, because I was there, that there was no fraud. Remote viewing is real. It works.

To me, the value of remote viewing lies not in so-called practical applications like performing services for business, industry, government, and science; or aiding in the recovery of lost children, assisting the FBI on kidnap cases, or helping to fight terrorism; or even contacting UFOs or spiritual beings. The value of remote viewing rests with the experience itself.

Remote viewing is like stopping to smell the flowers, drinking a goblet of fine vintage wine, or making love. Through experience, we become who we are. Through remote viewing, we realize (make real) the true nature of ourselves as sentient beings.

If remote viewing is going to be part of my future, it will be to serve in some way to promote increased first-person experiences of remote viewing and the discovery of who we are as human beings and the meaning that has for humankind.

Part Two:

Scientist, Explorer, Spiritual "I"

Chapter Five

Monroe World—
The New Land of Hemi-Sync

In 1986, a couple of years before I retired from the army, I began building a house near Nellysford, Virginia, very close to The Monroe Institute, a nonprofit organization founded by Bob Monroe. In the intervening years since we first met in 1977, Bob had been softly suggesting that I could join the staff of the Institute. He never made a direct offer but rather hinted that there might be a position available if I was so disposed. This open door, coupled with my own internal Guidance, led me in the direction of The Monroe Institute as army retirement neared.

Family life on Fort Meade had been great. The kids had rotated in turn through the elementary, middle, and high schools. There were school bands and recitals, after-school sports, a broken arm, and a bicycle accident that led to a few knocked-out teeth. When all the kids were old enough to go to school, in the mid-eighties, Joan had gotten a job.

Those were the burgeoning days of computers in the workplace, and Joan had landed a position with a growing company. She had become a valuable company asset and slowly had become more and more interested in her work and less interested in home life. I began to feel uncomfortable with the marriage as time passed. Perhaps I was jealous or felt abandoned, as she seemingly lost interest in family life. As military retirement approached, our lives drifted farther apart.

As I explained before, I relinquished my position as operations and training officer for the remote-viewing unit in the summer of 1987. I went on terminal leave from the army and left Fort Meade in December 1987, and we moved into the new house I had built in Virginia. I was officially retired from the army in February 1988.

Shortly after we moved to Virginia, Joan and I separated. She moved back to her job in Maryland. The separation led to an amicable divorce after being married twenty years. Although we have both remarried, we remain friends. She has since advanced her career and become an information systems manager for a large retail chain. She has my respect and gratitude for all the affection we shared during our twenty-year marriage and for our three beautiful children. I will always love her.

A New Career

Retiring from the army and moving to Virginia without a specific job offer might seem like a risky thing to do. But I had grown to trust Guidance as expressed through gentle feelings and a sense of divine-right-action. It was not as though I heard a booming voice say, "Retire from the army, move to Virginia, and get a job at The Monroe Institute." I just knew in my heart it was the right thing to do.

An understanding of the technology time window is important here. In the mid- to late-eighties, desktop office computers began to change the workplace forever. Personal ownership of a computer, a concept shared by only the most forward-looking entrepreneurs, became possible. I took to this new computer era with great enthusiasm. I bought a home computer and learned how to operate a variety of systems and to write my own applications programs. My electronics training from earlier years helped too. Guidance obviously had more on my agenda at the time than clandestine technical surveillance devices.

This new age of technology made widespread application of computerized electroencephalography, popularly referred to as "brain mapping," a reality. I found a fledgling company in Colorado called Lexicor Medical Technology that had developed a 24-channel, computerized EEG recording and analysis instrument. This remarkable-for-its-time system worked in conjunction with the latest in desktop computers—an IBM-compatible 286 with a 20-megabyte hard drive and 8 megabytes of RAM. I realize that such figures sound ridiculous by today's standards, but back then it was state-of-the-art.

Bob Monroe and I discussed the possibility of getting such a device for the Institute and using it to measure brainwave changes in people listening to Hemi-Sync. Ever since my experience "through the Flavor Straw" back in 1977, I had been curious. What was it about Hemi-Sync that made this journey possible, and how was it that Bob ever came up with this sound technology?

Bob had told me at the time that my specific experience was the result of my metaphysical upbringing and my intent. But my curiosity went further. Do the Hemi-Sync sounds alter brain activity and consciousness?

Bob assured me that this was probably true but there was no objective evidence to demonstrate such changes. But now, with the advent of desktop computers, such measurements would be possible outside a multimillion-dollar medical diagnostic facility. Bob sent me to Colorado to check out the Lexicor device.

During this same period of time (I still did not have a new job after my army retirement), I programmed my home computer, which was equipped with a stereo sound card, to produce complex binaural beats—the stuff of Hemi-Sync. I packed up my computer and took it to Bob to show him how computers could be used to produce his Hemi-Sync sounds. He was skeptical at first; then he asked me to "dial in" a few different binaural-beat patterns.

The short version of the rest of the story is that I did not leave with my computer. Bob was truly amazed. For years, he had been mixing together many layers of sounds from analog tape through a multi-channel audio mixing board. This method took hours and hours of work. With a computer, such mixing became obsolete as such combinations could simply be programmed into the sound card.

When I came back from Colorado and explained to Bob how the Lexicor device worked and what it would reveal, I recommended that he get one for the Institute. He asked me if I could operate it and the computer we would need to buy. I assured him that I could. It was only then, in June of 1988, that Bob actually offered me a job at the Institute.

After a provisional ninety-day hire, during which I set up and began to use the Lexicor, Bob offered me the position of research director at the Institute in September 1988. He was in fact inviting me to join him in a scientific journey on a course charted to discover the why and how of Hemi-Sync.

The rest of this chapter describes the journey from Bob's intuitive foundation in the 1950s and 1960s to the rapidly evolving field of neuroscience at the dawn of the twenty-first century and our current understanding of the Hemi-Sync process.

In the Beginning

Originally, Bob was interested in sleep-learning and wanted to develop a way to prolong those lighter stages of sleep wherein most sleep-learning seemed to occur. He experienced his first conscious out-of-body escapade only after many Hemi-Sync sleep-learning experiments.

Ever since the late 1950s, first Bob Monroe and then the Institute have been identifying propitious states of consciousness and developing various Hemi-Sync signals to induce them. The process of developing effective Hemi-Sync binaural beats has been as complex as the functions of the brain itself.

Under laboratory conditions, Bob Monroe originally tested many subjects for their subjective and objective responses to binaural beats, and recorded the effect on them of each binaural beat frequency. Then binaural beats were mixed and subjects' responses were again recorded.

After many months—years in some cases—test results began

to show population-wide singular responses to specific mixes of binaural beats, which laid the foundation for what are now called Hemi-Sync focus levels. The Hemi-Sync technology was eventually patented.[14]

Bob tried to describe Hemi-Sync as an auditory-guidance system that uses sound pulses to somehow *entrain* beneficial brainwave states. He said that Hemi-Sync seemed to be able to heighten selected awareness and performance levels while creating a relaxed state.

But could this be true? And if it was, how did all this work? Could sound pulses somehow *entrain* the electrical activity of the brain? Resonant entrainment of oscillating systems is a well-understood principle in the physical sciences—but was it the mechanism behind Hemi-Sync?

Although Bob found that Hemi-Sync, actually the well-recognized phenomena of binaural beating, enables focused states of consciousness and, for some, provokes the realization that they are more than their physical bodies, little was known about the mechanism—the so-called neural underpinnings of the process.

In the early years, it was assumed that the mechanism behind the consciousness-altering effects of binaural beats was somehow related to the frequency-following response. It was postulated that prolonged exposure to binaural-beat stimuli influenced brainwaves to the point of altering ongoing EEG through *entrainment* of the perceived rhythmic pulsing.

Since an auditory, frequency-following response could be measured at the brain's cortex, it was theorized that such entrainment imposed some sort of pattern on the nonlinear, stochastic resonance of brainwaves by means of the frequency beating of the auditory stimulus. Some erroneously called this "entrainment of the frequency-following response." This of course makes little sense, because a "response" is, by definition, a reaction to something and not in itself causative.

---

[14] a. Patent Number: 3884218; Issue Year: 1975
b. Patent Number: 5213562; Issue Year: 1993
c. Patent Number: 5356368; Issue Year: 1994

The Bob Monroe Research Lab

Even before I became the research director, I was fascinated with the concept that Hemi-Sync altered consciousness. I assumed this meant that the sound patterns somehow changed brainwaves. At first, I thought that Bob must have based the Hemi-Sync frequencies on his own brainwave states. So I began searching for some documentation of Bob's brainwave state during his out-of-body adventures.

I found it in the *International Journal of Parapsychology* and the *Proceedings of the Parapsychological Association.* The *Journal* article reported a study of Bob Monroe's brainwave state during two brief, self-induced out-of-body experiences. The recorded brainwave state resembled Stage One sleep, but Charles T. Tart, the principal investigator, reported that this identification was somewhat ambiguous because of exceptionally high variability in Bob's brainwave patterns.[15]

The *Proceedings* article said that Bob also reported two brief out-of-body experiences.[16] He had awakened within a few seconds after each one, which allowed for correlation of physiological recordings with the experience. Brainwave patterns immediately prior to and continuous through the first experience were roughly classified as a borderline or hypnagogic state, a brainwave pattern containing bits of slowed alpha rhythm (indicative of drowsiness) and theta activity (a normal sleeping pattern).

This pattern persisted through the time period Bob reported as his first out-of-body experience and was accompanied by a sudden fall of systolic blood pressure lasting seven seconds, the estimated length of the out-of-body experience. The second out-of-body experience appeared to have been accompanied by similar brainwave patterns.

The two studies of Bob's out-of-body experiences showed that

---

15 "A Second Psychophysiological Study of Out-of-the-Body Experiences in a Gifted Subject," *International Journal of Parapsychology* 9 (1967): 251-258.

16 W. Roll, R. Morris and J. Morris, eds. "A Further Psychophysiological Study of Out-of-the-Body Experiences in a Gifted Subject, Robert A. Monroe," *Proceedings of the Parapsychological Association*, 6 Nov. 1969: 43-44.

his escapades seemed to occur in conjunction with a prolonged and deliberately produced hypnagogic state (Stage One sleep). Such sustained states are not normally seen in the laboratory. Additionally, the preponderance of theta rhythms and the occasional, slowed alpha showed an intriguing parallel with brainwave states reported for advanced Zen masters during meditation. (The major achievement of these two studies was to demonstrate that the out-of-body experience can occur in a laboratory setting and is thus amenable to scientific investigation.)

So if Bob based the Hemi-Sync frequencies on his own brainwaves, hypnagogic theta with reduced alpha would be the logical place to start. When I asked Bob about this, he laughed and said that there was probably something to all this but that he had started developing Hemi-Sync long before he had had his first (conscious) out-of-body experience or had his brainwaves measured.

Early Understandings

If a tuning fork designed to produce a frequency of 440 Hz is struck so as to cause it to oscillate, and is then brought into the vicinity of another 440 Hz tuning fork, the second fork will begin to oscillate. The first tuning fork is said to have *entrained* the second, or caused it to resonate.

For one oscillating system to be capable of entraining another, the second system must be capable of achieving the same oscillating frequency. A 440 Hz tuning fork will not entrain a 300 Hz tuning fork because the second tuning fork will not vibrate at 440 Hz. Also, for one oscillating system to be capable of entraining another, the first system must have sufficient power or amplitude to overcome the homeostasis (stable state) of the second, and the first must be at a constant or fixed frequency. The tuning fork is an ideal example because it produces an oscillation of constant frequency and amplitude called a standing wave.

I postulated that the physics of entrainment applied to brainwaves as well. The electrochemical activity of the brain results in the production of electromagnetic waveforms (brainwaves) that change frequencies based on neural activity within the brain and can be objectively measured with sensitive equipment, the EEG. I wondered if Hemi-Sync could actually change this activity.

It seemed to me that caffeine, nicotine, and alcohol could alter brainwave activity. The senses of vision, touch, and hearing also provide easy access to the neural functions of the brain. Each of these senses responds to waveform activity within the surrounding environment and transmits information to the brain. Do the senses of sight, touch, and hearing, by their very nature, provide a fertile medium for entrainment of brainwaves? A strobe light flashing at 10 Hz will entrain occipital brainwaves to its frequency. Could the sound technology Bob Monroe called Hemi-Sync entrain the brain in the same way?

The strobe-entrainment effect involves only one of the sensory channels. The sense of kinesthetic touch is another. In one interesting experiment, I found a researcher had set up a standing wave of a desired frequency in a waterbed. The resultant tactile signals were seemingly effective in entraining the subject's brainwaves to the selected frequency.

In the case of Hemi-Sync, is the sense of hearing providing the neural avenues by which entrainment signals can be introduced into the electromagnetic cranial environment? Brainwave researchers had measured a low-amplitude, frequency-following response to binaural beating, but this volume-conducted reflection of the stimulus beating does not represent ongoing or dominant brainwave activity. I needed to learn more about brainwaves.

There is a popular notion that one can tell what a person is thinking by measuring brainwave patterns. This is like saying that one can tell what information is in a computer by simply measuring voltages present at various points, which of course is impossible. A more realistic analogy would be the telephone.

A telephone has three states of consciousness: State one is standby—the telephone sits waiting to be used. State two is ringing—the telephone is actively soliciting attention. State three is talking—the telephone is being used. All of these states of consciousness of the telephone can be determined by measuring the line voltage of the telephone wires. Direct access to the telephone itself is not needed in order to know what it is doing.

If 48 volts of direct current are present on the wires, the phone is in state one, or standby; if 100 volts of alternating current, the phone is in state two, or ringing. When there is a modulated 10-volt direct current on the phone wires, the telephone is in state three, or talking (being used).

These telephone states of consciousness, so to speak, are discrete in that the telephone cannot be in more than one state at a time. It is waiting, ringing, or talking. But measuring line voltage and determining that the telephone is in state three (talking) does not reveal what is being said over the telephone.

The same is true of brainwaves. Measuring brainwave frequencies and associative patterns and detecting REM sleep (dreaming) does not reveal the dream content. Only by awakening the subject and asking for a description of the dream can the experimenter discover this.

Brainwaves themselves exemplify arousal levels. They represent the electrochemical environment through which perceived reality is manifest. They do not reveal subjective or cognitive experiential content.

Recent Comprehension

My research into the literature revealed that the human ability to *hear* a binaural beat appears to be the result of evolutionary adaptation. Many species can detect binaural beats: The frequencies at which the beats can be detected depend upon the size of the cranium. In the human, binaural beats of up to 20 Hz can be perceived when carrier tones are below approximately 1500 Hz.[17]

The sensation of hearing binaural beats occurs when two

[17] Carrier tones are the two sounds played via stereo presentation, one to each ear, that produce binaural beating.

coherent sounds of nearly similar frequencies are presented, one to each ear, and the brain detects phase differences between these sounds. In an open environment, this phase difference would provide directional information to the listener, but when presented with stereo headphones or speakers the brain integrates the two signals, producing the binaural beat. From the available literature, I discovered that binaural beats originate in the brainstem within the contralateral audio-processing regions of the brain called the superior olivary nuclei. Binaural beating is perceived as a fluctuating rhythm at the frequency of the difference between the stereo (left and right) auditory inputs.

This auditory sensation is neurologically routed to the reticular formation in the brainstem and simultaneously volume conducted to the cortex where it can be objectively measured as the frequency-following response. As I stated earlier, this does not necessarily indicate a change in ongoing brainwave activity. A complete understanding of all this was going to require some research on my part.

Hemi-Sync and Brain Function

I thought that an understanding of a possible neurological mechanism was important as foundation for the observed effectiveness of Hemi-Sync technology. I wanted to replicate the frequency-following response studies of other researchers to be sure, for myself, that binaural beats did in fact produce this EEG anomaly. This would also provide me a journey into the realm of academic research, a place I had seemingly not been before.

Hearing-acuity researchers had defined the "frequency-following response" as a brainwave-frequency response (measured by EEG) that corresponds to the frequency of an auditory stimulus. Previous hearing-acuity research had demonstrated a frequency-following response to binaural beating—proof that the sensation of binaural beating has a neurological efficacy.

However, a frequency-following response to binaural beats in brainwave frequency ranges usually associated with reported altered states of consciousness (e.g., theta states) had not, at this point, been objectively demonstrated using appropriate evoked-potential EEG protocols.[18]

I thought that further study of frequency-following response would be vital in understanding the obvious effectiveness of the Hemi-Sync process and maybe would even lead me to a possible neurological mechanism.

The Frequency-Following Response Study

Following is a detailed description of an experimental procedure. It's pretty interesting and underscores the seriousness of purpose behind the work at The Monroe Institute, but you can flip forward a few pages to the "Meaningful Results" section if you want.[19]

It would have been easy to use an EEG machine to collect brainwave data while I had someone listen to Hemi-Sync. A simple evoked-potential data analysis would show if Hemi-Sync engendered a classic frequency-following response. But the task was bigger than I had imagined.

By using just one subject and one binaural-beat frequency, I couldn't be sure that results weren't due to chance. I needed to use several subjects and at least a couple of different binaural beats. I finally wound up with seven subjects and a small experiment designed to objectively verify a frequency-following response to both theta and beta binaural-beat stimuli through the use of an appropriate evoked-potential protocol.

The study was designed to determine if a 7 Hz (theta) binaural beat would result in a 7 Hz frequency-following response in the brain, and if a 16 Hz (beta) binaural beat would engender a 16 Hz response. I chose these frequencies because they were similar to the frequencies usually embedded within Hemi-Sync patterns.

In order to see if the binaural beating stimulated a frequency-following response, I had to compare EEG recordings taken while

---

18 Evoked-potential studies use time-domain averaging of a number of EEG responses to mathematically isolate and identify stimuli that would otherwise be overwhelmed by ongoing brainwave activity.

19 An academic version of the frequency-following response study is provided on the companion CD-ROM.

listening to the beating with some other condition. Silence could be one (baseline) condition, but I also thought it would be interesting to see the effect of using a nonbeating (placebo) sound.

In more scientific terms, the hypothesis of the study was that subjects exposed to a binaural-beat stimulus would evidence increases in amplitude of time-domain averaged EEG in frequencies matching that binaural-beat stimulus (the frequency-following response) when compared to a silence-baseline condition.

Additionally, I expected an elevation in overall EEG amplitude (an arousal response, not a frequency-following response) in the case of a nonbeating stimulus (placebo) and the alternative binaural-beat stimulus.

This may seem pretty complex, but if my hypothesis proved valid, I would be able to see significant increases in 7 Hz and 16 Hz EEG amplitudes during comparable binaural-beat stimuli periods, as compared to the silence-baseline condition. And this result would, of course, imply the development of a frequency-following response to binaural-beat stimuli.

In order to be sure that I got reliable results in the study, I decided to use both male and female subjects who had no prior experience listening to Hemi-Sync. I wanted to ensure that they wouldn't be simply exhibiting some form of conditioned response due to prior experience.

Also, to control for subject expectation, the two-second experimental stimuli periods (7 Hz, 16 Hz, and a nonbeating tone) were arranged in an eighteen-episode Latin-square protocol, which arranges the stimuli so that the subject cannot predict what the next stimulus will be based on previous exposure.

In order to automate the whole process and take the experimenter (me) out of the loop, I used a computer to present the audio stimuli. I constructed a series of sound files that provided the various stimuli. Each sound file was automatically played in the Latin-square sequence through a stereo sound card to the subjects' in-ear stereo headphones.

To isolate the subjects from intrusive stimuli, they were tested in the booth in the Institute lab, which is an isolated, double-wall, soundproofed, and electrically shielded chamber. During the evaluation, subjects lay comfortably on a waterbed. To aid in the reduction of eye-movement artifact, a small, soft fabric bag filled with rice was placed over the closed eyes of the subjects. EEG recordings were made during the entire Latin-square protocol outlined above.

So, I had been careful to ensure this frequency-following response study was conducted with some due diligence. But what would the results show?

I found that subjects exposed to binaural-beat stimuli evidenced time-domain averaged EEG increases in frequencies matching binaural-beat stimuli when compared to the silence-baseline condition. Some elevation in EEG amplitudes in comparison to the silence-baseline condition was also seen in reaction to both the placebo stimulus and the alternative binaural-beat stimulus. All results were as set forth in the study's hypothesis.

There was no reliable evidence of a 16 Hz frequency-following response. Increases in 16 Hz time-domain averaged EEG amplitudes during the 16 Hz binaural-beat stimulus periods over the silence-baseline condition were statistically nonsignificant when the increases in EEG during the placebo and the 7 Hz binaural-beat stimuli were considered.

However, statistically significant ($p < .05$) increases in 7 Hz EEG amplitudes were demonstrated during the 7 Hz stimulus condition, which provided evidence of a 7 Hz frequency-following response during the 7 Hz binaural-beat stimulus periods even when the increases in EEG during the placebo and 16 Hz binaural-beat stimuli were considered in the statistical evaluation.

The following graphs show the anticipated arousal response to the placebo stimulus and the alternative binaural-beat stimulus as well as substantial EEG amplitude increases in the appropriate binaural-beat stimuli periods over the silence-baseline condition.

Meaningful Results

With this small study, I had objectively demonstrated a frequency-following response to binaural beats in brainwave

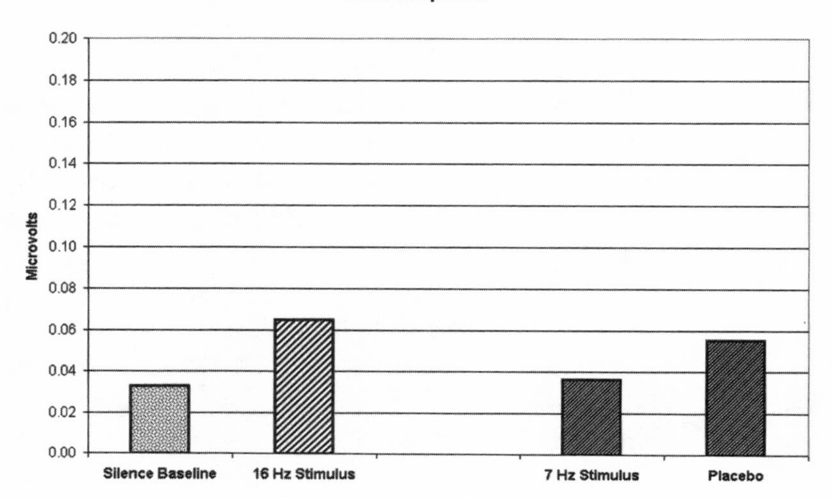

frequency ranges associated with discrete theta states of consciousness—the stuff of Hemi-Sync. This was a critical step in validating previous hearing-acuity research. This study also proved to me, personally, that binaural beats did in fact have a neurological impact.

But this only proved an auditory frequency-following response. It did not demonstrate that binaural beats have an ability to somehow

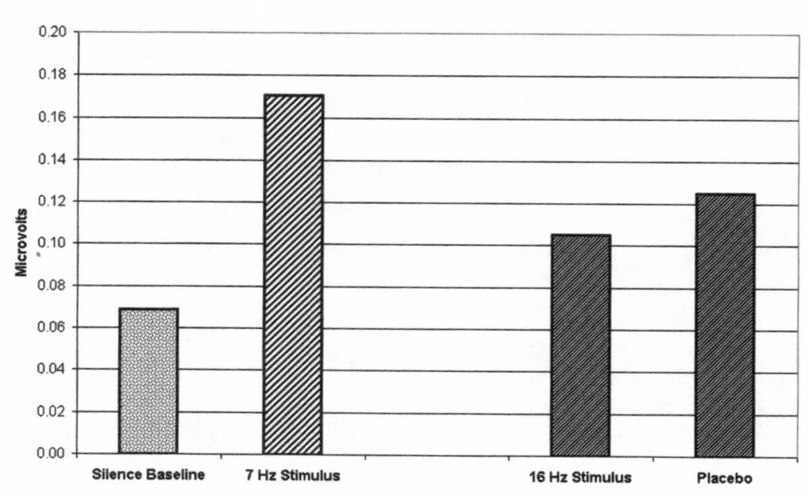

engender psychophysiological state changes, alterations in ongoing brainwave activity.

As I said before, decades ago it was assumed that the mechanism behind the consciousness-altering effects of binaural beats was somehow related to the frequency-following response. I wrote and spoke of this myself many times. However, at that point in my research, it was hard to even speculate that the very low-amplitude brainwave activity (represented by the frequency-following response) could in some electromagnetic inductive way modify ongoing brainwave activity. On the other hand, the mere presence of a frequency-following response to the binaural beats of the Hemi-Sync process in this study provided valuable evidence of the neurological impact of this stimulus.

Through further literature review, I found that there is no neurological effect-mechanism to support the notion that "entrainment" of binaural beating is responsible for alterations in brainwave arousal. The EEG signal strength of the measured auditory frequency-following response is extremely low, much too low to represent an overall ongoing brainwave state. Nevertheless, the frequency-following response to binaural beats remains an important aspect in understanding their potential state-changing effects.

Demonstrating the presence of a frequency-following response to the binaural beats in the theta range using evoked-potential EEG protocols provided me with some evidence of the neurological impact of the Hemi-Sync stimulus. So, what is the mechanism behind the observed changes in overall brainwave activity? With more recent research, I have taken a deeper look into the probable neurological mechanism involved in changing cortical arousal (ongoing brainwaves).

Neurology and Hemi-Sync

This is a rather in-depth look at brain activity as it relates to Hemi-Sync. You might want to flip forward a few pages to the section called "Altering Consciousness with Hemi-Sync."

Through further study of the available literature, I found out that ongoing brainwave activity is regulated by the brain's extended reticular-thalamic activation system. The neural-reticular formation is composed of a large, net-like diffuse area of the brainstem. The word reticular actually means "net-like."

The reticular activating system interprets and reacts to information from internal stimuli like feelings, attitudes, and beliefs as well as external sensory stimuli (like Hemi-Sync sound) by reactively regulating arousal states, the focus of attention, and levels of awareness. How we interpret, respond, and react to information, then, is managed by the brain's reticular formation stimulating the thalamus and cortex, and brainwave states of arousal.

So it seemed to me that in order to alter arousal states, attentional focus, and levels of awareness, it was necessary to provide some sort of information input to the reticular activating system. And therein appears to reside the neurological mechanism for the powerful consciousness-altering effects of Hemi-Sync.

If I understood the scientific literature, it would appear that Hemi-Sync provides information—the complex, brainwave-like pattern—that engenders cortical adaptation. The reticular activating system distinguishes the unique binaural-beat waveform arising within the brainstem as brainwave pattern information. If internal stimuli, feelings, attitudes, beliefs, and external sensory stimuli are not in conflict with this information (an internal, even unconscious, fear may be a source of conflict, for example), the reticular activating system seems to alter cortical arousal states to match the Hemi-Sync stimulus as a natural adaptive function.

In effect, as time passes the reticular activating system monitors the internal and external environment and arousal states, attentional focus, and levels of awareness to determine, from moment to moment, the most suitable way to deal with existing conditions. As long as no conflicts develop, the reticular naturally continues aligning the listener's brainwave activity with the information in the Hemi-Sync sound field.

The true mechanism, therefore, behind Hemi-Sync's ability to alter cortical arousal and consciousness is not brainwave "entrainment" but adaptation to auditory stimulation of the reticular. This understanding of a neurological mechanism as foundation for the observed effectiveness of the Hemi-Sync technology was so important that I wanted to study this process further. Ever since my adventure "through the Flavor Straw," I had been seeking to discover a practical explanation of how Hemi-Sync works.

Altering Consciousness with Hemi-Sync

Our state of consciousness can be described as a balance of cortical arousal level and subjective content. The reticular activating system in the brainstem is responsible for maintaining appropriate levels of arousal in the cortex as well as other specialized areas of the brain. And the subjective content (presumably, intracortical intercourse) of our experiences is dependent upon an individual's experience level, one's social-psychological conditioning, cognitive skills, and neurological development. I began to grasp an understanding of the power of Hemi-Sync.

The Hemi-Sync sound technology engenders the auditory sensation of binaural beating, and this rhythmic waveform can be objectively measured as a frequency-following response, providing evidence that it manifests within the brain.

Since this waveform is neurologically routed to the reticular formation and since the reticular activating system governs cortical brainwave amplitudes, Hemi-Sync binaural beats (through the mechanism of the reticular) thereby induce alterations in brainwave amplitudes or the arousal side of the consciousness equation. From this understanding, Hemi-Sync focus levels (Focus 10, Focus 12, etc.) become levels of brainwave arousal.

I have read numerous anecdotal reports of state changes (alterations in consciousness) encouraged by various low-frequency binaural beats. Listening to selected binaural beats seems to promote propitious states of consciousness in a variety of applications. It has been reported that binaural beating has different effects depending on the frequency of the binaural-beat stimulation.

I read that binaural beats in the delta (1 to 4 Hz) and theta (4 to 8 Hz) ranges are associated with reports of creativity, sensory integration, relaxed or meditative states, or as an aid to falling asleep. Binaural beats in the beta frequencies (typically 16 to 24 Hz) are associated with reports of increased concentration or alertness and enhanced-memory function.

Independent research has associated Hemi-Sync with changes in arousal leading to sensory integration, alpha biofeedback, relaxation, meditation, stress reduction, and pain management. I have read research reports linking Hemi-Sync with improved sleep, health care, enriched learning environments, enhanced memory, creativity, treatment of children with developmental disabilities, the facilitation of attention, and so-called peak experiences.

Further research validates Hemi-Sync's use in the enhancement of hypnotizability, treatment of alcoholic depression, the promotion of vigilance, performance and mood, increased intuition, improved reliability in remote viewing, telepathy, and out-of-body experience.

I found several free-running EEG studies that suggest that binaural beats may induce alterations in cortical arousal (ongoing brainwaves) and consciousness states. But I needed to do my own research. The only way I would know for sure how Hemi-Sync works was to find out for myself—something Bob Monroe had insisted on years ago.

Hemi-Sync and Brainwave Arousal

I decided to do two free-running EEG studies.[20] In the first study, I measured the neural accommodation (changes in ongoing or overall brainwave activity) associated with complex binaural-beat stimuli. In the second study, based on the same protocol, I measured changes in ongoing brainwave activity associated with placebo stimuli. By comparing the results of these two studies, I hoped to be able to validate the power of Hemi-Sync to alter consciousness.

20 An academic version of this report is provided on the companion CD-ROM.

As before, you can flip forward a few pages and see what I found out.

The hypothesis in the first study was that listening to Hemi-Sync for several minutes would modify ongoing brainwave activity in the direction of the binaural beat stimuli. That is, increasing the amplitude of delta-frequency binaural-beat stimuli while decreasing the amplitude of alpha-frequency binaural-beat stimuli would result in comparable changes in arousal as measured by free-running EEG.

I wanted to mimic existing, commercially available Hemi-Sync recordings, so the experimental binaural-beat stimuli consisted of mixed sinusoidal tones producing complex frequency patterns (waveforms) changing over a period of forty-five minutes. I first recorded brainwaves during a no-stimulus baseline condition. Next, I recorded brainwaves for each subject during six periods for the forty-five-minute sequence of changing binaural beats condition. Finally, I made an EEG recording during a no-stimulus post-baseline condition (figure 1).

I rejected the data from two of the subjects due to excessive movement artifact and used the remaining eighteen subjects' records for analysis. To determine statistical validity of the data, I

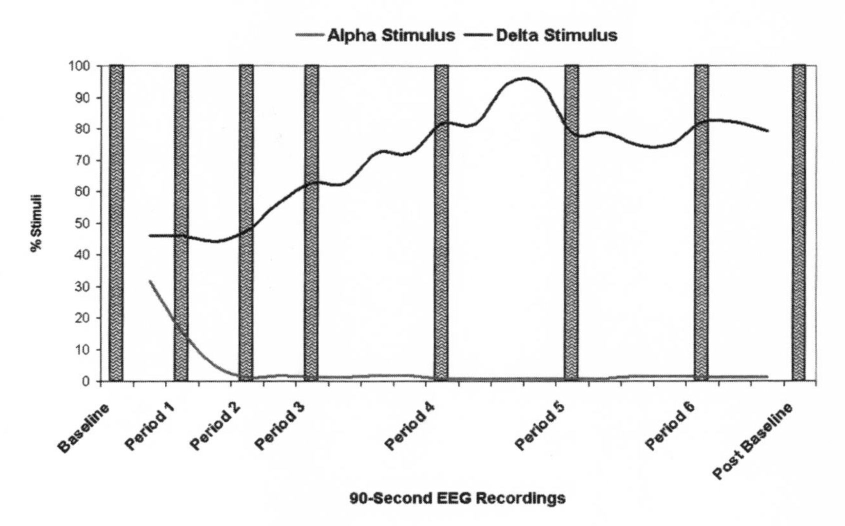

Figure 1

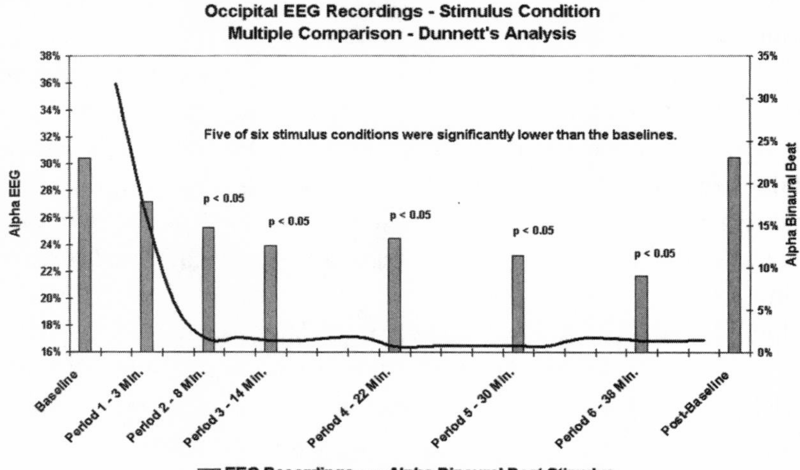

Figure 2

conducted a multiple comparison procedure following a one-way analysis of variance (ANOVA), Dunnett's Test, which compared the combined baselines (before and after) as a control mean with the binaural-beat stimulus periods. This analysis showed the reductions in the percentages of occipital alpha during stimuli conditions were significant (individually, $p<.05$, and together, $p<.001$) during five of six stimulus periods compared to baselines (figure 2).

Statistical analysis of the data also showed the increases in the percentages of central delta during stimuli conditions were significant

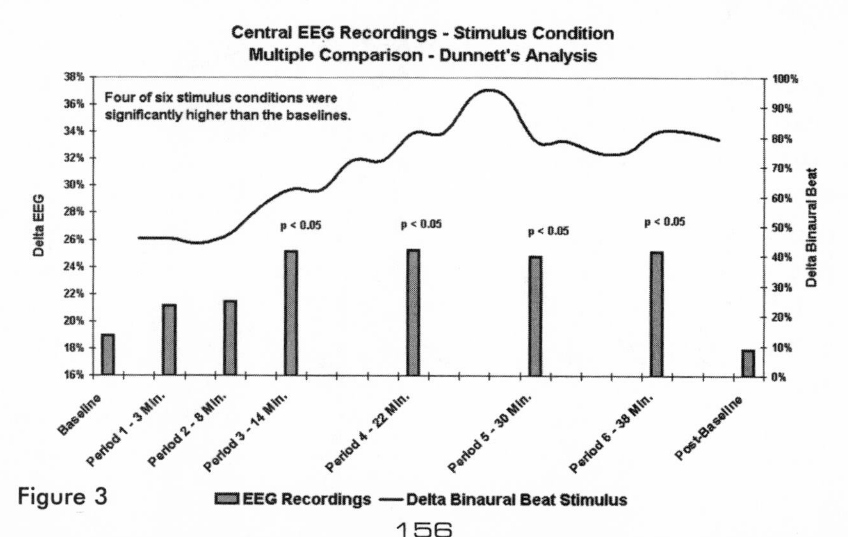

Figure 3

(individually, $p<.05$, and together, $p<.001$) during four of six stimulus periods compared to baselines (figure 3).

So, the results of this first study showed changes in brainwave activity during the stimulus periods when compared to the baseline recordings both with increased central delta and decreased occipital alpha. These decreases in alpha amplitudes, coupled with increasing delta activity, indicated reduced cortical arousal. The mounting changes over the time of the test and the course of the stimuli suggest a deepening trend of progressive relaxation and falling asleep.

A basic question raised by this first study was the role of Hemi-Sync stimulation in solely or directly causing the brainwave changes observed. Several of the subjects had had considerable previous experience with Hemi-Sync. Could it be that these subjects were naturally adept at altering levels of arousal or had acquired this ability through repeated Hemi-Sync practice? The deepening trend over time also suggests the need to take into consideration naturally occurring, progressive state changes associated with falling asleep. I designed a second study to address these concerns.

The hypothesis of the second study was that listening to monotonous tones (a placebo stimuli without binaural beats) for several minutes would result in habituation of the stimuli and a slowing of ongoing brainwave activity and a progressive state of relaxation.

The placebo stimuli consisted of the same sinusoidal tones used in the first study, except that they did not produce binaural beating. As in the first study, the volunteer subjects experienced a no-stimulus baseline condition during which a ninety-second EEG recording was taken. Next, each one listened to the same forty-five-minute sequence of changing tones during which six 90-second EEG recordings were taken at regular intervals. To reduce the influence of expectation, subjects were again blind as to the character of the tones. Finally, during a no-stimulus post-baseline condition, a ninety-second EEG recording was made.

A multiple comparison procedure following a one-way ANOVA (Dunnett's Test) comparing the combined baselines

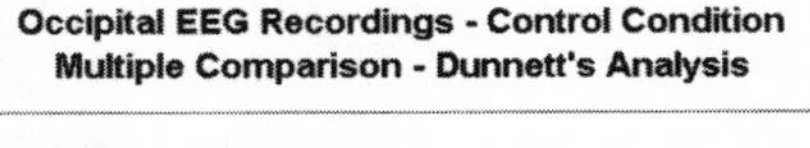

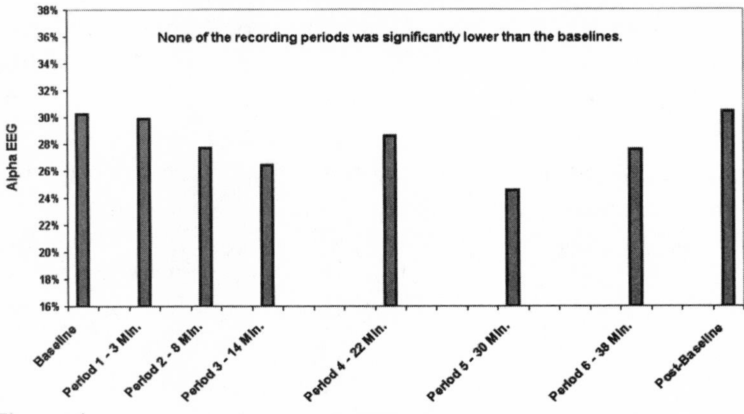

Figure 4

as a control mean with the placebo stimuli periods showed nonsignificant reductions in the percentages of occipital alpha during stimuli conditions compared to baselines (figure 4).

Statistical analysis showed the nonsignificant increases in the percentages of central delta during stimuli conditions compared to baselines (figure 5). The results of this second study, unlike the first, did not significantly distinguish occipital alpha and central delta brainwave activity during the placebo stimulus periods from the baselines.

Central EEG Recordings - Control Condition
Multiple Comparison - Dunnett's Analysis

None of the recording periods was significantly higher than the baselines.

Delta EEG

38%
36%
34%
32%
30%
28%
26%
24%
22%
20%
18%
16%

Baseline
Period 1 - 3 Min.
Period 2 - 8 Min.
Period 3 - 14 Min.
Period 4 - 22 Min.
Period 5 - 30 Min.
Period 6 - 38 Min.
Post-Baseline

Figure 5

EEG Recordings

The hypothesis of this placebo study expected observed decreases in alpha amplitudes coupled with increasing delta activity as a reaction to listening to monotonous tones. These changes, however, were not statistically significant, meaning that they could be expected to have happened by chance alone.

Meaningful Results

Together, these studies demonstrate that Hemi-Sync has a direct effect on brainwave activity, involving the interaction of binaural-beat stimulation with the basic rest-activity cycle, other sensory stimulation, and higher-order memory or attentional processes under the scrutiny of the reticular formation. All of these systems cooperate to maintain our homeostasis and optimal performance.

Our natural state-changing mechanisms, ultradian rhythms, individual differences, prior experience, and beliefs all contribute to the effects of and response to Hemi-Sync. But for me the bottom line, so to speak, was that these two studies provided statistical observations demonstrating changes in cortical arousal in response to Hemi-Sync. I had my proof.

Ever since my adventure "through the Flavor Straw," I had been wondering how Hemi-Sync worked. These studies showed me that the power of Hemi-Sync to provide an environment conducive to personal explorations beyond our physical senses was real, not snake oil, or self-fulfilling prophecy, or just wishful thinking, but real—real, that is, at least in terms of modern neurology.

But did this mean that the binaural beats of the Hemi-Sync process constituted an irresistible force that could really put the *whammy* on you, so to speak? No! And I think Bob Monroe explained it best:

> Hemi-Sync is like music. Imagine yourself out for an evening for dinner and dance. There you are, sitting at your table, having a cocktail, when the band strikes up a tune. Observing the couples around you, you see that some are getting up to dance, while others remain engrossed in their intimate conversations.

> You notice that you are tapping your foot to the beat of the music and your companion has stopped talking and is listening intently to the familiar tune. The waiter suddenly appears, and your attention and response to the music fall away as you focus your attention on savory menu items.
>
> What this all means is that music, like Hemi-Sync, only provides an inviting environment conducive to shifting your experience. The band music did not force or compel couples to dance. And Hemi-Sync cannot force or compel you in any way. Only you can change you. Your response to Hemi-Sync depends on you. If you willingly participate with the music, your experiences will be limited only by your own skill, expectations, and beliefs.

So was it Hemi-Sync that made my experience "through the Flavor Straw" back in 1977 possible? Or was it, as Bob had told me back then, that my experience was the result of my metaphysical upbringing and my intent? The answer to both questions is yes. Listening to Hemi-Sync apparently has the advantage of altering brainwave arousal, but one's subjective or cognitive experience of this shift is dependent upon one's beliefs, social-psychological conditioning, mental abilities or skills, intent, and perhaps even one's personal spiritual path or agenda.

Chapter Six

Through the Flavor Straw

I never forgot my reawakening experience "through the Flavor Straw" back in 1977 when I felt myself being gently pushed up and out of my body, away from familiar surroundings (understandings?), toward an eventual awareness of boundless white and the revelation that *I am*. This boundless-white realization was outside the limitations of the usual space-time orientation. So, while my senses told me that I rose out of my body and traveled some distance to a place where I found out that my spiritual self was ever-present, *my voyage was actually one of revelation.*

While I uncovered the neural underpinnings behind the Hemi-Sync process, I availed myself of the opportunity to use Hemi-Sync in realization of my own conscious being. I began by attending a Gateway Voyage program in 1978 at a retreat center in Richmond, Virginia. This was before any of the buildings or facilities of what is now The Monroe Institute existed (at least in the electromagnetic space/time continuum as we understand it).

The Hemi-Sync Programs

Gateway Voyage

Gateway Voyage is the Institute's basic, prerequisite program designed to provide the participant with tools to enable the development and exploration of human consciousness. The program I attended in Richmond was not nearly as comprehensive as the current program presented by the Institute.

In Richmond, we listened to a series of progressive, audio-guidance exercises recorded on cassette tapes using the Hemi-Sync technology. We also had group discussions and informal lectures—and, not least, free time for interaction with other participants.

Memorable for me was one tape experience during which I had a great adventure, and when it was finished I came back to my body and noticed that everything was very quiet. I didn't want to disturb the other participants, so I just rested quietly and waited for the trainers' instructions. After a while, I wondered if the tape experience was over, because I couldn't hear anything in my headphones.

Very slowly, I opened one eye and peeked to see if everybody else was still on tape. To my surprise, everybody was in the next room discussing their experiences. I was alone. I sat up, took off my headphones, and wandered in to join my fellow participants.

They all looked at me. The trainer explained that since a common fear that many had expressed was worry over what would happen if they got out-of-body and didn't come back when the tape ended, I had been used as an illustration that there was nothing to fear—that I would come back when the time was right.

I enjoyed the program so much I couldn't wait to do another once the new facilities on the new land opened. Two years later, I went to another Gateway Voyage program for still more great experiences.

On the second or third day of the program, we did an exercise called Five Questions. The idea of the exercise was to enter into Focus 12.[21] Once in Focus 12, the prerecorded voice of Bob Monroe would present five questions for the listeners to ask themselves in their own minds.

We were not told the questions before the exercise. We were told that the answers would most likely not be perceived as spoken or written words, but probably would be in the form of a series of pictures, or a sense of feeling or knowing, or—in their prime form—some sort of first-person experience. It would be up to us to translate such nonverbal communication into time/space words and physical pictures.

The questions presented during the exercise were:

1. **Who am I?**
2. **Where and who was I before I entered this physical being?**
3. **What is my purpose for this existence in physical-matter reality?**
4. **What action can I now take to best serve this purpose?**
5. **What is the content of the most important message that I can receive and understand at this point in my existence?**

As I asked myself question two in Focus 12, my intellect interpreted the question to be about a past life. The question could have just as easily been interpreted to be about a spiritual existence just prior to this physical life. But having understood the question as I did, my intent was to find out who I might have been in an earlier lifetime.

I had never really seriously considered the idea of my reincarnation. But in Focus 12 the question did not seem unusual, and I was willing to experience whatever—regardless of whether I

[21] During the three Gateway Voyage programs I attended, participants experienced various focused states of consciousness. Bob Monroe coined the following labels to provide a structure for novice explorers of these realms of consciousness: Focus 10, a "mind awake–body asleep" state; Focus 12, a state enabling expanded awareness of nonphysical perceptions; Focus 15, during which perceptions are expanded beyond time and place; and Focus 21, which provides access to other reality systems.

believed in the concept of reincarnation or not. When I was prompted by the voice of Bob Monroe during the exercise to ask, "Where and who was I before I entered this physical being?" I sent this question into the core of my being and awaited a reply.

Almost before I could finish asking, I saw a picture of a bearded man on a ship. I was told, as the expression goes, or came to know or experience or remember, that this was in the 1800s and that I was the captain of this ship. I was dressed in dark-colored woolen clothing and wearing a cap. I had a black, medium-length beard and was slender. The ship was sinking and, as captain, I had seen to the safety of my crew and was dutifully going down with the ship. As I pondered this vision, wondering what else I could learn, Bob Monroe's voice broached the next question and I complied.

After the exercise, the participants returned to the conference room to discuss our tape experience. It wasn't until then that I realized the implications of my experience. As I shared my ship's captain experience with the others, I began to remember, in the back of my mind, the origin of my nickname. This remembering was peculiar, because it was as though someone else was telling the ship's captain story while I occupied myself with the memory of my nickname.

Years ago my parents had explained to me that I had been given the nickname Skipper because they were seriously into recreational boating during my infancy, and I had become the "skipper" of the family boat, which was actually named SKIPPER. My needs and desires as an infant became paramount, and all family activities focused on my welfare. In nautical terms, I was the captain, the skipper.

As a part of me continued telling the Focus 12 ship's-captain experience, more memories began whirling around in the back of my mind. Just at the point in the story where my mouth was talking about "going down with the ship," I began to wonder if drowning was a traumatic experience. This immediately brought a memory of snorkeling at the age of twelve or thirteen. I failed a snorkeling class at the YMCA because I had passed out under water. The instructor had told me that I was different from other people because I did not know, by means of a panic response, when I needed to take a breath. The instructor said that he flunked me out of the class for my own safety.

A similar incident occurred in a friend's swimming pool when I was sixteen. My parents told me after that incident that I should never try scuba diving or any underwater sports. My mom told me that "normal" people, when holding their breath, know when it is time to take a breath because they are overcome by an unrelenting need to take a breath and will do whatever is necessary to satisfy that need. I don't experience these feelings.

The memory of all this seemed to answer my wondering about drowning being a traumatic event in the ship's-captain experience.

That other part of me finished telling the story to the group, and I raised my eyes, allowing the group back into my awareness. Several others told of their Focus 12 experiences in the Five Questions exercise. Then someone asked me, "Captain Atwater, did you see anyone else on the ship with you?"

He addressed me as captain out of respect for my military rank, but before I could answer his question, my thoughts flashed through the composite of what was happening—the past-life vision, my nickname Skipper, not drowning, and the respected captain. I finally answered the question, "No, I didn't see anyone else." But the underlying importance of his utterance did not escape me. I remain thankful for his question today. Guidance can seemingly come from all of God's angels.

Although my most memorable experience in this Gateway Voyage was the Focus 12 Five Questions exercise, others have their peak or most meaningful experiences in Focus 21. In the conference room after the Introduction to Focus 21 exercise, one participant started describing his experience by saying, "I went up through the colors and began to visualize a scene with people or beings in white robes. I was so excited! This was Focus 21. Several of these robed beings came forward in turn, presented to me a large open book with the open pages facing me. It was obvious that they wanted me to see what was in the book, but I pushed them aside because I was so excited about being in Focus 21. I didn't want to miss . . . ." He stopped mid-sentence and a bewildered look came over his face.

It wasn't until that moment in the conference room that he realized what had happened. He was so anxious not to miss anything in Focus 21 that he pushed aside the information being offered to him. The lesson here is one of willingness, openness, and acceptance rather than a goal-oriented demanding or controlling attitude based on ego-relevant expectations.

Guidelines

The theme of the six-day Guidelines program, which I have attended twice, is to assist the individual in learning methods through which conscious contact (a unity experience in the form of communication) can be established with one's Total Self—or Inner Self Helper (ISH), or Guidance, or Non-Physical Friends, or Universal Consciousness.

Remembering the elation of their Gateway Voyage experiences, many come to Guidelines filled with expectations. But this is an entirely different program with a consciousness horizon far beyond those of the Gateway Voyage. Once the participant realizes this, they open to what the program has to offer.

Working primarily in Focus 21, the program encourages the practical application of communications with one's true nature. With practice, I learned to quickly and directly access whatever information I needed. The goal is to make such lines of communication as direct and natural as possible. During a business meeting, for example, one can calmly and serenely access the communication skills learned and apply them within the context of the situation.

Also included is direct training relating to the out-of-body state and to the use of healing *energy* for oneself and others. I had my own personalized session during the program in a specially designed isolation chamber in the lab, which is where my travels "through the Flavor Straw" continued, which I'll get to in just a bit.

Lifeline

During the six-day Lifeline program, I gained familiarity with both Focus 22, where humans still in the physical have partial consciousness, remembered as dreams, delirium, and patterns induced through chemicals, and with Focus 23, a level inhabited by humans who have recently exited physical existence and have not adapted to such change.

From there I experienced Focus 24, 25, and 26—the Belief System territories where those who have exited the physical are residing in a particular belief system. I then went on to Focus 27—the Reception Center, Way Station, or Park, representing a *process* designed to ease the trauma and shock of the transition out of physical reality and assist in evaluating options for the next steps in growth and development.

I became familiar with these levels and then offered assistance to those I met in these realms. I also helped those I met come to know they survived physical death by inviting them to accompany me to Focus 27. Some call these activities *rescues*.

During several of the exercises, I kept passing by a guy in Focus 25 who seemed to be repairing a sink drain. After seeing him on a few exercises, I finally stopped and asked him what he was doing. He said that he had to get the sink fixed because there was an electrical short and somebody might get hurt. I wondered if a *rescue* was in order.

I asked him if he wanted to take a break and come with me for a while. He said he would, and I moved off toward *my favorite place* in Focus 27. He followed, and when we arrived he began looking around the kitchen and noticed that, although there was illumination, there were no light fixtures or light switches. I asked him what he thought about that and if he liked the idea. He said he thought it was just fine and began to relax a bit.

I told him I wanted him to meet someone who would show him many other wondrous things. I asked if he would like to do that. He nodded his head, and I turned to the waiting Guide and gestured willingness and receptivity. My new friend glanced toward the Guide as though he had not noticed him before and smiled as if greeting an old friend. They joined hands and became what I can only describe as a ball of soft light. This radiant oneness seemed to dance to music—a melody I could not hear—as it expanded beyond my perception.

Exploration 27

Exploration 27, which I attended twice, is a series of planned visits to Focus 27 to obtain information, data, and direct experiences related to this different nonphysical world. I experienced the unique energy field of Focus 27, had opportunities for extended communication with the *residents* there, and developed relationships that provided useful information. The program included explorations for the retrieval of historical data regarding Focus 27, including the investigation of *artifacts*.

A. J. Honeycutt, Bob Monroe's stepson and a stalwart example of thirty-something manhood, was one of my fellow participants in the second Exploration 27 program I attended. Beneath his sculptured physique and brusque mannerisms, A.J. hid a depth of understanding. You could see it in his eyes. He had his mother's eyes, the eyes of Nancy Penn Monroe.

A.J. Honeycutt

During the program, in the state of consciousness called Focus 27, A. J. visited a nonphysical version of the Roberts Mountain Retreat. He began *looking around* and found familiar articles, pictures, and knickknacks in all their proper places. In what he perceived as the kitchen area, he started thinking about small repairs that were necessary. To his astonishment, he found that this nonphysical version of the Roberts Mountain Retreat needed no repairs.

A.J. explained all this to us in the conference room after his experience. It illustrates that these nonphysical realms are not objective realities but convenient projections of our own idealized expectations. It is probably more practical not to think about *places* in nonphysical realms but rather *processes*.

In Focus 27, the Roberts Mountain Retreat *process* might include methods and practices for experiencing aspects of *All That Is* beyond the Earth-life system. We overlay these experiences on mental projections of physical matter reality in an attempt (many times unsuccessfully) to mentally integrate meaningfulness.

I also explored beyond Focus 27, into previously uncharted territories referred to as Focus 34/35. At this level it is nearly impossible to relate experiences in human terms. Metaphorically, I found myself inside a great oneness, which appeared to me as a crystal geode. The message here was that just as the geode is *one* thing made up of many individual crystalline forms which are dependent on each other to create the unity of the geode form, so too is humanity *one* thing made up of each of us and by which humanity itself is defined.

If you can't get your mind around that, you'll just have to visit Focus 34/35 and "find out for yourself," as Bob Monroe would say.

Heartline

The six-day Heartline program came into being as a result of Laurie Monroe's experience of the universal love energy communicated through her from Bob and Nancy Monroe.

Laurie, Bob's daughter, was about eight years old when he began having the consciousness-expanding experiences described in his book *Journeys Out of the Body*. As a child, Bob's out-of-body stories amused Laurie, for she herself experienced such adventures regularly, as many children do. Together, she and Bob grew to understand the greater spiritual implications of the out-of-body experience.

Laurie played an active role in the early years of Hemi-Sync research and development. Being a part of all of this through the years must surely have been her chosen course, her divinely appointed purpose in life. Today, a heart-centered Laurie dedicates herself to continuing the work of her father, to maintaining a local parent organization, and to establishing a global network so that people all over the world can experience the Hemi-Sync technology. She truly believes that the Hemi-Sync process will bring to humankind a knowing that we are more than our physical bodies and that in this knowing, life itself will be enriched here and beyond.

Skip with Laurie Monroe

Heartline offers new approaches for removing the obstacles to love's expression in everyday life, as well as methods for exploring deeper levels of Self—for discovering one's true self-essence. This highly interactive experiential process uses a variety of exercises beyond the program tapes.

For me, however, Heartline represented something special, for I read Conversations with God by Neale Donald Walsch during this wonder-filled weeklong retreat. Neale's forthright treatises, or, as he put it, an uncommon dialogue, touched me deeply. With each turn of a page, my heart filled with emotion and my eyes wept. Here in this book were the truths, the principles by which I had been living, and amazingly someone else knew these things.

As I read through chapter after chapter, I kept asking myself in the back of my mind, "Who is this guy, this Neale Walsch, and how does he know all this stuff? Is this really a conversation with God?" Ultimately, I guess, I wondered if my contact with Guidance was in fact a conversation with God too. The truth never changes; it is and always will be. Thank you, Neale.

I attended the Heartline program because I was serious about looking within. For me, Heartline was about realizing heart space: self-love, self-trust, and nonjudgmental acceptance. It was about allowing, understanding, and moving beyond feelings into the transcendental.

As humanity moves into knowing that we are indeed more than our physical bodies, so, too, do we need to understand that we are more than our emotional bodies, our personalities. To accomplish this, it is necessary to explore those areas within us that hold us back from self-trust and self-acceptance. The Heartline program teaches a willingness to let go of the energetic shields we hold to protect ourselves from (falsely perceived) threats.

Heartline is not about renouncing the rational self. Instead, it is an invitation to that part of oneself to open, allow, and welcome the heart, the feeling connection, to come into balance. In this way, humanity can move into a greater wholeness and expanded awareness of its true spiritual identity.

The Heartline affirmation is:

> I am in touch with the source of all life and I am open to receive all energy from this source. My purpose is to know and be love. My intent is to know the fullness of life, the joy of life, and the love that I am. I deeply desire to know, to be, to understand, to experience, and to express the love that I am and the absolute good that I bring forth. I ask that the light of the source surround me, enfold me, and embrace me. I ask that the love energy flow through me now. From this day forward, I am better able to be the love that I am and to know that I have no limitations. For I am this energy—I am love. And because I am love, I live each moment of this day in heartfelt gratitude and deep, abiding appreciation for All That Is.

In the Lab

When I was hired to work in the lab back in June 1988, it marked a significant shift in direction for research at The Monroe Institute. Never before had anyone been employed at the Institute to do quantitative inquiry into brainwave states engendered by Hemi-Sync. Unpaid volunteers running an extended version of the Explorer Program conducted the ongoing lab effort.

Explorer Program

The program involved the use of experienced Hemi-Sync users in the *exploration* of what Bob called locales—other dimensional realities. Bob had been experimenting with this concept for a number of years, and by the time I arrived on the scene, Dr. Rita Warren and her husband, Martin Warren, were running the lab and the Explorer Program.

Martin and Rita Warren

Rita, a brilliant, highly educated woman and retired university professor, applied her intellect and education to the task at hand with the expected precision. But there was something more. Rita's compassion for humanity and respect for every spirit-soul with whom she worked established a standard of excellence for work in the lab renowned to this day. Martin Warren, "the miracle man," referred to himself as a lifelong student of *The Course in Miracles*. To me, he was not the student but the teacher, the shining example, the model for living one's life by the principles of everyday miracles.

Bob Monroe was fond of saying that Hemi-Sync should provide "something of value." In vigorous pursuit of this concept, he developed a set of questions that Rita and Martin were to ask every explorer. The questions pertained to such things as how to solve the energy crisis (remember the gas lines of the 1970s), cures for chronic diseases, and the ultimate nature of reality.

But things at the Institute were changing fast. With the advent of the Guidelines program, Bob wanted to provide every participant the opportunity to experience a personalized session in the isolation booth in the lab. Bob asked Dr. Darlene Miller, a retired clinical psychologist who worked in the Programs Division at the Institute, to develop a format for these sessions.

Darlene and the Warrens had been close friends for a number of years, and a collaboration of these "experts in the field" was bound to yield a perfect solution. The Warrens brought to the table their years of experience with the explorers. And Darlene had her work with program participants, a career as psychologist, and an inner spirit wisdom evidenced in her soft-spoken ways to contribute. Her every carefully chosen word seems to be lovingly nurtured before it is allowed to grace the listener.

Skip with Darlene Miller

Over the years, the questions posed to the explorers (Bob's list) never yielded any consistent answers or reliable solutions. The explorers, however, found something of value for themselves in the Hemi-Sync booth sessions in the lab. In their explorations of consciousness, they found themselves—their true nature as spiritual beings. For those with a deeper interest, I recommend the book *Cosmic Journeys* by Rosalind A. McKnight, one of Bob's original colleague-explorers.

Darlene decided that the personalized sessions that Bob wanted to include in the Guidelines program should be intended to produce something of value for each participant by allowing them to explore their own personal resources. With Bob's approval of Darlene's plan, she and I got together and established a structure for doing individualized Hemi-Sync exercises.

Darlene labeled this the Personal Resources Exploration Program, or PREP.

PREP Sessions

Participants and graduates of the Guidelines program are eligible to participate in the PREP, a personalized session conducted in a specially designed, secluded cubical in the lab at the Institute or, more recently, at Roberts Mountain Retreat. Hemi-Sync frequencies and verbal guidance provided by a trained facilitator (monitor) support them throughout this unique experience.

Before PREP sessions, the participant and the monitor discuss the intent of the session and plan an agenda appropriate to the participant's goals. Sometimes people go into a session with goals and expectations. Sometimes these goals are achieved and expectations are fulfilled, but most of the time what is realized (as in, "made real") is something entirely different, of greater importance than can be imagined.

The use of physiological monitoring is especially beneficial to facilitation of PREP sessions. The monitor can tell when the participants are relaxed, when they "move" from experience to experience, and when to ask questions about the experience. Participants get a complete report of their physiological changes during their session at the end.

I am one of the monitors for PREP sessions at the Institute. Over the years, I have assisted hundreds of participants to shift their conscious perspective and explore a realm of knowledge seemingly available beyond the limitations of their physical senses. The affinity I have for this process comes from several sources.

My original training as a counterintelligence special agent introduced disciplined interviewing techniques. Later, I monitored thousands of remote-viewing sessions over the decade I spent in the Star Gate program. My own psychic experiences provided an empathetic understanding of the challenge posed when asked to objectify, describe, or report nonphysical experiences. But most importantly, above all else, is my profound respect—my gratitude for being chosen to enjoin these participants in the realization of spirit.

For the most part, participants come to a PREP session under the impression that the session is exclusively *for* them. After all, it is called the *Personal* Resource Exploration Program. For me, however, these sessions are unity experiences, times when the delusion of separateness from spirit fades and the silhouettes and shadows of darkness vanish in the light of knowingness—in the realization of *All That Is*.

Many times, these experiences are seemingly very personal for the individual. I say "seemingly" because, for the most part, the reported information may represent a truth for all humanity and is not all that personal or unique to that individual. To illustrate, Jim Szpajcher gave me permission to share a transcript of one of his booth sessions.

PREP Session Transcript
Before Exploration 27 Program
November 6, 1998
Time: 15:00 hours
Monitor: Skip Atwater
Subject: Jim Szpajcher
Elapsed Time: 76 minutes

(Resonant tuning)
(Pause)
Skip: Remember your resonant energy balloon and your affirmation, beginning, "I am more than my physical body," and move on gently to Focus 10, using the method you've learned.
(Pause)
Jim: I'm in Focus 10 now. The energy that I call "Blue" is here. I'm going to ask it what I need to learn today in Focus 10.
Skip: Very good.
(Pause)
Jim: I'm being shown a group of my, hmm, people from my I-There. There's a lot of them that I know already, sitting out amongst these trees, kind of in a woods or an orchard, or something. They're all just grinning and talking to each other, and I'm being shown that they are with me today. They're very laid-back. The message that I'm getting is that they are with me whenever I need them to be.

I've approached the three soldiers, military types, some of my past: the Airman, Jaques, the French soldier, and Hank, the Confederate soldier. I'm asking them, "What is there that I need to learn today?" and if they have anything for me.

[Note from Jim: In some of the hypnotic regression work I've done, I have "memories" of having lived from 1920 to 1942, being killed in World War II as a bombardier in the Royal Canadian Air Force. I also have "memories" of being a young French soldier who, at the age of sixteen, died in 1812, in the battle of Borodino before Moscow. And I have "memories" of having lived from about 1840 to about 1905, surviving the U.S. Civil War, then going west to ranch and farm in Oklahoma.]

The message that I'm getting is that I shouldn't take it too seriously, this business of military lifetimes, that war is an accelerated, speeded up style of experiencing life. And it's a way to cram a lot of experience into a short period of time. It's important to learn the lessons but not to get hung up on the emotions.

I'm thanking them and moving back with the rest of the group. They're waving at me as if to say "Hi," and I'm ready to go to Focus 12 now.

Skip: Very good. Using the method you've learned, expand once again to Focus 12.

(Pause)

Jim: I'm in 12 now, in a small darkened room that's like a small amphitheater, and I have before me three of my I-There group, the ones that I consider to be members of my Ex-Com [Executive Committee].

There are three individuals here. There's the one that I call Caesar, the one that I call Chin, and the one that I call Princess. The message that I'm getting is that what we are doing is important, in terms of my progress, and there's a lot of work left to do.

(Jim laughs.)

Jim: So, they're telling me to lighten up and not be so serious.

Skip: Lighten up; to get enlightened?

Jim: Um-Hmm. I get the impression that they are finished with me today, so I'm ready to move on to 15.

Skip: Very good. Open your heart, and from your heart expand into Focus 15. Affirming, and stating from your heart your willingness to learn, to know, to understand, to experience, and to love.

(Pause)

Jim: I'm in 15 now. The energy that I call "Blue" has changed into Rex, my "guide-dog," which is how I recognize him. We're walking along through a panorama of stars. Looking at, in the distance . . . basically the creation of galaxies, looking back into time.

[Note from Jim: Rex showed up initially as a blue energy during my Guidelines program when I asked to meet my ISH (Inner Self Helper). When I threw a rote at the energy to display itself to me in a way I would understand, a German shepherd dog ran up to me. When I tried to understand why my ISH was showing up as a pet dog, he appeared at my left knee with a seeing-eye dog harness and later gave his name as Rex.]

(Pause)

Jim: I'm watching a slow-motion movie of the development of the universe right now. I'm getting the impression that it's important to watch the galaxies as they are developing, and as time is moving on, the understanding that I'm getting is that everything is important. The job that I do, as small as it is in the whole scheme of things, is important, 'cause it all fits in somewhere. It's like I'm getting a message that there is a plan, and we all have our roles to play in it.

(Pause)

Jim: Rex has got up, and he's . . . looks like he's walking over to 21, so I guess I'll follow him along.

Skip: Very good. Once again, through the colors, into the free dom of the White.

(Pause)

Jim: I'm in 21 now, and Rex and I are moving over to a . . . it looks like a crystal city hanging in the void. There's a big building that looks like a cathedral. It's all transparent crystal. I'm walking into it and sitting down. There are rows of benches, or pews. It's very restful. I'll stop for a minute and absorb some of the energy.

Skip: Yes. Welcome and express your gratitude.

(Pause)

Jim: One of the members of my Ex-Com, the guide that I refer to as Chin, who looks like an ancient Chinese sage, has walked out and sat down beside me. Almost like an act of companionship. And the three of us, Rex, Chin, and myself, are looking around at the beautiful, prismatic colors that seem to light up within the walls of this crystal building; cathedral-like.

The message I'm getting from Chin is that the way to learn, and the way to acquire, is to go and experience things as often as I need to. To learn and understand them. To go out, and not be afraid of making mistakes but to repeat the lessons as often as I need to, to learn. And this should be done in a spirit of happiness. He smiles at me. Now he's walking away. Rex and I are just going to pop over to my cave in 21 and pick up some energy.

[Note from Jim: In my visits to Focus 21, I have found a little cave with a fire in the middle, which is like a small campfire. This represents a small part of all the light energy which is available to me, and I have often visualized absorbing light energy from the fire while moving through Focus 21.]

I'm ready to move on to the park in 27.

Skip: All right. We'll move, first passing through 23, for a brief stop in 25. Pass through 23 for a brief stop in 25.

Jim: Okey-dokey.

Skip: Here, in the belief-system realities of Focus 25, take a look around and see if there is anything for you here, before moving on.

(Pause)

Jim: The view that I have here in 25 is of thousands and thou sands of bubbles suspended in a light-green light, almost like bubbles in a light-green water. And I see myself moving amongst them. I'm checking out to see if any of them have any attraction to me, or me to them.

An arm has reached out to me and dragged me into a bubble. I'm in a Stone Age, caveman-style area with people dressed in skins. It looks like a group of people that, if they were North American Indians, I would call it the Happy Hunting Grounds, but this pre-dates them. This is very old. The fellow that drew me in is introducing me to several others of his friends and acquaintances there. They are welcoming me. The landscape is fairly rolling. It looks like early spring, because there are no leaves on the trees yet, but the grass is greening up nicely. These people look happy. The group that I'm with right now is all males. They are showing me to a small campfire, where some of them have been working on arrowheads and spearheads.

(Time elapsed to this point: 45 minutes)

It's like they know that they've passed on and they are trying to work hard to get ready for their next life, for their next go-around, by learning how to make tools. It's interesting. I never quite thought of that approach before, from that time period.

Skip: You might like to ask Guidance why it is that you've been brought to this world.

Jim: I've thrown the question out as to why I was attracted to here. And I feel a very strong resonance with one of the men. I have the impression that he and I are associated in the same I-There. He's greeting me like a very close friend. I feel that he's familiar, but he seems to respond to me a lot closer than I am to him. He's just giving me a great big bear hug.

I'm getting a time from him. It looks like he's in a time that's about ten or twelve thousand years ago. I'm trying to get a sense of where. All right, I get the impression of either north-central North America or north-central Europe, after the glaciers left. Both of them look as reasonable places. His skin is fair, so I'm getting the impression that it's north-central Europe. Hmmm. I'm being shown an area that would correspond to Romania, Hungary, somewhere in that area. He's inviting me to join him, but I'm telling him that I can't stay there, that I have to move on to other places.

[Note from Jim: I got the name "Grock" or "Groc" for him. Afterward, Skip pointed out that Robert Heinlein had used that word in *Stranger In A Strange Land* to mean knowledge or enlightenment, as in "I grok that."]

Skip: Does he understand the concept of other places?

Jim: He seems to, because he's saying that we will meet again. He's giving me a very clear impression that he feels he needs to be where he is, right now.

Skip: And so be it.

Jim: I'm thanking him, and acknowledging him with gratitude, for introducing himself to me. I tell him that I will remember him and perhaps seek him out again. He's smiling and waving at me. Rex and I are leaving, and we've just stepped out of that thought-bubble. That was a bit of a surprise, that one.

Skip: Hmm. Interesting concept of making tools for the next life. Some cultures bury their dead with food and tools for the journey, and here we find a culture who is preparing for the next life by making tools.

Jim: Yes, they seemed very much more sophisticated than I would have initially given them credit for. These people weren't dummies. But they had a very fixed belief system and they felt that what they were doing was the right way. And I give them all credit for their approach. Especially the one who seems to have been part of my link. I'm floating through the bubbles again here in 25. I've gone into one—hmmm. This looks like a medieval style of an existence. There's a bunch of knights standing around in armor, with horses. It looks like there's a town fair, a pageant of some sort. There are ladies here, damsels, all dressed up in their long-gowned finery. There's a festival on in this town.

(Pause)

Jim: Hmm. This knight that has greeted me, and there's a lady in a long, blue gown, a light blue gown. They tell me—he's welcoming me to his place, to their place, there. I have an impression that this is one of my personas as well. The lady that's on his arm seems to be his mate, of some sort. She's very friendly to me. I'm wondering if she isn't some persona of my wife's.

[Note from Jim: I got the names Michael and Anna, and when Anna greeted me, she held my hands in her hands, looked into my eyes, smiling, and said, "It's nice to see you again." She had a twinkle in her eyes, like she knew something that I had forgotten. I got a very strong echo of my wife when I looked in her eyes. I felt certain that she is a member of my wife's I-There.]

There's a castle on the edge of town. It's not very large. It looks like one of the older styles that was used as a secure hold, as opposed to a palace of some sort. The time period in this thought-bubble seems to be in the late fall, after the harvest has been brought in. They seem to be holding some sort of Thanksgiving-style, harvest-type festivities. These people seem to be aware that they've passed on. I'm looking for any semblance of a church, or anything. I see a stone, small country church with a spire on it, but it doesn't seem to play a major role in the existence of these people right now. It's like a big outdoor banquet. There's food on the tables, fruit, meat.

This fellow in armor is blond. I'm getting an impression of northern Europe, or northern England—not as far as Scotland, but somewhere in northern England or northern Europe, from a period about 700 to 800 years ago, 1200 or 1300 A.D.

I just asked if they wanted to go somewhere else, the man and the woman, and they laughed like it was one of the funniest things they had heard in a long time. They are where they want to be right now, so I'm thanking them for showing me their place. Rex and I are going to leave that thought-bubble.

(Pause)

Jim: There's a fellow who's showing up. I've seen this guy before.

[Note from Jim: I had a brief glimpse of him at the end of a tape during my Guidelines program. He showed up for about three seconds, striding purposely toward me, then Bob Monroe's voice had interrupted and called us to go back to C-1, and I lost the image. This time he showed up in Focus 25, outside a "thought-bubble," in the light green of the Focus level, as if he was trying to track me down before I got away.]

He looks like he's a tall, Viking-type person, with a cape of some animal skin. Marching toward me. He has a message for me. I'm trying to listen to see what it is. He's telling me that He is Me, that he is part of me.

[Note from Jim: At this point, this man had grabbed me by the shoulders with both hands, and was forcefully looking into my eyes, saying, "I am you. I am you. *I am you!*"]

He's big. He appears to me to be over six feet tall and looks to be in his early twenties, very strong-looking, very vigorous, very fit, very capable. And he's telling me that it's important that I not forget that he is me.

I've got my hands on his shoulders, acknowledging him as me, as part of me.

I'm asking for a name, but the name I'm getting is "Wolf," and I don't know if it relates to the animal, or if that's his name, or if that's his persona, but it seems to fit, all of that, somehow.

I'm asking him if he wants to take me to where he is from, in that area, or if he wants to come with me. He's taking me with him, to a village.

[Note from Jim: At this point, we had entered his thought-bubble.]

Hmm. The buildings seem to be made out of, basically, wood frames, covered in animal skins, like tents of some sort. Not like the American teepee but as rounded huts, not quite as big as the yurts that the Mongols had, but skin-covered, huts. There are maybe twenty of these in his village. There are children and women, other men. This is his place, he's telling me. He's a member here.

He tells me I should come back and visit. Hmm. I'm getting the impression that he has done something almost like vision quests, and has seen me, and come looking for me. He has been chasing after me for some time. I'm thanking him, acknowledging him and giving him gratitude. I'm telling him that I'm thankful to have met him and that I will remember him, that we will visit again. Rex and I are leaving that thought-bubble.

I'm going to move onto Focus 27 now.

Skip: Yes, very good.

(Pause)

Jim: I'm in 27, at the park. There's a man in a toga. An older man, balding. There are several others with him, but he's coming toward me. He's welcoming me to the park. Hmm. And he's also telling me that this week coming up he'll have a chance to show me around Focus 27, and that he's looking forward to this week coming up.

There's a group of people from my I-There surrounding him, and they are all grinning and smiling. My Roman guy—I'm getting the name "Claudius," I don't know if that's his real name but it's the first name that popped into my mind when I thought of how to address him. They are all grinning and laughing. They're saying, "Welcome to Focus 27."

[Note from Jim: At this point, I protested to them that I had been to Focus 27 before.]

"You just think that you've been here before." They're laughing. The understanding that I'm getting is that this coming week will introduce me to Focus 27 Proper. That's quite a reception. I wasn't planning on that one.

[Note from Jim: I was booked for Exploration 27 November 7th to 13th, which was starting the next day.]

Skip: Did you smile back and say "Thank you"?

Jim: Absolutely. Yes, indeed. Thanks, guys. They're waving at me now. They're heading off back into some other buildings. They are telling me that I'll see them again. So, I think I'll start my way back down now.

Skip: Yes, very good. Moving back down through 25.

Jim: I'm in 25. I'll head for 21.

Skip: Move slowly, making sure of your touchstones quite well. Moving from 25 down to 21, passing through 23.

Jim: I'm in my cave in 21, by the fire. Rex is grinning at me, as much as a German shepherd can. I'm absorbing some energy. I'm ready to work my way back down again from there.

Skip: All right. Just hold on here, and we'll move slowly once again. We'll move back to the point where we began. Follow the sounds, slowly, easily, back to the point where we began. Back to level 10, back to Focus 10.

(Pause)

Jim: I'm in Focus 10. My Blue energy is back in front of my eyes.

Skip: Very good. Anchor on the Blue energy. Anchor in Focus 10. Now, counting back. Counting back to Focus 1: nine, eight, seven, six, five, four, three, two, and one. Open your eyes. Can you see the light in the room there?

Jim: (Deep breath) Yes.

Skip: All right. Very good. Move your arms, move your legs, wiggle your toes. Everything still connected down there?

Jim: So far.

Skip: (With humor in voice) Good. That's a real good sign.

Jim: Umm-Hmm.

Skip: Now if you'll just relax for just a minute, I'll be right in to get those electrodes off your fingers. Just relax, and I'll be right there.

Jim: Excellent.

Personal Explorations through the Flavor Straw

When I first met Bob Monroe, I was in search of training techniques for the army's remote-viewing unit, and I had seemingly thousands of questions I wanted to ask Bob about Hemi-Sync. But as we had lunch on that springtime afternoon so long ago, I was also curious about the boundless white space I had visited during my "Flavor Straw" experience. When I asked Bob about this, he told me that the only way for me to know was to find out for myself (a comment he provided to many). In other words, I needed to explore this area on my own and not depend on what others may have to say about it.

It seemed to me that PREP sessions in the isolation booth would be ideal for explorations "through the Flavor Straw." While I have been the monitor for *others* (the purpose of my italicized emphasis here will become apparent later) hundreds of times since I became research director at the Institute, dozens of times I have been the explorer in the booth—expanding my conscious awareness into the knowingness of *All That Is*.

During these growth periods in my life, Teena Anderson, my colleague in the lab, was also my counselor and confidant. A motto at the Institute is, "I am more than my physical body." Teena, however, professes strongly that she is *not* her physical body. This spirit-centered being monitored my PREP sessions.

In preparation for one of these sessions, Teena and I talked about the fact that for some time I had been having mental visions, dreams, or experiences that I recognized as recurring mental visions, or trips, from my childhood. I was wondering why these episodes were once again drifting into my consciousness. I had also been having stomach problems ever since I retired from the army, and I was seeking some insight into possible metaphysical causes of these symptoms. I set learning about these topics as my goal for a PREP session on April 11, 1989.[22]

---

[22] An audio recording and transcript are available on the CD-ROM accompanying this book.

My questions about recurring visions from my youth seemed to be answered with an explanation of a "calendar of time" and the fact that these events aren't always coexistent from a temporal perspective. Apparently, events of our perceived past are not fixed and can be altered by present activities and the future present as well. My awareness of this happening was experienced as recurring visions of what I perceive as the temporal past but in reality are as yet uncompleted events. All that exists is the present. What we call the past is information (as in, in-formation, not solid). What we call the future forms by the laws of probability, intent-consciousness, and present activities (which, of course, becomes part of the past *in-formation* a moment from now).

Teena Anderson

During the session, I was reminded (put into my right-mind) that the question of purpose doesn't make sense. I also realized that, rather than using "who, what, why, when, or how," I should simply say in my mind "explain," to solicit the answers to questions I (or an aspect of myself) may have. Apparently, the use of the interrogatives limits the response by confining the answer provided to the boundaries of a belief that we are somehow separate from this knowledge. "Explain," on the other hand, simply means to make obvious what is already known and imposes no belief limitations.

When I sought answers concerning my colitis, I uncovered an aspective expression of myself that appeared to me as a black bird. Guidance offered this black bird and its nest-tending concerns as a metaphor. The black bird was concerned about losing its identity as a nest tender and principal family caregiver when its offspring outgrew the confines of the nest and their dependency. The nest-tender personality or aspect was, in a sense, facing death—and wasn't facing this transition comfortably.

I was unable to resolve the issues surrounding Nest Tender during this session because my bladder filled up to the point of physical discomfort and I couldn't continue with the session. This theme, however, continued for several years in many sessions.

Just two weeks later, I had the opportunity to do another PREP session. Before the session, Teena and I discussed the nest-tender aspect from my previous session. During the session, something wonderful happened. I discovered another aspect of myself that I have come to know as "the Flower." An unusual energy pattern also made itself known. It flooded my consciousness and spoke with a voice of its own while I remained in the background, mindful of all that was happening.[23]

The nest-tender metaphor appeared as a mouse, and the suggestion was that Nest Tender was sleeping. I was told that offspring activity (children) and spousal influences contribute to upsetting Nest Tender. But my attention was quickly drawn away from this line of inquiry.

I began to focus on realizing (making real) an alternate aspect or personality within me, the Flower. In the days previous to this session, I had been discussing the idea of totem symbolism as a viable expression of life's patterns. During the session, this notion emerged and I began my search for an alternate aspective expression or animal totem that was appropriate.

My analytical approach was abruptly set aside and I found myself releasing the issue to Guidance, a la Florence Scovel Shinn.[24] It was then that I discovered the Flower. Part of this wonderful discovery included experiencing a new form of communication. My

---

[23] An audio recording and transcript are available on the CD-ROM accompanying this book.

[24] Widely known in the first half of the twentieth century as an artist and illustrator, metaphysician, and lecturer, Florence Scovel Shinn helped thousands through her great work of healing. She once advocated an affirmation that went something like this: "I turn this problem over to the Christ within, and I go free." Florence explained that turning issues over to this Guidance within was actually gifting in much the same way that a child, taking troublesome problems to a parent, does not burden the parent by asking for help. Rather, the parent is grateful for the opportunity to assist the child and sees the opportunity as a gift from the child.

thoughts and words separated, and I began to hear myself speaking in a rather unusual voice. I was fully aware of what was happening. The experience did not frighten me.

During prior sessions, I had been noticing various kinesthetic sensations, tickling, and pressure in various places, especially in my nose. The rhetoric that I heard during programs at the Institute involved the concept of *controlling* these kinds of vibrations or feelings. Before this booth session, Teena and I had decided that control could be identified with ego and that perhaps expressing willingness to experience these sensations might be more appropriate.

We had talked about ego being afraid of the unknown—of whatever it could not control. So, when I began to have these kinesthetic sensations during the session, I silently welcomed the feelings and the experience. I invited the tickling and the vibrations and expressed my genuine gratitude for the event. In retrospect, I think these expressions of acceptance are what led to the experience of the unusual *energy voice* from within.

The essence of being a flower appealed to me. This aspective expression was not based on relationships with others either by judgment or expectation. The flower reaches for the light and in so doing demonstrates to all the elegance of its beauty. The flower centers its consciousness not on its stem and roots but on the blossom, on the radiation of its beauty and in sharing that beauty with all that come to it. So, in effect, even when the plant dies, its beauty, its consciousness, lives on in the joy that it has shared.

I was reminded too that, beyond expressing the flower essence within me, I could seek out the *flowerness* in all around me. The session ended with a bit of knowing beyond all of this, which may have been a hint of things to come. Guidance seemed to be affirming the appropriateness of me focusing on becoming the flower while at the same time reminding me that there is a greater expression that one might call the garden. This hint came at the end of the session and at the time I didn't fully appreciate its value.

I now think Guidance was reminding me that to perceive one's self as a sole flower reinforces the illusion of separateness. Awareness of one's identity as the whole garden realizes (makes real) our true nature. Does that make God the gardener? Or is there no separateness there either?

This whole session was capped by a very interesting experience. Without disclosing the contents of my session, I had made an audiocassette copy of the narrative and sent the tape to Fay, my fiancée, in North Carolina. Unknown to me, this beautiful woman had sent the following little story to me on the same day. Our correspondence crossed in the mail. Here's the story she sent:

> Suppose you'd known for a long time that you were a weed. When you were just a little sprout, before anyone had told you that you were a weed, you'd known something of what flowers feel like. And as you grew, you felt you'd like it better if you were a flower. But you learned to be satisfied living as a weed nonetheless—most of the time. You learned to bend a little so as not to take up too much sun, and to eat and drink and breathe not quite so much so as not to take too much nourishment from the flowers around you. It's only in spring, when the flowers start to bloom, that it's hard to be weed-like. Then, when the warm breeze comes, you feel a stirring, a hope, a wish for just a taste of blooming, but you can't of course because you're a weed.
>
> Now suppose that one day a lovely creature walks into your field looking for flowers. And suppose she walks straight up to you and says, "What a strange and lovely flower this is hidden from the light!" For a moment you would not believe her. But oh, you would want to. So you might begin softly to look and feel around yourself. And what if you discovered that this had all been a silly mistake—that you were not a weed, but a flower after all.
>
> Well, that's what it feels like. A little sad that I spent so much time as a weed when I didn't have to. A little in shock. A little exposed. Excited, in a quiet way, to discover what I'm all about. I don't know much about being a flower, yet. But it's me, and I love it, and I'm giving it all I've got.
>
> Author Unknown

The story was accompanied by a drawing of a flower looking at a reflection of itself as a weed, not realizing its true nature because of the image of itself that it saw.

After we received our respective mailings, Fay and I were astonished by the serendipity. It brought us closer together (as if we were ever really separate in the first place).

I thought long and hard about this session and the circumstances surrounding it. Even today, Fay and I speak fondly of the memories it has left with us. A month later, I did another PREP session that turned out to be a major breakthrough.

Teena and I had discussed my intent for this next session, as we had done for the previous work. I wanted to ask Guidance about Fay, to explain this new and wondrous relationship to me.

I met Fay when she came to the Institute on a Saturday morning for a prearranged tour of the facilities. The minute I saw her, I thought I recognized her. As the tour progressed, we wound up in the lab. Fay and I were standing in the doorway of the isolation booth while I explained the soundproofing, the floatation bed, and the physiological monitoring. I gradually became aware of the rest of the world fading away. Within just a few seconds, Fay and I were seemingly alone.

Although my mouth kept spewing out the construction details and technical attributes of the booth, I was alert to the fact that things were not at all as they seemed. As Dorothy said in *The Wizard of Oz*, "I have a feeling we're not in Kansas anymore." This strange place we fell into seemed to extend beyond all space and time. It was truly the proverbial forever. Just as gently as it had come over us, it was gone. We looked at each other and, without speaking, joined the others on the Institute tour.

The next significant activity was lunch. We ordered takeout and got some croissant sandwiches with dill-flavored potato salad from the Blue Ridge Pig, a local rustic café in Nellysford. Several Institute staff members and those taking the tour sat around the lunch table, socializing and getting to know one another. Fay started talking about moving out to Seattle to work for Lou Tice and his Investment in Excellence program. It seemed that this move was inevitable.

I couldn't take my eyes off her. She was so beautiful. I longed for the taste of her lips on mine. Unexpectedly, I heard myself thinking, "Why are you leaving me now that I have found you, after so long?" Fay looked at me and blushed with embarrassment, then looked away. She must have heard my thoughts.

After lunch, I asked my fellow staff members at the Institute if I had said anything unusual at lunch. They reported that I had not. Fortunately, Fay canceled her plans to move to Seattle, and our relationship quickly blossomed. But I still wanted to ask Guidance about Fay. Who was she? What was the overpowering attraction? It was something greater, deeper, and more profound than sex. What could it be?

I also wanted to understand more about this unusual energy voice that spoke the truth from somewhere inside my heart. The energy-voice experience had touched me deeply. It was intensely personal. I felt as though I was exposing myself, the true me without any social masks behind which I could safely hide. Teena and I talked about using affirmations of willingness to encourage more contact with the energy voice.

My trust in Teena, my monitor, was vital. And my bride-to-be, Fay, with whom I shared these adventures, was perhaps finding out more about me than she had imagined.[25]

In answer to my questions about Fay, I found myself in what appeared to be a bedroom scene. At the time, I thought this was too silly and too filled with sexual innuendo to be real. But then I was shown a heart-shaped pillow and told that this symbolized Fay as the epitome of the expression "a heart of gold." (Later, during a visit to Fay's house in North Carolina, I was intrigued to find out that she indeed had a heart-shaped pillow with white lace on her bed.)

I consider this session a breakthrough because of the intensity of the experience with the energy voice. The experience was very physical. I experienced the unconditional love of my total self. I found out more about the flower aspect, the garden, and tending the garden. And I discovered that asking to understand is a rather narrow concept.

---

[25] An audio recording and transcript are available on the CD-ROM accompanying this book.

Guidance told me not to limit myself (by asking to understand) but to express my willingness to experience love—in so doing I will come to know *All That Is*. What is valuable is experience, and Fay with her heart of gold was to be just such an experience.

As the months passed, I continued my explorations of reality through personal experience. In the summer of 1989, a close friend of Fay's shared her worries about her son Adrian. She told Fay that his dream was to be a military officer after he graduated from college, but that he kept reinjuring his hand or arm, resulting in numerous doctors' appointments and physical therapy sessions. Adrian's parents worried that when he took the physical exam for military officers he would be rejected. Fay had been telling her friend about my work at The Monroe Institute, and Adrian's mother wondered if I could do anything to help him.

Fay asked me if, while I was guiding someone through experiences in the isolation booth at the lab, I could ask about Adrian. But most of the folks that I worked with in the lab were having personal growth experiences and were unaccustomed to responding to questions about others. Occasionally, I did monitor and question adept explorers on a wide range of topics, but I was reluctant to bring a personal agenda into my workplace. I felt that I would be misusing my position at the Institute, not to mention that people were paying for lab sessions for their own benefit. Without telling Fay of my concerns, I suggested that it would be helpful to have a picture of Adrian and that I needed to be assured that I had his parents' permission to look into his condition. A picture was provided and permission was granted.

I set *the problem* aside for several weeks. Now and then, Fay wanted to know if I had asked anyone about Adrian. I told her that I hadn't but, for some reason, I couldn't bring myself to tell her I was uncomfortable asking anyone about Adrian, given my position and responsibilities. I tried to evade her inquiries by implying that there hadn't been anyone with sufficient talent in the lab recently or that, after all, there probably wasn't anything anyone could do. On my birthday, August thirtieth, in 1989, she asked again, and I listened to myself tell her that I felt I should probably do the session myself.

I was startled to hear myself say this. Throughout my life, I have always been very PSI-experiential and encouraged the same in others, but the idea of doing a remote medicinal investigation seemed somehow beyond my expertise. I had no medical training, and my extensive extracorporeal experiences had always focused on personal issues. With soft-spoken authority, something inside me whispered an assurance: This was something I was to do. On August 31, 1989, I met with Teena and prepared myself for a session in the isolation booth in the lab at the Institute.

As I held Adrian's picture, Teena and I talked about how I might focus my intent on investigating the issues surrounding Adrian's injuries and perhaps how I might be of some help. We decided that I should use the affirmation of willingness to become one with Adrian, so that by becoming one with him I would then know him and the issues surrounding his injuries. In practical terms, this meant that as I moved into an altered state of consciousness I would hold foremost in my mind the assertion that I was eager to become one with Adrian.

I settled into the warm waterbed in the isolation booth, and Teena hooked up my fingers to the physiological monitoring devices. When the lights in the booth were turned off and the soothing Hemi-Sync sounds began, I drifted away.[26]

Later I called Fay and described the session to her. I was concerned about giving the audiocassette recording of the session to Fay's friend, not knowing if the information would be useful. Also, I had never revealed my personal PSI activities to this friend. As it turned out, I didn't need to worry. When Fay told Adrian's mother that I had described him washing a black car, she said that Adrian had a black car, a graduation gift, which he washed frequently and meticulously. And Adrian's mother immediately recognized the vintage 1950s kitchen that I had described as the grandmother's kitchen.

Cautiously, Fay told her that Adrian had been influenced by a maternal authority figure and was perpetuating his injury as a way

[26] An audio recording and transcript are available on the CD-ROM accompanying this book.

of protecting himself from ridicule in case he was unable to live up to the expectations of others.

Adrian's mother realized exactly what had been happening. Adrian had been away at college in the same city as his grandmother and was expected to make regular visits, during which he was subjected to taunting sarcasm about where he was headed in life. Throughout Adrian's childhood, his grandmother had constantly modeled an aristocratic aloofness, never letting anyone in the family forget that they would never achieve an equivalent status in life.

Without telling Adrian about my session, his parents told him that he shouldn't feel obligated to visit his grandmother's house anymore. They also told him that they wanted him to be happy in life and choose for himself whatever he wanted to do. Regardless of all the family planning about joining the military, they didn't want him to feel pressured (and keep injuring himself) if he really didn't want to be an officer. Adrian told his parents that he really did want to be an officer and that he had made up his mind to join the military. Adrian's mother thanked Fay for the information.

When Fay and I married on April 14, 1990, Adrian came to the wedding and I met him in the flesh for the first time. Fay and I have continued as family friends with Adrian's parents over the years. We have never spoken about this episode of our relationship.

Today Adrian has completed his military service, having been a very successful and respected military officer. He has a wife and children and is entering an ambitious civilian career. He has outgrown his need to follow the expectations of others, and his proud parents applaud his every achievement.

Even though I don't think Adrian's parents ever told him about my session, perhaps someday Adrian and I will see each other again and talk about our unusual liaison so many years ago.

More than a year later I did still another session in the booth that exemplified a typical booth session, like others had experienced, filled with knowledge and revelation. By this time, I had encountered the energy voice many times and was close to becoming one with the source, the voice itself.

Before the session, Teena and I talked about my intent and my goal for the session. Having done so many PREP sessions, I had learned that, rather than detailing some ego-based narrow goal, it was best to go into a session with the intent of being open to experience whatever was most beneficial. That's what I did. During the session, the energy voice intervened only slightly. It was as though I was becoming more attuned to its knowledge and my regular voice spoke the truth.[27]

My favorite part of this session was experiencing the freedom of not clinging. I had a fear of letting go of things around me, a fear of loss of all that I thought I had worked for throughout my life. Metaphorically, if one wants to reach out and grab more, one is forced by circumstance to loosen one's grip on whatever one already has.

Confronted with this seeming dilemma, I turned to Guidance. Seen through the eyes of Guidance, there is no dilemma: ". . . one always has everything and there is no more or less and so there is no reason to fear loss of what cannot be lost." Metaphorically again, the only thing one loses when releasing one's grip to receive more is the burden, the perceived millstone of personal possession.

When I reflected on the deeper significance of all this as it pertains to my exploration of reality through personal experience, I was reminded (was put back into my right-mind) that affirming willingness to receive is inappropriate because we already have; willingness to learn is inappropriate because we already know; willingness to be is inappropriate because we already are. What it all comes down to is the spiritual I Am.

Another PREP session served to remind me (so I wouldn't be out of my mind, so to speak) of the limitations of our physical-world perceptions, which I call the "Other" session.

The energy voice had been coming through during my PREP sessions with some regularity, and I cherished this experience, feeling that it was deeply personal. In a very private talk with Teena, I spoke softly with her about the personal nature of this

---

[27] An audio recording and transcript are available on the CD-ROM accompanying this book.

experience for me and of how strange I thought it was that people who had similar experiences shared such an intensely personal event in public.

I clutched my hand to my chest and tears welled up in my eyes as I spoke of how personal, how spiritually moving this energy voice experience was for me. Wisely, Teena suggested that the next time I did a PREP session, I ask Guidance (meaning the energy voice) about my feelings and the concept surrounding people sharing this experience in public.

During my next PREP session, I set this subject before Guidance by placing the intent foremost in my thinking. As I moved into Focus 12, I reviewed the deep appreciation I had for the energy voice and how very personal this experience was for me.

I then requested that Guidance explain how it was that some people having similar experiences could do so in a public forum and allow others, people in the audience, to communicate with the energy voice. I added a sidebar to this request by expressing up front that I felt such a notion for me seemed ludicrous, even blasphemous.

I waited several minutes for an explanation but got nothing. I wondered if I had made myself clear, if I had structured my intent properly. Teena suggested that I ask again. I repeated my request to Guidance. "Explain how people having energy-voice experiences can do so in a public forum and allow other people to communicate with the energy voice, given the extreme personal nature of the experience."

Again I waited several minutes, but the only reply I got was, "We don't *understand*." Since I had learned in earlier PREP sessions that the word "understand" is not generally within the vocabulary of Guidance—conceptually, Guidance cannot not understand—I knew that this reply meant that my query was unintelligible. Teena suggested that I ask even again, and so once more I repeated my request.

"Explain how people having energy-voice experiences can do so in a public forum and allow others in attendance to communicate with the energy voice, given the extreme personal nature of the experience. Explain how they share with other people this deeply spiritual reverie."

Guidance replied, "What is an *other?*"

Well, that did it. I was dumbfounded, amazed by my own limiting viewpoint and my naiveté. Accompanying these four words was a huge message. From the perspective of Guidance—the level of reality through which Guidance operates—there is no concept of *other*. At this level, all is one.

So, from a practical standpoint, when an audience member asks a question, the energy voice doesn't perceive such a question as coming from a separate individual, as there is no such thing as separateness. My realization (what was made real) was that my concerns about sharing my experience in public were based on my limited viewpoint in seeing myself as separate from (nonexistent) others.

In one sense I am an individual, but I as an individual can never be separate from the family of man. In the same manner, by definition nothing can be separate from creation. If it exists, it's God's work. All is one.

Throughout the following year, I did a number of additional PREP sessions in the lab at the Institute. The energy voice showed up only occasionally to clarify my interpretations of experiences I was having. I seemed to be integrating the knowledge of the energy voice. I was realizing (becoming aware of the realness) my true spiritual identity.

These and other PREP sessions have helped me find answers to many questions. Sometimes our human earthly orientation limits our perceptions, but these sessions allowed me to explore a greater spiritual reality beyond the confines of my physical body. By September of 1991, I began having wonderful PREP sessions filled with the usual wisdom but without the semblance of my friend, the energy voice.[28] But in more recent years, my PREP-session exploration of reality has taken on different dimensions.

My sister Sue died in June 1996, and even though her passing was the expected result of a long-term illness, it impacted me more than the deaths of my parents. On some level, we expect our parents to die. When siblings die, it's different.

---

[28] An audio recording and transcript of a typical session without the energy voice are available on the CD-ROM accompanying this book.

I had come to know through out-of-body experience and spiritual insight that what we call death is but a transition from one realm to another. I see birth and death as doorways through which we, as spiritual beings, pass from experience to experience. So I see death not as a tragedy but as a welcome release from the confines of the physical body.

Nonetheless, a few days after my sister's death, I sensed a whisper of soft-spoken authority from within. It was a call to action, understated but of profound, compelling strength. I was told to use the skills that I had mastered in the Lifeline program at the Institute to help my sister.

Teena no longer worked at the Institute, and it had been a long time since I had done a PREP session in the booth. But there was no doubt about what I was being called to do. I asked Mark Cento, the Hemi-Sync audio engineer and my colleague, to act as monitor on this PREP session.

The impact of this session was so meaningful that it justifies including the full transcript here.[29]

PREP Session Transcript
Recorded June 1996
(Note that italic print within the quoted text indicates energy voice communication)

Skip: [I see] a tall, seven-year-old, blond girl with curly hair sit ting on a long wooden bench with, um, dark-wood finish. [It] reminds me of a bench that might be outside of like a courtroom or something, you know. Like a long park-bench type but solid wood with sides that come up and [a] well-sanded and finished. And there's a . . . I presume it's my child sister, uh, on the bench there. [The image is] nice, full, rich in color.

[Note from Skip: Even before the formal beginning of the session, I seemed to be getting information about my sister.]

Mark: Do you feel like staying with this image a bit, or would you like to move to Resonant Tuning?

[29] An audio recording is available on the CD-ROM accompanying this book.

Skip: I'll just kind of watch this and let you go ahead and continue your cross fade and [I'm] going to just melt into this a little bit.

Mark: Okay.

Skip: [It's] just kind of an indication to me that there's something waiting for me, so . . . I'll just proceed slowly. [I've changed from] feeling like I was sunk down way deep in the waterbed to being more like floating on top of the waterbed now.

Mark: Would you like to begin your Resonant Tuning at this point?

Skip: Sure, that's great.

(Resonant Tuning and the subsequent pause were not recorded.)

[Note from Skip: I phased out-of-body and found myself traveling somewhere.]

Skip: Got here through an image of a reddish-brown pyramid. And I flew around it to an archway door [and] sailed through the archway door into a tunnel matrix which led to outside. And I'm in this outside area which first is a, a, a park. And I can hear children playing and [I can] see flowers and, uh, swings and kids and things.

[Note from Skip: I phased back to my body in the booth, feeling a need to report my adventure.]

And then I was going somewhere down country roads and bushes in an outside area. And then I thought I'd better stop and describe this. So let me continue with that. Kinesthetically, this feels more like [Focus] 15 than [Focus] 10. But let me, let me let go for a minute and I'll be back.

(Pause)

[Note from Skip: I easily moved back to my sister and began to describe my perceptions.]

[I see a] golden, curly-haired, seven-year-old child on a mahogany bench. And it has . . . this mahogany bench is ornate and has side panels on it that are decorative and shiny mahogany. That is a continuing perception, as though she's just sitting in the background. This other place that I have gone to . . . I was confused as to whether I was going to that place [again] but that seems to be separate, like a sidebar, like that's still there waiting. [I'm going now to] this other place. I went from the recreational grassy area in the park with the swings and the playful kids and the flowers.

My sister Suzan

Now . . . and [now] I'm approaching what seems to be a classroom kind of a thing with antiquey [sic] wrought-ironish [sic] school desk-type things but it's in an outside area, like an outside camp, like you go to camp in the summer. So it's like this outside classroom. Let me check it out [and see] what's going to go on here.
(Pause)
[There's a lot] going on at once here. [I'm] having a little bit of difficulty getting any continuity here. School-type seats. Wrought-iron, ornate backs; ornate, shiny, black, wrought-iron backs to the seats but with those kind of desk things in front of you like you have in a school where the lid hinges up. I . . . it's really a weak visual. I keep shifting between being behind them, being over them, and sitting in them too. I don't know if they're empty or not.
[While all this is happening I'm also perceiving that] there's something going on about fish and then there's an American Indian bracelet with feathers on the bracelet. [They're]not . . . it's decorated with feathers but the feathers are silver, you know, like they make Indian jewelry with silver stuff. But they're . . . the little decorations are, are decorations of feathers but they're made of silver. And there's something also with fish.

Mark: Keeping in mind the images that have been presented to you, would you like to move forward to perhaps ask Guidance what this is for?

Skip: Yeah, that's a good, good idea. Let me ask [Guidance] what in the hell I'm doing here anyway.

(Pause)

[Guidance provided an answer to my question.]
I think I'm supposed to show the little girl [that I saw] sitting on the bench this place. And I'm supposed to bring

her to this place. That this is where she's supposed to go and she's sitting on the bench back wherever and I'm supposed to bring her to this place because she's supposed to be [or] come here to this kind of campground classroom.

Mark: Take a moment to go ahead and do that, and I'll wait for you.

Skip: Okay. I'm getting a lot of kinesthetics too. Um, like lots of rolling, spiraling, rolling around, and lots of body kinesthetic stuff here. [It's] a real roller-coaster ride here. Let me go find the little girl again [and I'll] sit down and talk to her and see if she wants to go to this other place. I think I had better move up in focus level here.

Mark: Okay. Just simply be guided to where you need to be going.

Skip: Cool.

(Pause)

I feel pressure, like swimming under water pressure. [Like] when you can feel the pressure around you. There; now that's being relieved. Um . . . um . . . that's better. [I'm having] muscle twitching and jerking. [It's a] familiar energy to me. Again, [I] don't feel like I'm in the waterbed. [I] feel like I'm laying on a flat piece of plywood. [There's] lots of jerking happening. [I] feel like a real jerk, as they say. [There's] something shaking me up. (Sigh)

Mark: As you relax into the feeling, focus once again on the young girl. (Mumble)

[Note from Skip: I phased out-of-body and the energy voice of the past immediately began to speak.]

Skip: I have . . . *She's on the bench over there. She's morphing into different aspects. She's not only the little girl. She's more a, than . . . than . . . than . . . than.* (Gasp) Where did she go? Okay, she's . . . Let me see if she wants to go to the other place. Um, I'm back now.

[Note from Skip: Just as quickly, I was back in the booth, reporting.]

Um, she seems to be a little bit afraid of me when I approach her, and she becomes different things. Like she is trying to hide or something behind these different things.Let me . . . I'm going to go over to her again, sit [down], and presume that it is my child sister and call her by her name and see what happens.

(Pause)

[Note from Skip: Once again, I found myself out-of-body with my sister and the energy voice began to speak intermittently. My sister agreed to go with me. Together, we flew into the pyramid, through the tunnel, out into the park, and over to the class area.]

Now a, a spiritual being not a girl or an animal, but a spiritual being and, and, and we will now go to, to . . . to . . . .

(Long pause)

We're, we're now . . . we're now. She's sitting in, she's sitting in the *chair in front of . . . I'm standing behind her in the class now. She's there in the cla . . . cla . . . classroom, no room, class outside class. She's in the chair . . . chair. She's . . .* she's in the chair. (Swallow) She's, she's in the chair in that class place now. And I don't know what else is going on here. Let me see if I'm supposed to do something else now. (Sigh)

[Note from Skip: I phased back to my body in the booth and became aware of the physical world.]

Oh, I'm back in the booth now, okay. I've got a bladder now. Okay. Oh, I hear the [Hemi-Sync] tones now, okay. Ugh. Okay, let me relax again and see, see what the situation is here.

(Pause)

[Note from Skip: I asked Guidance if there was something else that I should know or do and was given a a visual metaphor.]

Um. I'm watching [in my mind] somebody with a . . . I don't know what you call it. It's one of those . . . The vision I have is a folded paper. When you're a kid, you fold up paper in . . . to make this foursquare kind of a mouth thing. And you open and close it two different ways and then you're supposed to ask a question and thenit tells you your fortune or something. And you open and unfold the answer or something. I don't know what that's all about. I guess I'll ask.

(Short pause)

Some bizarre answer like . . . I just heard myself say a bizarre answer. The message back from Guidance is that this little thing is a symbolic [sic] of . . . The answers that you find depend on the choices that you make. And then I heard myself say [that] this is a bizarre answer and Guidance kind of laughed at me and says [sic], "That's what I'm trying to tell you."

[Note from Skip: I think Guidance was saying that it was for to me to decide if there was more for me in this experience with my sister.]

So this little thing about . . . you manipulate this thing with your fingers and then you open it up [means that] the answers you get depend on the choices you make.

Okay, I'm going to go and find that pyramid and go check on my sister again.

[Note from Skip: I easily phased out-of-body and flew back through the pyramid to the class area and my sister. I could feel the *energy* of the energy voice with me but the strange-sounding voice only leaked in a couple of times.]

There it is. It's got a flag on top of it now. [I'm going] around through the side, down through the tunnel, out to the playground, down the road, the classroom. *I get the impression.* I'm right on the edge here. I'm going to try and stay on this side of the edge.

I get the impression that she's okay in this place. She's not expressed as a child-self here. She's more of a total being here now. And by total being I mean she appears like an adult being now instead of a child being. And I keep saying [in my mind], "Well what's this class about."

And the answer is, "This isn't for you."

And [I'm] trying to say, "Well, what's the matter, can't I find out too?" And it's like, it's not that it's a secret, it's just not; it's just not for me. It's not like . . . to say I don't need the information that she's dealing with. That would be one way of saying it. But it's like [if] I walked into some college campus and walked into a, a class on nuclear physics I would know right away, well this isn't for me.

I think I'll go down the hall and find out something more interesting. It's like I'm just not *aligned with whatever she's trying to process in this class act* . . . Whoop.

Uh, uh . . . It's really hard to stay on this side. It's . . . she's, she's . . . It's not for me. There's no other explanation. Let me ask [Guidance] if there's anything else I need to do right now for her.

(Pause)

The message is to remember this place, this classroom

place [to which] I brought her. Remember this place. So let me look around. Okay.

Mark: Are you feeling the need to move beyond . . . ? (Mumble)

Skip: No. I'm feeling the need to come back because my bladder is filling up.

Mark: Okay.

Skip: So . . . I think I can get back to this place here. I know how to get down through the pyramid and, and through the portal and down the tunnel into the outside and then down the road to the right, over the stream to where the classroom area is. I can get back here again. I know wherethis is. If that's what they meant by remember. The bed is getting soft again.

Mark: If you'll count with me and come on back now.

Skip: Okay.

Mark: I'm simply going to fade out the [Hemi-Sync] tones.

Skip: Cool.

I felt good about this rescue mission. It gave me a sense of well-being and peace. I had helped Sue find her way beyond a plateau and on to an expanded experience of growth and development. The experience was so real for me that I had no doubts whatsoever that I had visited the realms beyond death's doorway.

But I wondered about the pyramid I had seen. It hadn't *emerged* in the way of the symbolic pictures that are common to some of my explorations. I remembered a seemingly physical orientation as I flew around the pyramid and down into a tunnel. This seemed very real—physical—but I had never experienced such a scenario. As time passed, I forgot about the pyramid and the tunnel underneath leading to another world.

Two years later, though, the mystery deepened.

In August 1998, Beyond Productions, an Australian company working under contract for the Discovery Channel, invited me to help make a documentary about ancient rituals. Knowing of my work with sound and consciousness at The Monroe Institute, they asked me to electronically monitor the brainwaves of someone reenacting an ancient ritual, in hopes that I would be able to produce data—changes in brainwave patterns—objectively demonstrating changes in consciousness related to the rituals.

As background: Ancient cultures used sound and music—music, rhythmic drumming, chanting—in religious ceremonies and to promote psychological and physical health. Pythagoras, Plato, and Aristotle thought that sound and music had special properties. Renowned classical and romantic composers viewed music as a powerful means of influencing consciousness and culture itself. And the idea that auditory stimulation can affect moods and consciousness is widely accepted today.

Beyond Productions wanted me to accompany its film crew into a cave beneath the Sun Pyramid in Mexico. At the time of the request, I didn't remember the pyramid scenario in the PREP session I did to help my sister, and I didn't think about the parallels until months later. Sitting here at the keyboard describing these events, I realize that all this was Guidance, sailing through life's adventures, navigating each moment, and keeping me on course within God's well-charted journey.

The Sun Pyramid, which was extensively excavated in the first decade of the twentieth century, is part of the ancient city of Teotihuacán, Mexico. Originally, it was approximately 215 by 215 meters at the base and about 63 meters high. It was enlarged later to a final size of 225 meters along each side. Its importance is indicated by its central location within the ancient city.

In 1971, archaeologists discovered a cave under the pyramid. Artifacts revealed that the cave was used for rituals focused on the netherworld and that musical instruments were used during such ritual activities. Ritual practitioners listened to the sound waves resonating from the walls of the cave and believed that this gave them a window to the world beyond death. (Some scholars believe that the Sun Pyramid was constructed over the cave to take advantage of its special characteristics during these rituals.) The public is not generally allowed into the ritual cave, so I felt privileged to be asked to participate in this experiment.

I did measure the brainwaves of one of the four ritual participants and was able to record significant changes relating to the conduct of the ritual. This adventure was eventually aired on The Learning Channel in September 1999. But more importantly for me personally was the fact that I was able to physically replicate part of the journey I had taken when I had helped my sister. Here I was, going underneath a pyramid, passing through a tunnel into a cave that reportedly was a gateway to the netherworld.

Months later, I realized that this physical experience answered my concerns about the pyramid in my out-of-body rescue of my sister. The pyramid in my PREP session experience had been real, although not made of physical matter. Perhaps ancient seers encouraged the building of pyramids as passages to the spiritual realms—the crude, physically constructed pyramid forms being symbolic—based on their own out-of-body experiences.

My exploration of reality through personal experience, my travels "through the Flavor Straw," rekindled so many years ago with Bob Monroe, continues today. I enjoy attending the Institute programs and occasionally doing a PREP session in the booth in the lab.

Through life's process, I have *realized* the rhetoric of my childhood. We are never separate from spirit. Things are not physical or spiritual. We are, always. We sometimes have physical experiences. I realize, therefore, it is not especially necessary to enter a focus-level state to commune with my spiritual self. I am that being and all it takes is a simple shift in perspective to access all that I AM.

My ventures "through the Flavor Straw" have helped answer some of those persistent questions that were originally presented in the Gateway Voyage program. Who am I? Where and who was I before I entered this physical being? What is my purpose for this existence in physical-matter reality? What action can I now take to best serve this purpose? What is the content of the most important message that I can receive and understand at this point in my existence?

At this point, the answers seem to be:

1. I am a spiritual being.

2. I am and always will be more than this physical body—I am a spiritual being.

3. My purpose here is to experience the awareness of All That Is.

4. There is nothing I can do that does not best serve this purpose.

5. The most important message for me (seemingly) changes from day to day. If I had to come up with the message for today, as I'm sitting here at my keyboard, it would be, "All is love." Coupled with previous insight, this yields "I AM = Love," or simply, "I am love." Cool.

The Out-of-Body Experience

Many who have read or heard of Bob Monroe's three books naturally associate The Monroe Institute with the out-of-body experience. These same enthusiasts assume that The Monroe Institute teaches people *how to* get out of their bodies, so to speak. And these same people think that the Bob Monroe Research Lab does out-of-body research, whatever that is. These assumptions are misplaced, but I do feel it is appropriate for me to comment on what has come to be called the out-of-body experience.

Over the years, Bob Monroe and I quietly discussed his out-of-body experiences in personal conversations away from public scrutiny. Years ago, Bob wrote about encountering a faraday cage while in the out-of-body state. He wrote that he was unable to penetrate the walls or get inside. When I asked him about this, he said that in later years he tried again and found that he was easily able to pass into and through the faraday cage.

Bob Monroe

Bob explained that his first encounter with the faraday cage was limited by his belief system. He believed, based on his earthly knowledge, that a faraday cage was impenetrable and that belief was so strong it carried over into his out-of-body experience. Learning to overcome his beliefs enabled Bob to explore far beyond the often-narrow confines of Earth-life expectations.

In another private conversation with Bob, I asked him about the concept of an *astral* body or second body apart from the physical body we occupy in the waking state. Bob smiled and said that he realized that in his books he left the impression that when out-of-body we retain a bodily form very similar to our physical facade. He went on to say that he no longer experienced himself in that way, that he thought of himself "more like a spot or point of light."

Based on Bob's experience, he felt that the notion of a second body was a habit or carryover perception from the Earth-life system of beliefs. To him, the humanoid form was simply "local traffic" on the interstate. Our true form includes humanness and more, much more than we can know if we limit our beliefs to the Earth-life system.

The very concept of an out-of-body experience suggests that we survive physical death. Couple this with a deep-seated common yearning, a nostalgia for something that seemingly eludes us, a heartfelt longing to return "home" or perhaps to our true identity, and it is easy to imagine the possibility that when we eventually die, each of us will travel out-of-body to our point of origin in a spiritual domain. This is indeed an intriguing notion.

The out-of-body experience (this side of dying) has often been viewed as something that happens *to* us. Many wonder why some people seem to have such experiences while others do not. Is it possible to learn how to have an out-of-body experience? What can be done to prepare for or encourage the experience?

The manner in which the out-of-body state is imagined actually limits the experience. What is needed is a whole new understanding about ourselves (and human consciousness) that will allow us to realize who we really are and recognize the validity of our experiences.

There is no magic key. There is no magic pill, no magic incantation, and no magic Hemi-Sync frequency that will bring about an out-of-body experience. The only thing that will bring about the out-of-body experience is your own personal growth and your own personal processing so that your *view of eality will change*. Once your view of reality changes—when your perceptions change—you will be consciously aware of your out-of-body experiences and even more.

I am really saying that you are having these experiences already. But because you have compartmentalized your consciousness, you are seemingly unaware; you do not realize what is already happening. You need to change your perceptions of reality so that you can begin to recognize the true nature of your existence. This realization is inevitable. You can begin working on it now or simply wait until your body wears out or is fatally injured and you leave it behind. Even then the delusion of separateness remains available.

Find your personal truth. Throw away the ideas and opinions of others that seem strange to you. The only opinion that counts is the one that you hold. Be honest with yourself.

Examine your inner beliefs. Think about who you really are. Are you the car you drive or the house you occupy? Are you the clothes you wear? Are you the day's hairdo? Are you just your body—or is there something more that entices you?

Embrace humanity. See yourself as one with all, without the perceived barriers of race, religion, sex, or economic level. Go within and embrace the feelings of those around you. Empathize with the pain and suffering and rejoice at the joy and love. Marvel at the wonder of an emerging perception of reality that was here waiting for you all along.

Confront your fears. In regard to the out-of-body experience, ask yourself, "What am I afraid of?" If you don't get an answer, realize that many fears are unconscious. Use your fear as a reminder (to put you back in your right-mind, so to speak) that you have forgotten who you really are. All fear is based on the notion that you are not a divine expression of God I Am, which, of course, is baloney.

Integrate your consciousness. If you are not recognizing your true nature, you may have compartmentalized your consciousness into just one expression of you, your body. As a result, you believe your mind is in your head and that all there is to your divine essence is your physical body. This is your reality. It's all you have to go on.

Well, I've got news for you. It's all a matter of perspective. You can begin to realize these other parts or expressions of yourself by first looking for them in others. Smile.

Claim your power. Elect yourself president of all you survey. You are the only one in charge of your own perceptions.

An out-of-body experience isn't something that happens to you. It's just another way of being, an alternative available so that you might know, might recognize who you really are. The true out-of-body experience you seek includes the realization that you are and always have been and always will be greater than your physical body in both physical life and beyond. This being the case, Guidance—your spiritual self—has always been and will always be one with you.

Life is not something physical and death something spiritual. Substantive reality is inclusive. God is really big! The secret to remembering your true identity is simply realizing *All That Is*.

Realizing All That Is

Imagine that you have the opportunity to recognize a realm greater than earthly life, a spiritual reality that has been there all along, even though you may not have been fully aware of it. Death provides such an opportunity, but I'm not suggesting here that you keel over midsentence.

Instead, pretend that you have died and seen your way through the many diversions of such a wondrous experience. You once again become aware of the oneness, a profound awareness you have experienced so many times before.

For imaginary purposes, make believe that after the death process you find yourself sitting around something like a campfire. Actually, you are the campfire, but for this little story to work you'll have to pretend that you are sitting around in a circle with all other enlightened souls.

All souls always have been and always will be sitting around the campfire. All are *enlightened* souls aware that they are there; they know the warmth from the light of the flame and don't perceive themselves to be separate from it.

Continuing the story, there you are, existing in the light of God and consciously recognizing *All That Is*. You are actually the whole campfire scene, the flame, the souls, the camaraderie—in the sense that the *campfire* is a phenomenon rather than an object. But for the purposes of illustration, think of yourself as an enlightened soul sitting around the circle. Gaze upon your fellow souls and once again realize the oneness of your being together there as you have always been. Okay, have you got it?

The flame from the campfire illuminates *All That Is*. In the presence of the light, souls see clearly. Beyond the circle of souls there is a forest. It too is part of *All That Is*. Interestingly, you notice that the light casts shadows of the enlightened souls into the forest.

A shadow, of course, has no substance. Yet the light of the iridescent flame creates these dancing silhouettes from the oneness of souls. Or is it the souls themselves who create their own silhouettes, shadow puppets of their aspirations?

The closer you are to the light, metaphorically speaking (realizing you are truly one with the light), the more distinct and more defined your silhouette—the more it seems very different than the light and separate from your true identity. If you assume a position some distance from the light (in truth, this is not possible, but you can imagine such a circumstance), the more diffuse your shadow and the less clear is your perception of who you really are.

Remember that the shadows themselves have no real substance. They are something akin to intellectual hypotheses, wonderings of God, "what ifs" in a preexisting realm of *All That Is*. The silhouettes are soul caricatures produced by the light. They are strangely nonsubstance and yet a part of *All That Is*.

At our imagined spiritual campfire gathering, the way of knowing is the realization of oneness! Through this realization we come to know *All That Is*. Of course, in our non-space/time spiritual reality, we always have and always will know *All That Is*. But let's get back to the storyline.

Recognizing that in the light of *All That Is* there are shadows, you begin to think about what you know while staring at one of the silhouettes seemingly dancing about in the forest beyond the circle of souls. Can you experience this shadowy realm?

In the literal blink of an eye, you remember that you can momentarily experience the shadow, the nonsubstance part of *All That Is*. For when you blink, the light of *All That Is* slips ever so briefly from consciousness and you become aware of the shadow aspect.

In our physical bodies, an eye blink is a very quick event. So accustomed are we to blinking that we hardly notice it or think of it as a momentary loss of awareness of the surrounding visual field. Of course, the whole idea of moviemaking is based on this physiological behavior. Singular still pictures are shown by a movie projector with a shutter that "blinks" so rapidly that we experience smooth, "moving pictures," as they are so appropriately called.

If a blink is so quick in the physical world, think how fast it would be in the non-space/time spiritual domain. It would literally take "no time" at all, as though you never even did it, which is why I'm explaining all this within the venue of this storyline.

You recognize that in spirit you are already aware of all this. But right now, within this thing you call your lifetime, you are in the middle of a blink. You have closed your spiritual eyes to the light of *All That Is* and you are experiencing one (or more) of those shadow puppets dancing in the forest beyond the circle of souls basking in the light of God.

In a very short time, the blink will be over and you will remember the *campfire*, where you have always been and always will be. In fact, since a blink takes "no time" at all in spiritual terms, you already realize this.

So there you are, existing in the light of God and consciously recognizing *All That Is*. You gaze upon your fellow souls and once again realize the unity of your being. The flame from the campfire lights up *All That Is*, including the forest beyond the circle of souls. The light creates dancing silhouettes in the forest. You know *All That Is* and, because there is no space/time, you never blinked. You have always known *All That Is*, and you always will.

You realize that, during the *time* that you never blinked, a mere shadow of your soul was mysteriously unaware of the world of substance, of *All That Is*. This wisp of consciousness thought that it was alone, separate somehow from *All That Is*. So convincing was this illusion that this aspect thought of itself as "real" and "physical," even though it was just a silhouette without substance. This "you" spent a great deal of *time* collecting imaginary "material" goods and believing that someday it would die—whatever that is.

There were moments, however, little reminders of *All That Is*, while all this was happening. Because you realize *All That Is* as you always have, even this wisp of yourself experienced such knowingness (Guidance). Overwhelmed as this "you" was by its perceived life circumstances, these experiences of *All That Is* seemed like messages or communication (Guidance) from *outside* yourself. But this cannot be, as there is *nothing* outside of *All That Is*.

You realize now, as you always have and always will, that when these shadowy profiles dancing in the forest glimpse *All That Is*, it serves as a marvelous reminder of the fact that they are but divine expressions of God I Am. The light of God shines through these window-experiences of *All That Is*, illuminating all shadows and unifying the separateness of a silhouetted existence. Guidance—opportunities to recognize who you really are. These are the moments (in "no time"), even while *blinking* into physical life, when the spiritual world of substance, true reality, prevails.

I'll leave you with this:

Open your heart. And with an open heart, speak the truth.

Say to yourself from your heart, "I reveal the truth and realize that I Am."

Put a smile on your face and carry love in your heart.

Show the world you know that you are a divine expression of God I Am.

See you around the campfire.

Author's Note

I am immensely interested in realizing the evolution of consciousness—the inevitable awakening of the human spirit, God I Am. Sharing our experiences with one another, "re-membering" who and what we are, promotes this realization. You can share your experiences with me via e-mail through my website, *www.skipatwater.com*, or by writing me in care of the publisher. Better yet, please say hello the next time you see me at a convention or seminar.

I also want the communication we've had through this book to continue. Readers who don't have a computer and cannot view the CD-ROM that comes with this book should find an agreeable friend with a computer. I have put some of the material onto videotape as well. You can order these videotapes online using a credit card at *www.skipatwater.com* or by phone at 1-877-692-7999 (US) or (214) 757-7900, Mondays through Fridays, 9 AM to 5 PM Eastern time. A company called CDStreet.com will process your order.

The Monroe Institute
62 Roberts Mountain Road
Faber, VA 22938
1-434-361-1252
www.monroeinstitute.org

Monroe Products
PO Box 505
Lovingston, VA 22949
1-800-541-2488
www.Hemi-Sync.com

Afterword

BY PAUL H. SMITH

Some people just turn up in the right place, at the right time, with the right preparation to make a difference in the world. I'm not talking here about those figureheads of change, the ones you see staring out of the cover of *People* magazine, who end up sitting on couches on late-night talk shows, the people who are ranked on all the social A-lists in big cities and let you know about it. Instead, I mean someone more humble in person and circumstances, yet perhaps more important—one of those class of people whom Fate, or God, or the Universal All (take your pick) seems to have singled out, molded, and then plugged into a critical node to serve as a change-agent, a catalyst. These kinds of people work quietly and mostly anonymously behind the scenes in those places where new ideas and determined humans combine in a way that can, conditions being right, eventually shift the world onto a whole new tack. The world seldom learns who these unsung world-changers are, and even the effects they cause sometime take years to be felt. But without them the world would be a poorer, duller place.

Every so often, though, one of them gets to tell his story. F. Holmes "Skip" Atwater is one of the lucky ones, and his story is compelling.

I first met Skip in 1983, when I moved my family next door to his in the row-house quarters where we both lived while stationed at the home of army spies, Fort George G. Meade, Maryland. I knew him as Fred back then, and I was struck by how easy going he was in an otherwise frantic environment of career-minded intelligence officers working in the high-stakes game of international espionage. Instead of a uniform like the rest of us, he always wore civilian clothes, which piqued my curiosity.

Three months later I found out that he was, like others on Ft. Meade, a spy-master of sorts. Only instead of electronic eavesdroppers or secret agents, Skip worked with army psychic spies. And before I knew it, I was one of them. For five years, besides being my neighbor and friend, he was my mentor, my trainer, my tasker, and my sounding board. Together with the rest of our friends and colleagues in the military remote-viewing unit, we discovered that there was much more to the universe—and to human beings—than we had ever before imagined.

And, I think, we did help change the world, if only just a little. It doesn't look much like it yet—the world is a big place, with a lot of inertia, and it takes awhile before a little push shows up as a significant movement. But thanks largely to the groundwork Skip helped lay in a series of government remote-viewing programs with odd sounding names like Gondola Wish and Grill Flame and Center Lane and Sun Streak, things now are starting to happen.

It is tempting to think that if Skip hadn't been in the right place at the right time, remote viewing as an operational intelligence discipline might never have been tried. I don't think that would be true, since at the time there were strong forces moving in that direction, and if Skip hadn't been there, someone else would have filled the vacuum. But luckily for the rest of us, Skip was there, properly prepared, and willing. He got to be the "pointy-end of the spear," as we sometimes called it in the army. The behind-the-scenes forces that were at work coalesced around him; he gathered people who had the talent needed to make the whole thing work (no one could have done it alone, and Skip would be the first to admit he shares credit with many others); and he eagerly turned to his assigned mission.

Here is where the preparation part came in. In the field of the paranormal it is easy to get carried away, to start "believing too much," to grow egotistical and a little megalomaniacal. It has happened to lots of folks and is not a pretty sight. Where someone else might have been irresistibly tempted to sky off into fantasy, chasing down phantoms and imagining powers that were not real, Skip's life experiences came together to help him resist that temptation and act as a speed brake to keep himself and the rest of us under control. He served both as ground and anchor. We speculated on some pretty wild things while assigned to be official government remote viewers. And some pretty wild things happened. But Skip kept us honest. Though he was willing to experiment—carefully—he also knew the value of strict protocols and the importance of keeping us planted firmly in the here-and-now when we were doing real-world projects that involved mentally going elsewhere or elsewhen.

Today, Skip remains unassuming to a fault. He bears no resemblance to the self-promoters and media hogs of the "pop" remote-viewing culture—folks who had a much smaller role to play in the remote-viewing saga than did Skip, yet who try all the harder to grab the limelight for themselves.

Skip's story is unassuming, too—which is not to say it isn't exciting, thoughtful, and mind-expanding. But he doesn't go out of his way to toot his own horn, and he presents incredible things in a gentle way that will no doubt be lost on those who are jaded by the chaotic, sound-bite sensationalism of media excess—those who have forgotten how to slow down long enough to think. The rest of us will find Skip's book a breath of fresh air, and a doorway to an endless universe of nothing but possibility—the human mind.

Paul H. Smith, retired army intelligence officer and remote viewer
President, Remote Viewing Instructional Services Inc.

References

Bem, Daryl J. and Charles Honorton. 1994. *Psychological Bulletin*. American Psychological Association (January).

Braud, William G. 1975. "PSI Conducive States." *Journal of Communication:* 142–152.

McMoneagle, Joseph. 1993. *Mind Trek: Exploring Consciousness, Time, and Space through Remote Viewing*. Norfolk: Hampton Roads Publishing Company.

Monroe, Robert A. 1971. *Journeys Out of the Body*. Garden City: Doubleday.

Radin, Dean I., Ph.D. 1996. "Towards a Complex Systems Model of PSI Performance." *Subtle Energies and Energy Medicine Journal* 7, no. 1: 35–69.

Roll, W., R. Morris, and J. Morris, eds. 1969. "A Further Psychophysiological Study of Out-of-the-Body Experiences in a Gifted Subject, Robert A. Monroe." *Proceedings of the Parapsychological Association* 6 (November): 43–44.

Schnabel, Jim. 1997. *Remote Viewers: The Secret History of America's Psychic Spies*. New York: Dell.

Targ, Russell, and Harold E. Puthoff. 1977. *Mind-Reach: Scientists Look at Psychic Ability*. New York: Delacorte Press/E. Friede.

Targ, Russell. 1994. "Remote-Viewing Replication: Evaluated by Concept Analysis." *The Journal of Parapsychology* 58 (September).

Index

A

B

Hampton Roads Publishing Company

. . . for the evolving human spirit

TO VIEW THE CD

Insert the compact disc into your CD-ROM drive.
Wait for autorun to launch the program.
If autorun does not launch, run x:\start.exe
(where x= your CD-ROM drive).

Minimum System Requirements:
Windows 98
Pentium II or higher
32 MB RAM
CD-ROM drive
800 x 900 color resolution

Hampton Roads Publishing Company
publishes books on a variety of subjects including
metaphysics, health, complementary medicine,
visionary fiction, and other related topics.

For a copy of our latest catalog,
call toll-free, 800-766-8009,
or send your name and address to:

Hampton Roads Publishing Company, Inc.
1125 Stoney Ridge Road
Charlottesville, VA 22902
e-mail: hrpc@hrpub.com
www.hrpub.com